THE HUMAN FACE OF THE BOOK TRADE:
PRINT CULTURE AND ITS CREATORS

Printed by Peter Cole
In Leaden-Hall
In Effigiem Nicholai Culpeper Equitis
Cross fecit in Aquafort

Nicholas Culpeper (1616–1654): portrait frontispiece to his *Pharmacopoeia Londinensis* (1653), reduced from 135 x 94 mm (see p 75)
(Reproduced with the permission of the Wellcome Institute Library, London)

The Human Face of the Book Trade

Print Culture and its Creators

Edited by

Peter Isaac and Barry McKay

ST PAUL'S BIBLIOGRAPHIES
WINCHESTER

OAK KNOLL PRESS
DELAWARE

PRINT NETWORKS

This series, edited by Peter Isaac & Barry McKay, publishes papers given at the annual Seminars on the British Book Trade

1. *Images & Texts*
2. *The Reach of Print*
3. *The Human Face of the Book Trade*

© St Paul's Bibliographies & the Contributors 1999

First published 1999 by
St Paul's Bibliographies
West End House
1 Step Terrace
Winchester
Hampshire SO22 5BW

Published in North & South America and the Philippines by
Oak Knoll Press
310 Delaware Street
New Castle
DE 19720

ISBN 1 – 873040 – 54 – 7 (UK)
ISBN 1 – 58456 – 003 – 7 (USA)

British Library Cataloguing in Publication Data
is available from The British Library

Library of Congress Cataloging-in-Publication Data
The human face of the book trade: print culture and its creators /
edited by Peter Isaac and Barry McKay.
p. cm. -- (Print networks; 3)
Includes bibliographical references and index.
ISBN 1-873040-54-7 (UK)
ISBN 1-58456-003-7 (US)
1. Book industries and trade – Great Britain – History. I. Isaac,
Peter C.G. II. McKay, Barry. III. Series.
Z325.H83 1999
381'.45002'0941 – dc21
99 – 30585
CIP

Composed in MONOTYPE *Bulmer* by Peter Isaac & Barry McKay
Printed in England by St Edmundsbury Press, Bury St Edmunds

Contents

The background of the front cover is an engraved portrait of William Buchan
(1729–1805) from a plate in *Wonderful Museum* (1803)
(Reproduced by permission of The Wellcome Institute Library, London)

Contributors

Iain Beavan, Senior Curator in the Heritage Division, Aberdeen University, is a member of the University's Cultural History Group. As well as managing the University Library's digitization projects, Dr Beavan maintains an active research interest in the print culture of Northeast Scotland, and in the early history of Marischal College Library.

Stephen Brown, Master of Champlain College, Trent University, Peterborough, Ontario, recently spent a year at the Institute of Advanced Studies in the Humanities of Edinburgh University, working on William Smellie's MSS letters and papers. He is at present preparing microfilm and database editions of these papers, together with a biography of this gifted printer.

Graeme Forbes is currently a sub-librarian at Napier University, where he has worked since 1986. He has worked in several libraries since qualifying at Sheffield University's School of Librarianship. He is Head of the University Library's Acquisitions, Record Management & Supply Division, including the responsibility for the Edward Clark Collection. He also teaches librarianship in the University's Department of Print Media, Publishing & Communication.

Peter Isaac, Emeritus Professor of Civil & Public Health Engineering of the University of Newcastle upon Tyne, set up the research group on the History of the Book Trade in the North in 1965, and, in 1985, began the compilation of the British Book Trade Index. He was President of the Bibliographical Society 1994–1996, and is now President of the Association of Independent Libraries.

Philip Henry Jones has, since 1970, been a member of the lecturing staff of the College of Librarianship Wales (now part of the University of Wales Aberystwyth). His FLA study in 1977 was on the Welsh printer-publisher Thomas Gee; he is now engaged in a detailed study of the Wrexham firm, Hughes & Son, 1820–1920. The major work *A Nation and its Books*, which he edited with Eiluned Rees, was launched at the National Library of Wales in November 1998.

Warren McDougall, an Honorary Fellow of the Faculty of Arts of the University of Edinburgh, is editor of the eighteenth-century volume of the projected *History of the Book in Scotland*. He has microfilmed, and is currently indexing, the archive of Charles Elliot, the eighteenth-century Edinburgh bookseller and publisher.

Barry McKay, an antiquarian bookseller who specializes in bibliography and the art and history of the book, has been, for several years, engaged in research on the book trade in Cumbria. He is at present transcribing the day-books of the printers and booksellers John Ware & Son of Whitehaven 1799–1806, and is investigating the sources of the chapbook wood-cutter 'R M'.

Paul Morgan has worked with antiquarian and early printed books first in the Library of the University of Birmingham and then in the Bodleian Library, Oxford. He has published many studies of the English provincial book trade, bookbinding, and Warwickshire history.

Michael Powell, Librarian of Chetham's Library, has published on the local history and bibliography of Manchester and its region, and has recently edited, with Terry Wyke and Chris Ford, *The Church in Cottonopolis: Essays to Mark the 150th Anniversary of the Diocese of Manchester*. He is a member of the Council of the Chetham Society and a former editor of the Lancashire & Cheshire Antiquarian Society.

Jonathan Sanderson is currently completing his PhD in the School of English at the University of Leeds. His thesis examines the publishing histories of Nicholas Culpeper's medical books during the middle decades of the seventeenth century, and the commercialization of the Culpeper brand-name in London's medical marketplace.

Brenda Scragg, of the John Rylands Library, has published several catalogues of exhibitions of that Library on the theme of nineteenth-century book arts and historical children's literature. Mrs Scragg has made a special study of the nineteenth-century book trade in Manchester.

Richard Sher is Professor of History at New Jersey Institute of Technology and Aassociate Chairman of the Federated History Department at NJIT and Rutgers University, Newark. He is currently engaged in a study of the book history of the Scottish Enlightenment.

David Stoker is a Senior Lecturer in the Department of Information & Library Studies, University of Wales Aberystwyth. Between 1970 and 1994 he undertook research into the history of the book trade and antiquarian communities in Norfolk. Following the fire in Norwich Library in 1994 he has concentrated upon quantitative studies of the provincial book trade.

Terry Wyke teaches social and economic history at Manchester Metropolitan University. He has written extensively on the history of the Northwest, particularly Manchester. His recent publications include *Mirth in the Mill: the Gradely World of Sam Fitton* (1995) [with Alan Fowler], and *A Hall for All Seasons: a History of the Free Trade Hall* (1996). He has recently completed a study of the history and economics of the *Cotton Factory Times* (1998).

Editorial

F OR MANY HISTORIANS of the book the path from the author's mind to that of the reader is a relatively straightforward economic and technical progress, but in the introduction to his fascinating paper on a complicated best-selling eighteenth-century author Rick Sher writes (see p 46)

I want to focus here on the importance of going beyond the bibliographical record whenever the sources permit. As much as bibliography... can tell us about the making, selling, and collecting of books,... it is constrained by its inability... to humanize the study of book history. By this I mean showing how stories about books are also stories about authors, readers, and members of the book trade, seen as flesh-and-blood individuals with their own interests, aspirations, motives, strengths, and weaknesses.

In this Professor Sher is reminding us that human idiosyncracies (the 'human face' of our title) intervene at every stage of the author-to-reader journey – we all have our own aims, both admitted and hidden – and human strengths or frailties may produce smaller or larger deflexions (or changes of direction). Rick Sher's human stories commonly call for access to private correspondence, which too seldom survives. The authors of several papers to the Sixteenth Seminar on the British Book Trade held at Napier University, Edinburgh, in July 1998, which form the third volume in the *Print Networks* series, have been fortunate in having such access, and so can give us a more rounded picture of their subjects.

Paul Morgan looks at two early book historians, each breaking new ground to sketch an outline of book production and its varied location. David Stoker shows how present-day electronic techniques allow us to refine, and even to redefine, the pioneer accounts of Cotton and Allnutt. Graeme Forbes describes the splendid Edward Clark Collection, now in the Library of Napier University, formed by William Maxwell, Edward Clark's successor as head of R & R Clark, to demonstrate the highlights of book-making.

The eccentricities of authors are readily accepted, for they are the 'creators' in our eyes, and Richard Sher brings to our view, in the physician William Buchan, a potentially best-selling author, spoilt by his 'conviviality'. But book-producers, too, could have their foibles, and William Smellie, a contemporary of Buchan who had edited his *Domestic Medicine*, is shown by Stephen Brown to have been brilliant but unreliable. Jonathan Sanderson, the British Book Trade Seminar Fellow for 1998, describes a power battle between a devious author and 'authority' personified in the College of Physicians, money being a prime mover.

The workings of the book trade in Manchester in the nineteenth century are illuminated by Brenda Scragg's study of that town's 'most prestigious bookseller', William Ford, while the less honest goings-on in auctioneering are the subject of the paper by Michael Powell and Terry Wyke. Peripatetic salesmen of part publications were among the nineteenth-century successors of the chapmen; Philip Jones shows something of the forceful activities of Scottish number salesmen in Wales, and assesses how these may have affected local Welsh-language publishing in the nineteenth century.

As was appropriate at a Seminar held in Edinburgh, Scotland received attention with two papers on Charles Elliot, the eighteenth-century Edinburgh bookseller, based on his very full archive, now with the family firm of John Murray (Publishers) Ltd. Warren McDougall covers his dealings with the London trade, while I give an account of his parallel dealings with the English provincial trade. Iain Beavan's tale of the *Aberdeen Shaver* provides an unusual picture of the Aberdonian *Private Eye* of the early nineteenth century.

Barry McKay explores an unknown by-way of publishing, the shepherds' guides of the Lake-District fells, and the shepherds and others who produced them.

The study of The Book – one can almost feel the capitals – has become a 'respectable' academic field of research and teaching, but the wide range of participants at these annual seminars demonstrates that there is still a place for the amateur. Long may this remain true!

Peter Isaac, Wylam
April 1999

Henry Cotton and W H Allnutt:
two Pioneer Book-Trade Historians

PAUL MORGAN

IT IS A TRUISM that when a subject reaches maturity, its history begins to be studied and recorded; it seems to be also a fact that this historical work gets undertaken by senior people who have abandoned the attempt to keep up-to-date with current developments. The study of the English provincial book trade and myself fall easily into this category. It is exactly sixty years ago, in 1938, that I began collecting details about the Warwickshire book trade and have continued to do so ever since, except for 1939-1945. In the late 1930s there were few general works to help one; at that date, of course, one did not have John Feather's *Checklist*[1] or the *Cambridge Bibliography of English Literature* as guides, and, incidentally, it is remarkable how many particular English places have printing histories or bibliographies published before 1900, but there was a dearth of information for most areas. Eleven places were dealt with in E Gordon Duff's *English Provincial Printers, Stationers and Bookbinders to 1557* published in 1912, whose concluding words were[2] 'a cloud of obscurity still hangs over the subject, but the cloud has a silver lining. Think how much there still remains for us to discover'. Then if one consulted the second edition of Henry R Plomer's *Short History of English Printing, 1476-1900*, which appeared in 1915, one found a note[3] at the start of the chapter on provincial presses thanking 'Mr Allnutt's series of papers contributed to the second volume of *Bibliographica*' alongside Duff. Additionally, one might find in guides to reference books mention of a further promising source, *The Typographical Gazetteer Attempted by the Rev Henry Cotton*, two series, 1831 and 1866. At least, that is the course I took. Further investigation revealed that both men, like myself, had been at one time or another on the staff of the Bodleian Library in Oxford, so I thought it might be interesting to say something about these two contrasting characters before they sink into the mists of time.

REVD HENRY COTTON

The earlier of the two, and of whom more is known, was Henry Cotton, born in 1789 to a clerical family at Chicheley, Buckinghamshire.[4] He went to Westminster School and then Christ Church, Oxford, where he became a protégé of the Dean, Cyril Jackson, through whose probable influence he became, first, Reader in Greek at the age of twenty and then, in 1814, one of Bulkeley Bandinel's two Sub-Librarians at the Bodleian Library at a salary of £250–300. Here, as he wrote himself, he was 'Obliged... to be conversant to a certain degree with books of almost every kind, for the purposes of arranging, cataloguing, and assisting the researches of students'.[5] He has left a trace of his work, with which every cataloguer will sympathize, on the front endleaf of a volume with seven incunabula printed 1472–1480 bound together: 'Mem. This is the most tiresome volume I ever had to deal with. H.C.'[6] Cotton found he could not identify every place-name he saw in imprints so began taking notes of them, a habit he continued for nearly sixty years.

Like most graduate staff of the Bodleian at that time, he was in Anglican orders,[7] and in January 1818 was instituted Vicar of Cassington, a few miles north of Oxford, and in the summer married Mary Vaughan Laurence, daughter of Richard Laurence,[8] Regius Professor of Hebrew and Canon of Christ Church. Then in 1822 Cotton's mother-in-law died and Professor Laurence was appointed Archbishop of Cashel, in Ireland, and it must be assumed that he asked his daughter and son-in-law to accompany him; Cotton became his domestic chaplain and resigned his Bodleian post. He was to spend the rest of his life in Ireland, being appointed Archdeacon of Cashel in 1824 and later Dean of Lismore, where he died in 1879. Until he lost his sight about 1876, he continued to take notes and to publish books.

By the time he was 'unexpectedly called away... to clerical duties in a country-town of the south of Ireland' he had amassed 'a very considerable quantity of... information',[9] and consequently *The Typographical Gazetteer Attempted* was published by the Clarendon Press in 1825. It contained 188 pages of an alphabetical list of mainly Latinised place-names; those for which evidence of printing before 1501 existed were put in capitals, the others in italics. Continental European towns naturally predominate, but Britain and other continents get mentioned. To take three consecutive entries at random:

Canterbury, an ancient metropolitical city of England, chief of the county of Kent. The art of printing appears to have been first exercised here about the close of the reign of Henry VIII. John Mychell is the only printer whose name is recorded, and his first dated book, as given by Herbert, is of the year 1549. Not more than eleven or twelve early Canterbury books are known.

Canthurium, qu? – 1677.

Cape Town, chief town of the settlement of the Cape of Good Hope; which has been permanently occupied by the British since the year 1806. Printing has for some years been exercised in this colony, and among other publications, a *Cape Town Gazette* is now regulariy published in monthly numbers.[10]

Points that stand out in these very typical entries are firstly, Cotton was under no pressure to be concise; secondly, no actual books are named but only a date; thirdly, overseas entries and names of newspapers are frequent. Entries vary greatly in length. Many English towns get mentioned, as *'Newcastle-on-Tyne.* A newspaper was published here as early as 1639',[11] which may be news to Professor Isaac; presumably the proclamations issued by Charles I are meant. The number of entries for North American places is remarkable; perhaps dwelling in Ireland among the relatives of so many emigrants to America gave him opportunities of hearing about them. The general absence of named sources and titles is a great disadvantage; a location is occasionally given, like 'Bodl.' but not enough details to be able to find the book. An appendix of fictitious and pseudonymous place-names in imprints, together with a rather inappropriate chronological list of books printed on vellum, and an index conclude the volume.

Cotton did not cease his searching after publications; he must have spent a lot of time reading through catalogues and lists, but this did not fill all his time judging from the score or so of his other publications. Many were theological; two of permanent historical value are *Fasti Ecclesiae Hibernicae*, listing holders of appointments in the Church of Ireland, published in six volumes between 1851 and 1876, and his *The Bible and Parts thereof in English from the year MDV to MDCCI*, first edition published in 1821, with a second in 1852, still has its uses. He had prepared a second edition of *Typographical Gazetteer* by October 1830 and the Clarendon Press published it in 1831; it included

282 new entries and many had been expanded, while 180 had been given an earlier date. Two more appendices were added, a useful chronological index and a list of academies occurring in the titles of books. One imagines industrious evenings in remote Irish parsonages reading through catalogues and reference works, for the process continued so that a second series was published in 1866 when Cotton was 71 – some six years before his sight began to fail. Cotton must have acquired reference books as they came out and read them through, such as the second edition of John Martin's *Catalogue of Privately-printed Books* in 1854, and Robert Moffat's *Missionary Labours in South Africa* in 1842, for this volume is remarkable for the large number of places in Africa, Asia and America. Under 'United States', for instance, there is a separate alphabetical list of over 900 places 'for which a newspaper, if nothing else, was printed in or before 1850'. The preface includes an interesting short essay on 'The itineracy of the press', how presses moved around, from the Martin Marprelate tracts of 1558–59 down to the 'late fierce conflict' in America, when 'printers were often forced to fly with their presses', as well as printing on ships such as Sir William Parry's *Hecla* in the 1820s.

Cotton accumulated no mean library himself to judge from the Sotheby sale catalogue of 1868,[12] which shows a general collection of classics, early printed books, theological controversy and many editions of the Bible and Psalms. There were many published library catalogues and Oxford-printed pamphlets of his time. It also had no less than 128 copies of his own *Memoir of the French New Testament in which the Holy Mass and Purgatory was part of the New Testament* which had been printed in 1863 and possibly flopped.

Cotton was under no illusions about the scholarly standard of his *Gazetteers*: as he wrote in the Preface to the second series, they were 'mainly a collection of rude materials, the miscellaneous gatherings of a single individual',[13] and he saw no prospect of anyone else taking on the project. This is very true, but these volumes form a marvellous lucky dip with unexpected treasures turning up, though balanced by frequent disappointments. He also made a proposal to publish his life and all the remains of Sir Thomas Bodley in one convenient volume, which was submitted to the Delegates of the Clarendon Press in March 1822, but they rejected it on the grounds 'it will not sell'.

The general impression one gets of Cotton is of a well-educated, widely read, cultured clergyman, comfortably off, cheerful and active in publishing the results of his investigations, rather typical of his time. The published selection of his *Anecdota*, already mentioned, confirm this cheerfulness together with a rather gossipy interest in his Oxford contemporaries; the notebooks were started in 1814 and seem to have been discontinued after the move to Ireland.

WILLIAM HENRY ALLNUTT

On the other hand, the second subject of this article was self-educated, not comfortably off and of limited antiquarian interests. At the 1990 Seminar on the British Book Trade in Durham, Dr F W Ratcliffe named W H Allnutt's *Notes on Printers and Printing in the Provincial Towns of England and Wales* as one of the 'planks on which so much of the study of the provincial book trade has been built'.[14] William Henry Allnutt was born in 1849 in the parish of St Giles-in-the-Fields, London,[15] into a family that had originated in Ipsden, Oxfordshire, and Sutton Courtenay, Berkshire, as appears from his notes;[16] he named his own house *Ipsden* at 39 Woodstock Road, Oxford. In 1864 at the age of $17^1/_2$, he entered the service of the Bodleian Library as a non-graduate assistant,[17] when the salary range was £20–£130 a year; Cotton had received £250–£300 as a sub-librarian.[18] Not surprisingly Allnutt took on extra work; a notebook from the 1880s gives details of much transcription for others, such as Dr Dee's diary for J E Bailey of Manchester, and manuscripts for Prince Boncompagni and Osmund Airy; he also catalogued Hertford College Library, did work in Merton College archives and arranged the Cottrell-Dormer papers at Rousham.[19] Furthermore, he made transcriptions used in Surrey Archaeological Collections IX (1888), Somerset Record Society VIII (1891), and for the Worcestershire Historical Society in 1890. Not all his work has been named by any means, but enough to show that he must have had little time left for any personal interests from the free hours of a full-time library assistant. It must be pointed out that many, if not most, of his colleagues were also engaged in similar work – look at the publications of his friends W D Macray or Falconer Madan for instance.

Presumably he spent his first few years in the Bodleian acquiring skills in palaeography and Latin as well as passing the examination for Associate of

Arts, a status now obsolete. When he began to take an interest in the history of provincial printing is unknown, but his colleague W D Macray noted in 1890 that 'Mr Allnutt has long been engaged in preparing for publication a Bibliography of Provincial Presses to the year 1800'.[20] Like Cotton he must have become fascinated by the variety of imprints seen when cataloguing. His earliest publication on the subject seems to have been in 1878 when he delivered a lecture entitled 'Notes on printers and printing in the provincial towns of England and Wales' to the first annual meeting of the Library Association, held in Oxford in the October of that year and opened by H O Coxe, then Bodley's Librarian. It was fully reported in a local newspaper, so Allnutt had offprints of the talk prepared with a title-page; a list of about 300 entries and 230 places and dates was appended with an introductory paragraph:

> Several members... having expressed their willingness to assist in making the following list more complete it is now printed and circulated with the hope of obtaining the co-operation of those... possessed of earlier information... The compiler requests that... a full collation may be supplied, and especial care taken to give the IMPRINT *verbatim, literatim et punctuatim.* Private presses are not included in the list.[21]

The talk first surveyed recent studies such as Robert Davies on York, S F Cresswell on Nottinghamshire and J H Hinde on Newcastle upon Tyne, then showed the need for further investigation and gave an outline of the history of the subject. Allnutt concluded 'Archdeacon Cotton's *Typographical Gazetteer* having been compiled under specially disadvantageous circumstances, is naturally imperfect... the accompanying list will be found to supply an earlier date, in most instances'. Incidentally, Cotton was still alive, but blind, and died the following year; it is to be hoped that he was told about Allnutt's work. At the end there was some discussion, with Allnutt responding to six speakers and being thanked by George Bullen of the British Museum Library.

The talk, substantially the same as in the Oxford offprint, was duly printed more attractively by the Chiswick Press the next year in the Library Association *Transactions and Proceedings*,[22] but the 'Table of Places with their earliest Specimens of Typography' was much improved. In addition to the bare place, name of printer and date, the 'Book or Pamphlet, etc., Printed' and the 'Authority' are given, with the number of entries increased by about 75. These authorities, mainly published works, include eleven individuals such as J P

Earwaker of Manchester, G W Tomlinson of Huddersfield, and J Askew Roberts of Oswestry; Cotton was still the authority for about 30 entries.

Allnutt did not publish anything further on the provincial book trade for about twenty years when, in 1896–97, he contributed three articles on 'English provincial presses' to the short-lived *Bibliographica*.[23] The subject was treated chronologically with long sections for the sixteenth and seventeenth centuries and only short details for the eighteenth, giving date, place, title and imprint with brief notes. Extracts were offprinted with a title-leaf *Some Account of English Provincial Presses '1468' to 1750* (Oxford, 1896), of which only twelve copies were produced according to a note by Falconer Madan.[24] The earlier sections have been superseded by E Gordon Duff's Sandars lectures of 1911,[25] in which Allnutt hardly gets a mention. In 1896 also he wrote a note for the same journal on the Recusant press at Stonor Park in Oxfordshire in 1581.[26]

Allnutt's final two studies of provincial printing appeared in *The Library*, not to be confused with the Bibliographical Society's journal of the same name: in 1900 was published 'The King's Printer at Shrewsbury in 1642–43',[27] made good use of by William K Sessions in his greenback, *A World of Mischiefe* (1981). Lastly in 1901, two years before his death, he brought his survey down to 1800 in 'Notes on the introduction of printing presses into the smaller towns of England and Wales after 1750 to the end of the eighteenth century'.[28] This is an expanded and revised chronological arrangement of his 1879 alphabetical list, with improved descriptions of the books printed. As with his *Bibliographica* articles, it suffers from the absence of indexes of places and printers. Allnutt was simultaneously writing articles on bibliographical and antiquarian topics, but one suspects provincial printing was his real personal interest. He certainly collected examples himself and at least four have been traced in the Bodleian Library. They are:

> *The Returns of Spiritual Comfort and Grief, in a Devout Soul. Represented by an Intercourse of Letters, to… the Lady Lettice, Countess of Falkland* (Leedes: reprinted by Griffith Wright, for George Copperthwaite, 1760), (Bodleian, 1419 f.619).
>
> Benjamin Keach, *War with the Devil…* (Coventry: T Luckman [*c* 1763]) (Bodleian, 147 g.544, with note by Allnutt 'A title and preface of this work was given me by W D Macray with "Michms 1763" on title')

A bound volume containing four tracts printed by John Fawcett at Ewold Hall, near Halifax, Yorkshire, about 1798, with a full-page note on Fawcett by Allnutt, dated 26 February 1885. (Bodleian, 1419 f.611, bought 12 March 1897)

Sidney Melmoth, *Beauties of British Prose* (Huddersfield: printed by Brook and Lancashire, 1803). (Bodleian, 270 g.861, with the signature of Allnutt)

Allnutt resigned from the staff of the Bodleian in July 1896, but before discussing the rather sad circumstances surrounding this, it is necessary to put it into context. Allnutt had been appointed to the staff and had worked for 17½ years under the librarianship of H O Coxe, one of Dean Burgon's 'Twelve Good Men', who, though he spent 5½ hours daily on his library duties, and often 5 hours as well on his own interests or transcribing for others, 'Lacked the faculty of delegating to others'.[29] In 1882 he was succeeded by a very different type of librarian, E W B Nicholson,[30] from the London Institution, a scholarly philologist, but a young man of 33 full of feverish energy. Oxford University was in the process of being reformed, opened to all religious denominations, the curriculum revolutionised, more importance paid to examinations, and doctorates of philosophy on the German pattern introduced. Nicholson began revolutionising the Bodleian with frequent controversies and poor relations with colleagues, and within the University. Falconer Madan, a sub-librarian and his successor, after a few years communicated only by formal, written notes.

Allnutt was soon in Nicholson's bad books. According to a statement Nicholson prepared for the Curators of the Bodleian, he soon discovered Allnutt was not to be trusted out of sight of the Librarian's chair; he left his desk for long periods and kept private work there 'even when forbidden to do so'.[31] He also was often late in the mornings, did less work than the other assistants and took mid-morning breaks at the Three Cups Hotel in Queen Street; this last habit was unusual until the Second World War. Consequently Nicholson kept a watch on him and, on the 8 July 1896 found that at 12.45 the books had not been re-shelved in the section for which Allnutt was responsible and which should have been completed by 11.30. Nicholson had introduced a new system for this purpose. Nicholson searched for him in the Radcliffe Camera and in the Three Cups, without success, but at 1 pm came across him returning to the Library. Allnutt said he had been to his bank, so Nicholson proposed going there to check, so Allnutt then said that when he had got there he found he had forgotten his cheque-book and started to return when he met a friend, went for a drink with him and stayed talking. The untruth gave Nicholson his opportunity, so he wrote to Allnutt that he would be glad to receive his resignation or he would have to take the matter up with the Curators; permission would be granted to use the Library as an ordinary reader during normal opening hours. On the 11 July Nicholson wrote a detailed narrative for circulation to the Curators, including 'the cessation of £200 a year to an idle man... will be a great gain and I see no sign that it will be a cause of regret to the staff'. On the 22 July Allnutt came into the Bodleian to see W D Macray on a private matter and was asked to see the Librarian, where a letter of resignation was put in front of him to sign, which he duly did. Later the same day Allnutt wrote to Nicholson in a futile attempt to withdraw the resignation. Feelings had died down and in November Allnutt sent a receipt to Nicholson, adding he harboured no unfriendly feelings to him personally and did not wish to be thought in any way discourteous; Nicholson, basically a kind-hearted man, replied that he hoped to be 'able to suggest you for the purpose of cataloguing or weeding out gentlemen' s libraries as I did a week or so ago'. Allnutt retained the friendship of W D Macray and Falconer Madan judging from presentation inscriptions, though possibly not of some of his other colleagues who had complained he did not pull his weight.

Allnutt, now aged 50, had to turn to full-time cataloguing and transcribing. He had a small leaflet printed describing what he had done and could do with an impressive list of published work. Nicholson, who preserved every possible document, added it to the archive together with a copy of his reference for a post in the Clarendon Press in 1897, when the applicant was said to show an 'interest and more than usual intelligence in bibliographical matters', but his poor time-keeping habits did not make for success. The archive concluded with a letter from Allnutt to Falconer Madan, dated 5 December 1902, reporting that he was going into a London hospital for an operation and he wished to be remembered to 'all his old Bodleian friends and many kindnesses received from yourself'; a pencilled annotation reads 'died 2 March 1903'; he was only 56 years old.

CONCLUSION

Cotton had been a university graduate with an assured income, Allnutt a non-graduate on a low one; indeed, Compton Reade, writing in 1875, said Bodleian assistants 'were shamefully underpaid' and 'seldom or never rewarded by promotion'.[32] There was clearly a marked class division, as between fellows of colleges and college servants, which only recently has disappeared from the memories of elderly library staff. Allnutt enjoyed the friendship of Falconer Madan, a fellow of Brasenose, and of W D Macray, who had risen the hard way. One can only admire how both Cotton and Allnutt accumulated so much detailed information without the reference books and equipment available today – their publications are monuments to serendipity. Both had been cataloguers and must have taken notes as books passed through their hands, as I was advised by my chief in 1937. Thanks are indeed due to the prolixity of Cotton and the bare details provided by Allnutt for supplying so much basic material even if it is now largely superseded.

NOTES

1. John Feather, *The English Provincial Book Trade before 1850; a Checklist of Secondary Sources* (Oxford Bibliographical Society Occasional Publication 16, 1981).

2. (Cambridge, 1912), 128.

3. (London. 1915), 98 note.

4. *Dictionary of National Biography*; J Foster, *Alumni Oxonienses* (Oxford, 1888), part 2, vol 1, 302; F Boase, *Modern English Biography* (Truro, 1892), vol 1, 728–30; T D Rogers, 'Anecdota Cottoniana: selections from the notebooks of Henry Cotton', *Bodleian Library Record*, vol 12 (1986), 152–63.

5. *The Typographical Gazetteer Attempted* (Oxford, 1825), v.

6. Shelfmark: Auct. 0.2.21; I am indebted to Dr Alan Coates for this reference.

7. Permitted from 1813; see Sir Edmund Craster, *History of the Bodleian Library, 1845–1945* (Oxford, 1952), 28.

8. Rogers, 'Anecdota', 152.

9. *Typographical Gazetteer*, vii.

10. *Typographical Gazetteer*, 29.

11. *Typographical Gazetteer*, 107.

12. 31 Jan–3 Feb 1868; Bodleian (Mus.Bibl. III 8° 575 (1)).

13. Pp ix, xii.

14. Peter Isaac (ed), *Six Centuries of the Provincial Book Trade in Britain* (Winchester, 1990), 1.

15. Census 1891 (Oxford City Library, Fiche RG/12/116612+).

16. Bodleian, MSS Top. Oxon c. 232 and f.38.

17. W D Macray, *Annals of the Bodleian Library, Oxford*. 2nd edn (Oxford, 1890), 490.

18. Craster, *History of the Bodleian*, 45.

19. Bodleian, MS Eng. Misc. f.30.

20. Macray, *Annals*, 490.

21. (Oxford, printed for private circulation by J Vincent, 1878), 5.

22. *Transactions and Proceedings of the First Annual Meeting of the Library Association of the United Kingdom Held at Oxford... 1878* (London, 1879), 101–3, 139, App V.

23. 2 (1896), 23–46, 149–80, 276–308; 3 (1897), 481–4.

24. Bodleian, 25821 c.17.

25. See Note 2 above.

26. 3 (1897), 163–5.

27. *The Library*, 2nd ser, 1 (1900), 355–64.

28. *The Library*, 2nd ser, 2 (1901), 242–59.

29. Craster, *History of the Bodleian*, 148–51.

30. Craster, *History of the Bodleian*, 152–243.

31. Bodleian Library Archives c.473,'Resignation of W H Allnutt, 1896': I am grateful to the Bodleian Library for permission to examine and quote from these papers, and to Mr Steven Tomlinson for providing the reference.

32. 'The future of the Bodleian Library', *Belgravia*, 25 (1875), 180.

The English Country Book Trades in 1784-5

DAVID STOKER

WRITING THIRTY YEARS AGO, Roy Stokes pointed to a widely acknowledged geographical imbalance that required correction:[1]

The history of printing in many countries all too readily becomes the history of printing in a limited number of major centres. Nowhere is this tendency more marked than in England. The book trade in England is largely the book trade in London. This, at least, is how it appears through the majority of general accounts.

At this time there were in existence a few pioneering nineteenth-century studies such as those of Henry Cotton and W H Alnutt.[2] Likewise E Gordon Duff's Sandars Lectures for 1911 covered the earliest provincial presses and the book trade prior to the accession of the first Queen Elizabeth,[3] but coverage thereafter was extremely patchy. Little serious work was undertaken during the first half of this century, and interest in the study of provincial printing was not revived until 1959 with the publication of Paul Morgan's brief account.[4] In the same year Graham Pollard's Sandars Lectures dealt with the 'English market for books' and gave much valuable information about provincial bookselling.[5]

Thus Roy Stokes's assessment was largely accurate, and he went on to discuss how the situation might be remedied in future through the use of local records, and business archives:

A high percentage of such material must be related to 'local' as opposed to national activities... Our conspectus of the national book trade and the universal development of the book can then be revitalised by new attitudes based on newly discovered facts.

Stokes was showing a fair degree of prescience – for there has indeed been an enormous growth in scholarly interest in the provincial book trades since that time. The fact that this paper is being delivered during the sixteenth annual seminar devoted specifically to this purpose is itself a testimony to the range of work now undertaken, and our growth in understanding of this previously neglected area of our cultural life. There is now much published literature on all

13

aspects of the book trades outside of London from the beginnings of provincial bookselling until the mid-nineteenth century, and this may be an opportune time to take stock of what we have, and what remains to be done.

As predicted, much of the work undertaken in the last thirty years has been at the local level, providing a foundation upon which more analytic studies may be based. There are a growing number of detailed studies of the book trades in individual cities, towns, counties, and in a few cases accounts of whole regions. The last three decades have also seen the rescue from oblivion of several important provincial publishing houses or printing and bookselling dynasties during the eighteenth and early nineteenth centuries. Yet it is clear that a bias towards London and an under-representation of the role of the provinces in publishing history continues well into the twentieth century. Recent work by John Turner on the publishers Walter Scott of Newcastle and Arrowsmith of Bristol shows that they published works of lasting literary and cultural significance up to the First World War, yet neither firm features in the standard histories of publishing, so dominated by the London trade.[6]

Other work has focused upon the detailed study of particular aspects of the trade outside London, such as Cranfield and Wiles's two studies of early provincial newspaper presses.[7] There has also been a lot of work undertaken with respect to the Welsh, Irish and Scottish trades and their relations not only with England, but also with the colonies and indeed with one another. John Feather has also given the first significant attempt at studying the English provincial trade as an 'economic entity' during a discrete period – namely the eighteenth century.[8] Yet there are still plenty of gaps remaining in the jigsaw, and it is only once these are filled that there can be any comprehensive account of the provincial trade, and assessment of its importance can be made.

An understanding of exactly who was at work in the provinces and where, at any given time is a crucial preliminary to this work. The British Book Trade Index is gradually providing us with a useful overall index to the personnel in these trades in England and Wales during the period up to 1850, which is not limited to any area or sector, by collating local work and specialised studies. This will be particularly useful in tracking those printers and booksellers who moved around. For example, of the four printers known to be at work in Norwich in the spring of 1718 only two remained in the city in the face of competition. Benjamin Lyon turns up a decade later in Bath, and Robert Raikes moved on to St Ives, Northampton, and then to Gloucester.[9] Likewise, when in 1735 the Reverend Francis Blomefield wanted to employ a journeyman printer for his private press, he chose a man from Bailey's printing house in Bury St Edmunds. He chose Nicholas Hussey, who had previously been in business in Dublin.[10] Hussey subsequently ran away from his master and I should love to know exactly where he went.

However, the most obvious gap is in the provision of comparative quantitative data giving an overall picture of the spread of trades such as printing or bookselling, and indicating the relative importance of different places at different times. This would come from a census of the book trades if there ever were such. Even the bald numbers of printing and bookselling businesses in operation in each town at one time would provide useful comparative data, but the numbers of workmen employed would be even better. Such figures would put one town into an overall context with others elsewhere in the country. For example, a study of the book trade in Norwich during the eighteenth century provides a picture of fairly steady and largely uninterrupted growth and development. This takes no account of the significant decline in the relative economic importance of this city *vis-à-vis* the emerging industrial centres in the north, and ports such as Bristol or Liverpool which were prospering from the slave trade during the same period.

The objective of this paper therefore is to ask whether there is any reliable and comparable quantitative data that may be used as a framework within which other more detailed and often interesting sources can be used and interpreted. Detailed case studies based upon individual account books or surviving correspondence provide an important way of bringing the subject alive and introducing a human dimension. However there is also a need to put into an overall context.

The three fundamental sources for providing information about the names and addresses of provincial printers and booksellers for the whole country are:

Imprints of publications, which exist in fairly large numbers from the mid-seventeenth century.

Provincial newspaper advertisements, existing from the early eighteenth century.

Entries in local directories which date primarily from the last quarter of the eighteenth century.

Each of these sources has been used extensively in studies at a local level, but it is only during the 1780s that there is sufficient evidence at a national level to paint a picture of the trade as a whole.

PENDRED'S DIRECTORY

John Pendred's *The London and Country Printers, Booksellers and Stationers Vade Mecum* was published in 1785, and provides entries for provincial and metropolitan letterpress and copperplate printers, booksellers, stationers, binders, and also many other ancillary trades, such as collectors of stamp duties, paper and parchment makers and fellmongers. The work has certain limitations of coverage, which were outlined in Graham Pollard's introduction to the Bibliographical Society's reprint of 1955.[11] As far as London is concerned the directory is fairly detailed, and as complete as any other source. At the other extreme, the coverage of Wales, Scotland and Ireland is very poor indeed. If one accepted Pendred neither Edinburgh nor Glasgow had any booksellers at work in 1785. As far as provincial England is concerned it is noticeable that the further away from London one travels the less complete is Pendred's coverage. Many of these entries appear to have been compiled by copying them from William Bailey's *British Directory* of 1784, supplemented by files of country newspapers maintained by his neighbour W Taylor who operated as an advertising agent. Given the pedigree of many of the entries, it might be more accurate to extend the date range to 1784–5. Inevitably there are gaps, and errors in transcription, and by itself it would not provide sufficient data for any reliable comparison. Graham Pollard's assessment was that:[12]

> Pendred's aims were utilitarian: his sources such as came to hand: and his treatment of them was sometimes careless. Nevertheless he has preserved for us a substantial body of information about members of the book trade in 1785.

Pendred's directory does have two advantages not foreseen by Graham Pollard which now make it eminently usable for such a comparative exercise. The first of these is that it has been reprinted using a modern typeface thereby permitting the use of optical character recognition technology, and so has been relatively easy to convert into a computer file. The second advantage is that the provincial entries generally follow a standardised pattern, giving the name of town, county, mileage from London, and market day; followed by a list of surnames and trades of those operating in the book trades. Therefore, it has been a relatively straightforward task to scan the work, and with a minimum of editing, load it directly into a simple flat-file database. This may then be searched or sorted by any of the above-mentioned elements. The results of this process after editing are displayed below. Using this database it would be possible, for example, to identify and calculate the numbers of printers or booksellers working within a fifty, one hundred or one hundred and fifty mile radius of London.

Table 1: Entries from Pendred as digitised, and then transferred to a database table

ALRESFORD, (Hants, 57 MD Th.) Hart and Prangnall, Fellmongers.
   Upsdale, Bookseller, stationer and Sub-Distributor of Stamps.
ALTON, (Hants, 47 MD Sat.) Bristow, Fellmonger. Roe, Bookseller.
ANDOVER, (Hants, 65 MD Sat.) Maud, Bookseller. Pugh and Willis, Parchment-makers.
APPLEBY, (Westm. 268 MD Sat.) Wilkinson, Bookseller.
ARUNDEL,(Sussex, 56 MD Wedn. and Saturd.) Blanck, Stationer. White, Bookseller.
ATHERSTONE, (Warwicksh. 103 MD Tuesd.) Parker, Bookseller
AYLESBURY, (Bucks, 40 MD Sat.) Dagnall, Bookseller and Stationer. Nicholas, Printer. Wiltshire, Fellmonger.

No.	Cntr	Town	County	Dist.	Name	Trade 1	Trade 2	Trade 3
1	En	Alresford	Hampshire	57	Hart and Prangnall	Fellmonger		
2	En	Alresford	Hampshire	57	Upsdale	Bookseller	Stationer	Sub Distributor of Sta
3	En	Alton	Hampshire	47	Bristow	Fellmonger		
4	En	Alton	Hampshire	47	Roe	Bookseller		
5	En	Andover	Hampshire	65	Maud	Bookseller		
6	En	Andover	Hampshire	65	Pugh and Willis	Parchment-makers		
7	En	Appleby	Westmorland	268	Wilkinson	Bookseller		
8	En	Arundel	Sussex	56	Blanck	Stationer		
9	En	Arundel	Sussex	56	White	Bookseller		
10	En	Atherstone	Warwickshire	103	Parker	Bookseller		
12	En	Aylesbury	Buckinghamshire	40	Dagnall	Bookseller	Stationer	
13	En	Aylesbury	Buckinghamshire	40	Nicholas	Printer		
14	En	Aylesbury	Buckinghamshire	40	Wiltshire	Fellmonger		

There is not sufficient space to present all the possible results from this exercise, and so this paper will be restricted to coverage of letterpress printers, booksellers and stationers in the English provinces.

Beginning with the country printers Pendred identifies approximately 201 printers in 113 English provincial towns compared with 135 businesses in London. The reason for the approximation in these figures lies in dealing with the inevitable anomalies – such as trying to identify exactly what constitutes a provincial town.[13] It would appear from Pendred's directory that the main centre for English provincial printing at this time was Bristol with nine printers, and four newspapers.

In Table 1 above there is only one printer listed in a county town, but elsewhere Pendred gives many examples of printers working in market towns such as Bishop's Castle in Shropshire, Ilminster in Somerset or Leek in Staffordshire. Likewise there are printers in newly established resort towns such as Brighthelmstone (later Brighton), which was not yet the fashionable resort associated with the Prince Regent. There are also presses in new industrial towns such as Wigan or Burnley.

Pendred also provides lists of the country newspapers then in existence. By combining these figures with the number of printers, it is possible to draw up an approximate table showing the relevant importance of different centres of printing compared with their estimated populations.[14]

Table 2: The most significant centres of provincial printing according to Pendred

	No. of printers	No. of Weekly newspapers	Estimated population
Bristol	9	4	60000
Liverpool	8	2	52000
Birmingham	7	2	48000
Bath	7	2	23000
Newcastle	6	2	30000
Manchester	5	1	45000
Norwich	4	2	36500
Exeter	4	2	16500

From this it appears that Bristol is still predominant as a printing centre followed by Liverpool and Birmingham. Traditional cathedral cities such as Norwich and Exeter are beginning their gradual decline. There is no direct correlation between size of population and number of printers. At one extreme there is one printer per 3.3 thousand population in Bath compared with one printer per 9.1 thousand in Norwich. The two most populous provincial cities, Bristol and Liverpool both have approximately one printer per 6.5 thousand people.

Every English county except Rutland has at least one printer, although Bedfordshire, Berkshire, Hertfordshire and Huntingdonshire each have one only. The counties with the most printers listed are Somersetshire (within which Pendred includes Bristol) with 23, Lancashire 19, Yorkshire 13, and Warwickshire 11.

ESTC ENTRIES

As mentioned, a second valuable source for the names and addresses of those employed in the book trades is the information given in the imprints of contemporary publications. These are listed in the English Short-Title Catalogue (ESTC), which may be searched by year and country of publication. In so far as ESTC is listing publications rather than individual workmen, it may also be used to provide a fairly crude guide to the level of activity and comparative importance of towns and businesses. Only a proportion of publications have survived and only some of these have ESTC entries; likewise not all printers have their names in the imprints. However, in spite of these limitations this is undoubtedly the best single source of such information we have for the period, and the CD-ROM version of ESTC provides a great deal of material that can be used to supplement Pendred.

Extracting a list of all ESTC entries printed in England other than in London, for the two years 1784–5 is a relatively simple task. Out of 6446 entries for the British Isles 5372 (83%) were published in England, and of these, 1267 (24%) originate in the English provinces. There is however a considerable degree of approximation in these figures resulting from incomplete and occasionally inaccurate entries, and the problems of comparing multi-volume books, which only have one entry, with pamphlets and single sheets. Thus it would be most unwise to draw too many conclusions or to suggest that in

1784–5 provincial printing represented one-quarter of the whole printed output.

One hundred and seventeen towns are represented in this list, compared with the 112 listed in Pendred. ESTC records the names of only 143 individual printers compared with 199 in Pendred – presumably those most active in local publishing, but there are thirty-seven names in ESTC which are not in Pendred. The most significant difference between the two sources however lies in how they appear to rank centres of printing.

Table 3: The most significant centres of provincial printing according to ESTC

ESTC Entries	Town	Printers in Pendred	Estimated population
336	Salisbury	3	7 000
67	Newcastle	6	3 000
62	Oxford	2	10 500
47	Birmingham	7	48 000
45	Cambridge	2	10 000
43	York	3	13 000
40	Bath	7	23 000
37	Manchester	5	45 000
35	Exeter	4	16 500
29	Leeds	2	20 000
27	Bristol	9	60 000
27	Norwich	4	36 500

On the basis of the ESTC entries Salisbury was by far the most significant centre of English provincial printing, and this was almost entirely due to the output of one man, John Fowler, who does not even feature in Pendred's directory. The cities of Bristol and Liverpool, which, according to Pendred, had the most printers at this time, would nevertheless be ranked eleventh and twentieth respectively in terms of the numbers of ESTC imprints. Likewise Oxford and Cambridge, which both feature high in the ESTC largely due to the output of the University presses, would hardly have been recognised by Pendred.

Neither source is completely reliable, however. Several of the ESTC entries have assigned places of publication, some of which are highly questionable; or else the imprint was deliberately left vague or intended to mislead. Likewise Pendred sometimes fails to identify that a bookseller was also a printer – such as in the case of John Ferraby of Hull, thereby leaving the town with no printer. There is also a sizeable discrepancy between the personnel listed, but less so in terms of the locations. Overall, the degree of overlap between these two sources is represented diagrammatically in Figure 1 below.

OVERLAP BETWEEN ESTC AND PENDRED – PRINTERS

By combining the two sources it is possible to create a composite database of about 236 named provincial printing businesses working in 125 English provincial towns during 1784–5. These figures can be compared with a similar exercise based on ESTC entries between 1701 and 1725, which identified only about 66 named provincial printers working in 31 towns, and therefore indicate the substantial growth in the provincial printing trade during the middle years of the century.[15]

Figure 1: The extent of overlap between ESTC and Pendred for provincial printers

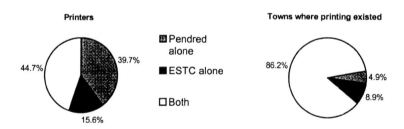

To what extent do these two exercise provide a complete or reliable picture of the extent of provincial printing at this time? The only apparent means of verification was to cross-check the entries against specific local studies. For this purpose the two East-Anglian counties of Norfolk and Suffolk were chosen, as the area known best to the author, the book trades of both of which have been covered in some detail.[16] For printers the combination of ESTC entries and Pendred gives a fairly complete picture of the established printing trade in this region, and there appear to be no significant omissions in these two counties. There may have been some very short-lived businesses not noticed, and there may be more gaps in counties more distant from London.

Do these figures tell anything useful regarding the numbers of those employed in the provincial printing trade at this time? Perhaps a figure of 236 businesses indicates an overall workforce in excess of 1000 individuals, but this is merely a crude guess. Provincial presses could be extremely varied in size. This is well illustrated by considering two of the Norwich businesses listed by Pendred.

The firm of William Chase & Co was the third generation of a highly prosperous printing and bookselling dynasty, which had been in business since about 1707. Various William Chases had printed and published the *Norwich Mercury* since 1715, and the firm had prosperous bookselling, auctioneering, and estate-agency interests, and was the official stationer to Norwich Corporation. When William Chase II died in 1781 he left diamond rings to members of his family and directed that six journeyman printers should carry him to his grave.[17]

At the other extreme, there was the business of Stephen White, which was later to be engagingly described by his apprentice Luke Hansard.[18]

> The Printing office was in the Garret, and consisted of one Letter Press and one Copperplate Press, and of Types, but small quantities of few varieties; but with these Types and these presses, I did learn accordingly. – My Master was but very rarely in the office; he was either engraving, or painting, or woodcutting, or fishing, or pigeon and rabbit shooting, or boatbuilding and rowing and sailing; anything but in the office; yet I esteem him to have been a good printer... I was proud in being compositor & pressman, corrector and manager, copperplate printer and shopman, book keeper and accountant to this chequered business.

Both of these examples were perhaps typical English provincial printing businesses of the period.

BOOKSELLERS

Pendred is not always clear or consistent between his designation of bookseller and stationer, and clearly entered them under whatever denomination he had found them listed or advertised. Indeed in most instances there was no clear difference between the trades outside the metropolis. Therefore the two terms have been taken to be synonymous for the purposes of this exercise.

Pendred lists approximately 300 booksellers and stationers working in 172 provincial cites and towns. Every English county is covered although Bedfordshire, Derbyshire, Herefordshire, Huntingdonshire and Rutland each have one name only, which in most cases sounds suspiciously low. The provincial city with most booksellers listed is still Norwich, with ten businesses, followed by Manchester with 7, Bristol and Bath each with 6 and Liverpool with five. Thirty-two booksellers are listed in Yorkshire, thirty in Lancashire, 18 in Norfolk and 17 in Somersetshire (including Bristol). By comparison Pendred lists about two hundred booksellers and stationers in London.

The task of isolating a complete list of provincial booksellers from ESTC imprints is somewhat more difficult and time-consuming than for printers. There are a number of potential complications. Firstly there is no separate index of provincial towns within imprints, merely a keyword index to the imprint field. Secondly, although there will usually be only one printer named, there are frequently several booksellers listed in one imprint. Also, many of the required tradesmen will appear in the imprints of items published in London as well in the provinces, and indeed occasionally in Scotland. There are many individuals whose names appear in the imprints of publications but who were not part of the book trade. Thus it is not always easy to decide who was a regular bookseller and who just happened to be concerned with the distribution of a local tract. Finally there are many booksellers with names missing from the imprints given in early ESTC entries, instead the formula '1 in Blackburn' or '2 others in Bolton' is used. However, only a small proportion of these incomplete entries relates to provincial imprints.

The only way to isolate entries with provincial booksellers only would be to work through the index of the 'Imprint All' fields looking for the names of towns, and then search for these terms. This would be a time-consuming task and prone to error. In the event it proved easiest to identify and download all the ESTC imprints for works published in England, Scotland, Wales and Ireland during 1784–5 into a single computer file. This file was then processed en-masse and broken down in such a way that the individual names could be isolated and inserted into a database. The Table below shows the results of this process.

Table 4: ESTC imprints after processing

ESTC No.	Place of Printing	Printed by, or for, sold by	First Name	Surname	Town
t103675	Oxford	sb	Avery	Shank	Abingdon
t104115	Oxford	sb	Avery	Shank	Abingdon
t052303		sb	Mr	Hemming	Alcester
t106571	Alnwick	pf	Alexander	Graham	Alnwick
n030221	London	sb	Mr	Roe	Alton
t190981	Aylesbury	pb	W	Nicholls	Aylesbury
n001588	Aylesbury	pb	W	Nicholls	Aylesbury
t031657		sb	T	Cockshaw	Barnsley

Of the 6446 records downloaded for 1784–5 2149 had no names in the imprint, merely a place of publication. The remaining 4297 records resulted in the creation of 8946 database records (in other words 2.08 names per imprint – although there were 1139 potential records where all the names were not given by the ESTC cataloguers, and so this figure would be more accurately expressed as 2.35 names per imprint).

Removing those that related only to printers (2262), which have already been dealt with, then reduced the 8946 records. Those that related only to London, Scotland, Ireland or Wales (5203), and those that only had very general imprints such as 'sold by the bookseller in town and country' or non-book-trade imprints such as 'printed for the author' (551) left only 803 records for named individuals who appeared to be English provincial booksellers. From this list of 803 records it was possible to identify 273 named individuals working in 130 towns.

The most prolific provincial booksellers in terms of the appearance on imprints were John & Joseph Merrill of Cambridge (50 imprints), Prince & Co of Oxford (35 imprints), and Fletcher & Son of Oxford (33 imprints). However considering only truly provincial towns and cities the most prolific names would be as shown in Table 5.

Table 5: The major provincial publishers according to ESTC entries

Name	Place	Imprints
Hazard	Bath	16
Todd	York	13
Wilson	York	13
Mills	Bristol	12
Simmons & Kirkby	Canterbury	12
Clarke	Manchester	12
Collins	Salisbury	12

It would not be difficult to identify the 'key' members of the provincial trade, responsible for a large amount of book distribution in the provinces, merely by identifying all names that appear on more than five or six imprints during this two-year period.

By combining information from ESTC with Pendred, it is possible to identify in the region of 434 booksellers working in 219 provincial town and cities. However, in this instance the level of correspondence between the two sources is significantly lower than for the corresponding exercise with printers. In fact only about one half of the entries are to be found in both sources. A few of the discrepancies may be due to differences in spelling (for example: the Bristol bookseller Miles listed by Pendred is probably the same as Mills on many ESTC imprints), but there is nevertheless a high level of difference between the sources.

OVERLAP BETWEEN ESTC AND PENDRED – BOOKSELLERS

Once again these results were compared with known information about bookselling in Norfolk and Suffolk, but on this occasion the resultant list is far from complete. The Norfolk market towns of Aylsham, Cromer, Downham Market and Harleston all appear to have had some bookselling business, but none of them is listed here. Likewise Bungay, Needham Market, Halesworth, Saxmundham, Debenham and Lavenham in Suffolk are missing. Important provincial booksellers such as Thomas Hunt of Harleston are not listed. The gaps do not apply merely to East Anglia. Booksellers were listed from the 1680s for towns such as Ashby de la Zouche, Coggeshall, Uttoxeter, and

Yeovil, yet none of these feature in this list one-century later. Thus the list of booksellers obtained is significantly less complete than that for printers.

Figure 2: Overlap between ESTC and Pendred for provincial booksellers

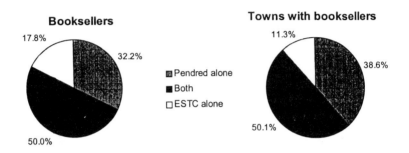

Many of the booksellers' names are identified by their appearance in only one or two ESTC imprints for these two years. Therefore, in order to compile a more comprehensive and reliable list, it may be necessary to throw the net a little wider and include five years, or perhaps a full decade. Nevertheless the exercise as it stands provides a significantly more detailed picture of the pattern, and extent of English provincial bookselling than any other source.

CONCLUSION

Taken together, the two lists described identify more than 600 printing and bookselling business throughout England outside London (some firms were of course both booksellers and printers). This may be a reasonable picture of the established book trade.

Yet the list takes no account of the hundreds of shopkeepers, stall-holders, chapmen and others who would have sold books at fairs, in tiny market towns or villages, or even door to door. It also takes no account of the mobile presses which may have been taken by wagon to major events such as public executions, or which might have accompanied itinerant players. These men were also in their way a part of the English country book trade, although they have left hardly any trace of their activities behind.

NOTES

1. Roy Stokes, *The Function of Bibliography* (Grafton, 1969), p168

2. Henry Cotton, *The Typographical Gazetteer Attempted* (Oxford: Clarendon Press, 1825), 2nd series 1866; W H Alnutt *Notes on Printers and Printing in the Provincial Towns of England and Wales* (Oxford: privately printed, 1878), and 'Notes on the introduction of printing presses into the smaller towns of England and Wales, after 1750 to the end of the century', *The Library*, 2nd series, 2 (1901), 242-59.

3. E Gordon Duff, *The English Provincial Printers, Stationers, and Bookbinders to 1557* (Cambridge University Press, 1912).

4. Paul Morgan, *English Provincial Printing* (Birmingham, 1959).

5. Graham Pollard, 'The English market for printed books', *Publishing History*, 4 (1978), 7-48.

6. John R Turner, 'Conditions for success as a provincial publisher in late nineteenth century England', *Publishing History*, 41 (1997), 63-73.

7. R A Cranfield, *The Development of the English Provincial Newspaper 1700-1760* (Oxford: Clarendon Press, 1962); R M Wiles, *Freshest Advices; Early Printed Newspapers in England and Wales* (Ohio State University Press, 1965).

8. John Feather, *The Provincial Book Trade in Eighteenth-Century England* (Cambridge University Press, 1985).

9. David Stoker, 'The Norwich book trades before 1800', *Transactions of the Cambridge Bibliographical Society*, 8 (1981), 79-125.

10. Francis Blomefield, *The Correspondence of the Reverend Francis Blomefield* (1705-52), ed David Stoker, (Bibliographical Society, 1992).

11. *The Earliest Directory of the Book Trade by John Pendred* (1785), ed Graham Pollard, (Bibliographical Society, 1955).

12. Pollard, *Earliest Directory*, xxiii.

13. Several of the provincial towns listed by Pendred would now be regarded as part of London, such as Deptford and Hammersmith. Likewise Berwick, which is in England, (but not Berwickshire) has been included, as have the Welsh-language presses in Shrewsbury.

14. These are the author's own estimates derived from the figures for 1775 and 1801 given in John West, *Town Records* (Phillimore, 1983), 310-31.

15. David Stoker, 'The Eighteenth-Century Short Title Catalogue, and provincial printing', *Journal of the Printing Historical Society*, 24 (1995), 9-35.

16. David Stoker, 'The Norwich book trades before 1800' and unpublished notes on the Norfolk trade; Tony Copsey, *Book Distribution and Printing in Suffolk 1534-1850* (Ipswich: The Author, 1994).

17. David Stoker, 'Prosperity and success in the English provincial book trade during the eighteenth century', *Publishing History*, 30 (1991), 1-58.

18. Luke Hansard, *The Autobiography of Luke Hansard Printer to the House 1752-1828*, ed Robin Myers, (Printing Historical Society, 1991), 9.

William Smellie and the Printer's Role
in the Eighteenth-Century Edinburgh Booktrade

STEPHEN BROWN

W ILLIAM SMELLIE was a printer in Edinburgh from 1752, when he entered the trade as an apprentice to the firm of Hamilton, Balfour & Neill, until his death in 1795. After service from 1759 to 1765 as a journeyman corrector to the press of Sands, Murray & Cochrane, the publishers of the *Scots Magazine*, Smellie set up as a master printer in partnership with the brothers Robert and William Auld. By 1767 William Auld and Smellie had joined John Balfour in a firm that was to be dissolved in 1771 to form Balfour & Smellie, a concern that continued until 1782 and was largely sustained through an appointment to print all the medical and legal dissertations for the University of Edinburgh. Smellie left Balfour to join William Creech in 1782/83, although he continued to print the theses for the University, and the copartnery with Creech ended in 1789, after which Smellie established a family printing business with his son Alexander. Smellie's printing firm in the Anchor Close continued until 1846, when the premises were taken over by *The Scotsman*.

Over the course of his career, William Smellie was employed to print works by David Hume, Adam Smith, Hugh Blair, Henry Mackenzie, Adam Fergusson, Lords Hailes, Kames and Monboddo, and Robert Burns, to name only the most distinguished. His name appeared on hundreds of imprints when we include the university theses in the count; or some thirty otherwise. He also held or sold the copyright or shares in a number of works of genuine commercial worth, in particular the *Thesaurus Medicus*, the *Medical Commentaries*, and his own *Philosophy of Natural History* and translation of Buffon. Of less monetary value but greater literary interest were his shares in the *Edinburgh Magazine & Review* and Maria Riddell's *Voyages to the Madeira and Caribee Islands*. Such are the facts, and in the case of the careers of most printers, there would be little of interest or significance to add. But such facts are perhaps the least compelling aspect of Smellie's career. His life in printing spans what were probably the most critical and exciting years in Edinburgh publishing history, a period in which the Scottish capital came to be the pre-eminent centre for learned publications in English. And although Smellie's printing firm did not thrive beyond his own energies and ambitions to become like that of his master Patrick Neill, a long-term influence in the Scottish trade, William Smellie was himself a crucial player in the establishment of the distinctively Scottish attitudes and practices which characterized British publishing in the late eighteenth and early nineteenth centuries.

My intention here is to explore the ways in which Smellie gave the role of the printer his own peculiar turn. He was a remarkable man whose intellectual gifts were immediately apparent to his contemporaries. From the first days of his apprenticeship until well into the final decade of his forty years in the trade, Smellie was singled out for special treatment by employers, teachers, publishers and patrons.[1] Throughout his period of indentures, he was permitted to leave the shop for two hours each working day to attend classes at the University where, it appears, most if not all his instructors waived their usual fees. Under these circumstances Smellie completed the courses of study in the arts, in Natural History, Moral Philosophy, and Medicine, especially distinguishing himself as a student of Latin, botany and anatomy. Still, he took no degree from any of the Faculties in which he studied. At the age of seventeen, Smellie won for his masters at Hamilton, Balfour & Neill, the silver medal of the Edinburgh Society for the Improvement of the Arts and Sciences for a perfect edition of Terence, the only occasion on which the prize did not go to the Foulis Press of Glasgow.[2] Smellie left his indentures six months early and as a journeyman with Sands, Murray & Cochrane was made the equivalent of the editor of the *Scots Magazine* for a period of nearly six years.[3] He continued to receive permission to take time away from his printing responsibilities to study medicine, using his increasing medical knowledge to improve the articles on medicine in the magazine. He was encouraged throughout this period of his life to become a practising physician by Dr William Buchan who offered to take Smellie into his practice as a pharmacist and medical apprentice and whose letters regularly praised Smellie's intellectual capacities and natural gifts for medicine.[4] Dr William Cullen and Dr Alexander Monro at the University of Edinburgh gave similar encouragement, but Smellie could not find a self-confidence equivalent to the belief others had in him. How remarkable, then, were

Smellie's talents; how justified his mentors in promoting his efforts? Two further examples make the case: Smellie taught himself French and Hebrew while working in his print shop in order to translate Buffon and to print Professor Charles Wilson's Hebrew Grammar. This was no ordinary printer. A classical education, a detailed understanding of the physical sciences, a love of medicine and a facility with language all made Smellie especially well qualified to print the great works of moral and natural philosophy published in Edinburgh; indeed John Balfour did very well by his partnership with Smellie, whose extraordinary knowledge of Latin enabled him to print and correct the University theses which financially sustained Balfour's business with a speed and accuracy not likely to be matched by any other Edinburgh printer. Smellie's facility with medical language further drew him to the attention of publishers like John Murray and William Strahan in London, and Charles Elliot and William Creech in Edinburgh. That Smellie was the right man at the right time as an Edinburgh printer in the 1760s, 1770s, and 1780s is confirmed by the projects which defined Edinburgh as a 'hotbed of genius' and which were shaped in some way by him as a corrector, editor or printer: the first *Edinburgh Review*, the *Scots Magazine*, the first edition of the *Encyclopaedia Britannica*, William Buchan's *Domestic Medicine*, the *Edinburgh Magazine & Review*, Dr William Cullen's *First Lines of the Practice of Physick*, Andrew Duncan's *Medical Commentaries*, the *History & Transactions of the Society of Antiquaries of Scotland*, James Hutton's *Chymical Dissertations*, Lord Kames's *Sketches of Man*, Buffon's *Natural History*, and Burns's Edinburgh edition are only a selection of the works which show his influence in some way.

But even when we take Smellie's talent as a printer, his gifts as a compositor, corrector and editor, along with his education and quick intellect, and add these to his business opportunities and partnerships, we still have only a very limited sense of his role as a printer in the Edinburgh trade. Smellie's achievements would have been more straightforward, his financial rewards more lasting and his renown less fraught, were it not for his personality and his politics. Smellie's obsession with printing – and it was an obsession in his youth when he worked long and even desperate hours – was rooted in his love of reading, and his access to learning both in the press and in the University convinced him that print was essential to a free society. While an apprentice, Smellie first read Addison, Swift, and Pope as he corrected them in the press.[5] His first encounters with Scottish history came in a similar way, and he continued to enrich his university courses with the eclectic contemporary reading he did in preparing the *Scots Magazine* for Sands, Murray and Cochrane. Smellie's letters throughout the early 1760s to William Tod, a fellow apprentice who had become a journeyman in London, and the Reverend Samuel Charteris, whom he had met at university, detail his reading. He is as keen a reader of novels as of natural science and is impressed equally by Laurence Sterne as by Linnaeus. Even in late life, Smellie continues to be attracted to novelty and invention, to youth and controversy. In 1792, he would share with Maria Riddell, a friend thirty years his junior, an enthusiasm for William Godwin,[6] and in the same year Smellie would write for Bell & Bradfute an appreciative but also slightly ironic Preface to the new edition he was printing for them of the *Wonders of Man,* an obscure work published only once before at London in 1704.[7] The *Wonders* is a bizarre and captivating text that uses the essay style of Montaigne to pursue an agenda reminiscent of Burton's *Anatomy of Melancholy;* its eccentricity and eclecticism appealed to Smellie, who may have brought the book to the attention of Bell & Bradfute, and initiated their interest in offering such a belated second edition.[8]

It should be clear by now that Smellie was too talented and too intellectually gifted to remain 'just a printer'. But how he would rise above his trade was not an easy determination for him. In his years as a journeyman, Smellie writes to William Tod, contrasting the highs and lows, the excitement and the drudgery of printing. To be the midwife to new work thrills the young Smellie and to see classical and modern authors reissued in reliable quality editions satisfies him; but he already shows a disdain for the busy work, especially the endless legal papers, which were the dull prerequisite for balanced books among the Edinburgh printing houses. But Smellie's control over the *Scots Magazine* quickly alerted him to the most liberating role a printer can play: actually inventing the text as it goes to press. Journalism or contemporary history as he defined magazines, reviews, and newspapers, Smellie recognized as providing the printer's role with genuine creative agency and political power. In corresponding with Smellie, both Tod and Samuel Charteris begin to refer to the *Scots Magazine* as 'your periodical', and Smellie too quickly assumes possession of the magazine as much in his fantasizing about his prospects as an editor of an ideal periodical, as in his actual labour in collecting, editing and printing this particular monthly. As I have indicated above, Smellie's hand is apparent in the increased volume and quality of the *Scots Magazine*'s medical articles. But as Smellie's tenure strengthens, he also begins to slip into the magazine his own original efforts. Throughout 1761 and 1762, Smellie writes to Samuel Charteris about his plans for a periodical to be called alternately 'The Man in the Moon' and the 'Speculator'. He describes essays he is writing and suggests topics for further articles (Robert Kerr tells us that two issues of the periodical were completed by Smellie); but when it becomes apparent to Smellie that any prospect of having his own periodical in the true sense is years away, he prints two issues of his Speculator as articles in the *Scots Magazine* in successive months in 1763. This first experience of the power an intelligent printer has to determine the shape of a published work quickly expands to become a primary factor in keeping Smellie happy – at least periodically – in his otherwise very demanding trade. After leaving the *Scots Magazine*, Smellie carried two lessons from this experience through the rest of his printing career: first, that periodical publications afforded a printer his greatest source of power; and second, that the democratization of learning was a printer's primary obligation to the community he served. Smellie's subsequent efforts in contributing to the final shape of the first edition of Buchan's *Domestic Medicine* and his remarkable performance in compiling, writing and editing the first edition of the *Encyclopaedia Britannica* attest to his first lesson; the *Edinburgh Magazine & Review* would confirm the second.

Of course, Smellie's talents particularly predisposed him to seeing the printer's role as being akin to that of the author as a maker of books in the fullest sense of that term. Smellie might more easily (and certainly more profitably) have enhanced his position as a printer by assuming the title and responsibility of publisher. That was the route preferred by most of his contemporary eighteenth-century printers who showed any ambition. Certainly Smellie had the friendly example (and encouragement) of William Strahan to follow, and he could observe the more competitive success of Alexander and James Donaldson among others in Edinburgh. But if Smellie fully appreciated the professionalization of the business of books in his unhappy dealing at various times with Bell & MacFarquhar, Strahan & Cadell, and William Creech, his temperament was disinclined that way. Authorship not entrepreneurship sustained his energies and fed his imagination, and while he cared passionately for literary ideas, he cared very little about literary properties. In fact, an examination of William Smellie's book-trade correspondence would suggest that he thought it the role of printers to antagonize their business partners. Each of Smellie's printing partnerships ends rancorously; it is only because of the trade's grudging acknowledgement of his skills and his specialist knowledge of languages, science and medicine that he moves on so easily to new arrangements despite his reputation. Smellie's bad faith broke Robert Auld's health; William Auld never forgave Smellie for his attempts to undermine the *Edinburgh Weekly Journal*; John Balfour believed that Smellie had promoted William Creech over him as bookseller to the Society of Antiquaries of Scotland; and Creech and Smellie ended their union, as John Murray had predicted, among the lawyers.[9] Even Murray complains in a letter written in 1778 that he has heard rumours that Smellie is 'no longer my friend but has turned my enemy'.[10] While both Balfour and Creech proved in their own ways difficult partners, the former in his lack of ambition in business, the latter in his excess of it, Smellie was from the beginning withholding at his best and destructively mischievous at his worst in all his partnerships. As a writer, Smellie always believed that the arousal of suspicion in a reader was fundamental to the pursuit of truth; unfortunately, he aroused the same feeling as a businessman.

At a distance, Smellie's behaviour is not without its lighter side. In 1787, as his relationship with Creech worsened, Smellie published a satiric poem in Latin with Scriblerian English commentary directed at a squabble in Edinburgh over improvements to the High Street.[11] Smellie co-wrote the piece with Charles Little and took the opportunity to slyly lampoon Creech through a crucial reference in one of the mock footnotes to the authors from Creech's most recent advertisement of new titles for sale. He then went one step further by promoting Charles Elliot's sales list in a subsequent footnote.[12] Some twenty years earlier, William Auld drew attention to Smellie's penchant for fiction-making both in the firm's Ledgers and in the newspaper they were printing for John Balfour; writing on 30 April 1770, he says:

I have just read your Paragraph in the Journal concerning Bowed Joseph and his Procession, which indeed is diverting enough if it brings no reflections; but no doubt you know the facts and can best know upon what grounds they are founded. If there was a <u>real</u> procession, what meanness not to take notice of it. If it is altogether imaginary, I hope you know from whom you got the Paragraph.[13]

William Auld's letter is prescient in many ways about Smellie's career. He identifies two serious problems here: first, that Smellie may have been too political in the naming of a notorious mob leader and thus giving credibility to a mob action, a journalistic gesture which might bring 'reflections' from important readers. But the second concern raises the possibility that Smellie has invented the whole episode, a manufacture all the more politically dangerous for being a fiction. As a writer and as a printer, Smellie liked to stir things up. He considered the virtue of History as a literary genre to be 'not the mere recital of facts' but rather narrations 'of that important kind which agitate and interest the mind'.[14] Smellie goes on to observe that 'events of this nature [ie that agitate the mind] do not frequently occur in history... It is not therefore surprising that we often find a difficulty in keeping our attention awake when reading history' (p 63). He concludes with this observation: 'History never interests us agreeably, unless we contract an attachment to some important causes, or to some distinguished characters' (p 64). This is a romantic sense of history with its notion of the great man and the noble cause, but more than this, it is a political definition of narrative and language. Smellie goes on to remark that while 'the most important end of history is to promote liberty and virtue' yet 'the circumstances which accompany all great events are so complicated, and the inconsistencies of human characters are so various, that a writer of ingenuity is enabled to place them in any point of view he chooses' (pp 64–5). Even more than romantic, this, Smellie's ultimate view of history, is also radical. It allocates a dangerous degree of power to the interpretation of historic events without diminishing the significance of those events. And to hold such views, as Smellie did, is to acknowledge and embrace the role of an effective public press in bringing about social improvement. Such a press should not be swayed in Smellie's words, 'by an affected fear of the laws, or a pretended delicacy with regard to established opinions' since 'we cannot confute a hurt, or answer an objection, that is not explicitly stated' (p 65). These somewhat liberal political notions about the power of language and narrative are very much rooted in what Smellie values most about natural science, namely the need to confront all systems with doubt. This he states directly as a credo in his notes for his *Philosophy of Natural History*:

> I only wish to render certain theories suspicious that the mind may have full liberty to examine some parts of the oeconomy of Nature that were formerly thought to be well known or exhausted.[15]

This operative relationship between suspicion and liberty is what separates science from theology in Smellie's mind, and causes the physician to eclipse the priest. All histories then, whether narrative, moral, philosophical or natural, are united and energized by their need to raise suspicions and be sceptical of any and all, but especially, of received truths. Finally, for Smellie the problem with an adherence to systematic truths is in the eventual need to justify the system that represents the truth so that in Smellie's words,

> under the plausible pretence of a regard to truth, and of being superior to vulgar prejudices, [one] may render the best cause doubtful, and the most respectable characters ambiguous.[16]

If the best writing, to Smellie's way of thinking, seeks to agitate and to create suspicion by way of provoking insight, understanding, and improvement, then the printer not the publisher or bookseller is the author's nearest ally. The crucial point of distinction here for Smellie is proprietorship. The printer facilitates the appearance of the author's work by rendering it accessible to the world without obvious vested interest. This is not the case with the publisher/bookseller. Smellie's business correspondence throughout his printing career is full of evidence for this distinction. From his first disagreement with Bell & MacFarquhar over the format of the *Encyclopaedia Britannica* in 1767, through his arguments with the Auld brothers over the *Weekly Journal* in 1771, to his disagreements with the Earl of Buchan over how far to go in antagonizing the University of Edinburgh and the Royal Society of Edinburgh in his *Account of the History of the Society of Antiquaries of Scotland* in 1782, Smellie finds himself coming up against the greatest resistance when he confronts, as a printer, ownership and vested interests. These experiences gave him a particular empathy for Robert Burns in his various clashes with Creech and Thomson over his poems and songs, and there is a nice symbolism in the appearance of Burns's most controversial work, *The Merry Muses of Caledonia*, under the liberated auspices of Smellie's Crochallan Fencibles.[17]

Still perhaps the best example of the political courage and commercial naivety of Smellie's idea of the role of the printer in an enlightened society is the publication history of the *Edinburgh Magazine & Review*. For in that instance Smellie the author found himself allied in Gilbert Stuart with a man who carried the concept of the writer as antagonist to its extreme;[18] while Smellie the printer was partnered in John Murray with a publisher and bookseller who understood the commerce of literary property better than any of Smellie's previous partners. Indeed, Murray seems fully to have understood how Smellie's politics affected his printing, an insight that appears everywhere in Murray's correspondence with Smellie and nowhere in Smellie's correspondence with any of his other business partners. In fact, in a letter to Smellie dated 28 January 1775, Murray chides Smellie for letting his time be taken up with the printing of pamphlets on town politics which generate no income, and were usually printed by Smellie entirely at his own cost, while he neglected to fulfil his contractual responsibilities for the printing of the *Medical Commentaries*, which provided a guaranteed source of income. Murray is remarkably patient with Smellie over a period of years, as he watches Smellie put politics and satire ahead of income in the priorities he sets as a printer. Smellie is engaged by Murray to print a number of things along with the ongoing *Commentaries* including Dalrymple's *Annals*, but it is the printing and distribution of the *Edinburgh Magazine & Review* which gives rise to the majority of their correspondence. Typical of Murray's frustrations with Smellie is this letter dated 25 September 1775:

> The Mag for last month did not arrive at London till the 8th of this, consequently the market was over. I have your advice the succeeding Mag & viz for Sept are shipped the 13th. This is too late, & in all probability will incur the same fate of the last. It is impossible for me to remedy this neglect, and indeed for this spirit of carelessness your Mag has lost all credit here. You ought also to have sent the ship's receipt; but do not now attempt it being too late.
>
> Your Guinea shall be paid.

On 11 December of the same year, Murray writes to Smellie about David Dalrymple, Lord Hailes's *Annals*:

This is to entreat you will write me of the state of the 'Annals' by <u>return of Post</u>. You are acquainted that the publication is fixed for the 1st of January and must conceive that I remain very uneasy till I am advised that 300 Copies are shipped for me in Order to be at London on time.

This Matter is of importance to me and I flatter myself you will not neglect it. The book is already called for and the opening the sale favourably here depends a good deal upon your exactness and Punctuality.

Through the early months of 1776, in January, February, March and again in April, Murray writes repeatedly on the same subjects without response from Smellie, who is all that time caught up in writing and editing the *Edinburgh Magazine & Review*, dealing with lawsuits arising from the publication, and printing pamphlets on local politics.

Even when the *Edinburgh Magazine & Review* has folded after August 1776, Murray finds Smellie no more capable of putting business ahead of politics. Murray everywhere complains about Smellie's utter lack of understanding or sympathy in matters related to the business of books. In mid to late 1776, they have a complete misunderstanding about the meaning of copyright over the sale of Douglas's *Elements of Euclid*. Then, on 29 May 1777, Murray complains about Smellie's failure to list the appropriate booksellers and publishers on the title page of the *Commentaries*, writing:

> You can write fully in a Magazine or in a newspaper; but to a correspondent, who by the bye is of most importance to your interest, it is below you to attend... I pray you never write to me till you have <u>leisure</u>; for your <u>letters in haste</u> are seldom worth 6d. Written at leisure they may be worth Gold.

Later still, on 17 June 1777, Murray writes to Smellie describing his anxieties brought on by William Mason's prosecution of Murray for pirating, but he ends with this exasperated utterance: 'But why do I trouble you with <u>exuberances</u> who like them so little'. And what was Smellie doing that so captivated his attention, his pen, and his printing house: once again, it was a pamphlet war surrounding a new crisis with the town council and Sir Lawrence Dundas.[19]

In September Smellie would publish a clever broadsheet, in which he took on the identity of an Edinburgh shopkeeper with a gift for philosophy and six hungry children, ironically to attack Council mismanagement. In the pamphlet wars as in the *Edinburgh Magazine & Review*, Smellie was joined by

Gilbert Stuart, and together they pushed Smellie's ideas about the role of the printer to its limits. Both men wrote confrontational but critically brilliant reviews for their magazine, reviews that aroused continual discomfort in Edinburgh. Here Smellie put into practice his notion that the public press was charged with the responsibility to raise doubts and suspicions about received ideas. In the contexts of literary reviews this often meant *ad hominem* attacks since in Smellie's words,

> when an author has acquired the reputation of ability by public suffrage, he is apt to assume an air of self importance and to expect an equal measure of praise from all his subsequent publications. The task likewise of dissenting from the opinions of such an author or of taxing him with folly or bad writing or a deficiency either in taste or sentiment becomes more arduous and more ungracious.[20]

But, nonetheless, arduous and ungracious Smellie and Stuart were in their treatment of James Harris, Robert Henry and Lord Monboddo among many others.

In the correspondence Smellie exchanged in the aftermath of the Monboddo affair there is a curious letter to John Maclauren, Lord Dreghorn. Maclauren had written two abrupt notes to Smellie cancelling his subscription to the *Magazine & Review* on account of the scurrilous treatment of Monboddo's *Origins of Language*. The law lords uniformly supported their fellow, regardless of their private opinions about his learning, and Smellie lost the favour of both Lord Kames and Lord Hailes over this episode. But it is Smellie's explanation of his role as printer that makes the letter to Dreghorn of interest here. Robert Kerr in his *Memoirs of William Smellie* prints the text but suppresses this crucial paragraph:

> The question must arise; why print articles contrary to the conviction of your own mind, and contrary to the sentiments of your heart? Timidity and a desire to preserve a solemn engagement to publish the first of every month, is all I can plead. I was averse from breaking an engagement with gentlemen whom I respected, and to whose opinions I thought myself obliged to submit; and when articles were sent there was little time for altercations or disputes. A mind of more fortitude might, perhaps, have refused to print.[21]

Smellie's apologies elsewhere in the letter are fulsome and tend mostly to excuse Creech and Elliot by declaring their complete ignorance of the content of the *Review* prior to its appearing in their shops. He takes full responsibility as printer, offering as his only defence his sense of the utter obligation a printer has to fulfil his engagements with his authors without regard to personal sentiment or monetary interest. Smellie's tone in the letter is necessarily contrite and submissive: he depended upon Hailes and Kames as patrons and was a friend and regular supper guest of Monboddo. Dreghorn presents Smellie with a first opportunity to salvage what he can of those relationships. But when we recall that Smellie had himself been the first to arouse Monboddo's wrath when he attacked the pretentious use of classical learning and latinate jargon in his review of Harris's *Philosophical Arrangements,* and when we remind ourselves that Smellie together with Stuart had refused to print a review written by Hume because it was not direct enough in its critique of Robert Henry, the claim to 'timidity' Smellie makes in his defence before Dreghorn is hardly tenable. Still, it is remarkable that in the midst of this desperate attempt to save himself and his business from the consequences of the Monboddo scandal, Smellie pleads in his defence that it is the paramount role of a printer to honour the intent of the author and to meet the expectations of his reading public, even when his own financial security and proprietorship are at risk. And at any rate, despite the conciliatory tone of Smellie's rhetoric here, his behaviour elsewhere suggests that even in this instance he would have been fully complicit with Stuart's inflammatory intents. After all, Smellie was not averse to writing pseudonymous letters to pompous medical students or posing as a wool merchant to undermine a pamphlet attack by a Dunfermline Tory. As William Auld's earlier letter about Bowed Joseph and the mob suggested, Smellie was capable of employing whatever means were necessary to evoke passion through the Press.

In the *Edinburgh Magazine & Review,* Smellie together with Stuart defined the confrontational, ironic and satiric kind of criticism that would become the hallmark of the Scottish style in the *Edinburgh Review* and *Blackwood's Magazine.* And Smellie demonstrated with this periodical and his own pamphlets, especially the Scriblerian tour-de-force, 'Behold yon pair',[22] how a printer of courage and intelligence could make his political points in the journalistic press without sacrificing literary excellence. If Smellie began his career as a printer celebrated for his skills as a compositor and corrector, he had now achieved notoriety for his gifts as a disrupter and instigator. But to take on such roles cost Smellie much in terms of patronage from his betters and business from his colleagues, so that in 1781 he could write to William Strahan describing a business now chiefly dependent upon the printing of theses.[23]

Smellie began the 1780s where he had left off after the failure of the *Magazine & Review* in 1776 by using public platforms, and especially his own printing press to attack the establishment in an alliance with the Earl of Buchan as a cofounder of the Society of Antiquaries of Scotland. He also firmly established himself as a force in natural history with his two great works, the translation of Buffon and the *Philosophy of Natural History* and published his most important pamphlet work on the power of juries.[24] However, despite a partnership with William Creech through most of the decade, Smellie suffered as a printer. By 1790 he was owed extensive sums from both Charles Elliot and Creech, which for quite different reasons he was unable to collect in his lifetime. The number of printers in Edinburgh had greatly increased and the old conventions of business under which Smellie had entered the trade had long since disappeared. The book business had become a source of great wealth for some of the Edinburgh booksellers and of mass employment for others in the trade, a state roundly acknowledged in Smellie's *Address to the Journeyman Printers of Edinburgh on behalf of their Masters*. The significant role Smellie had played in the 1760s and 1770s as a simple printer could not be repeated in this new industrial and business environment. Still, the political power of the printer in the periodical press, a role much cherished and developed by Smellie continued, especially in the Reform movements. We should note here that in 1788 Smellie drew up with Charles Elliott a proposal for a newspaper called the *Scottish Chronicle* to be edited and printed by Smellie. As in the case of the *Edinburgh Magazine & Review,* the *Chronicle* was to be unabashedly Scottish in its approach and content. As Smellie writes in the Prospectus, the 'one great object of the Scottish Chronicle is to make us acquainted with our own country'.[25] The newspaper was intended to pay especially close attention to 'Parliamentary proceedings and other national objects'. It was clearly to be a Whig publication inclined toward instigation.

Of course, where a printer like Smellie conceives of his role as political then, while he may often effect public reform, he will seldom achieve private fortune.

Proprietorship gets in the way of risk-taking and Smellie's well-known aversion to being a publisher or bookseller was a necessary prerequisite to being the sort of printer he aspired to be. Were he a bookseller and not a printer he would never have been capable of the extraordinary achievements of the *Edinburgh Magazine & Review*, because he would have thought more as John Murray did, and been predisposed to praise Monboddo and prosper.

NOTES

1. See Robert Kerr's account of Smellie's early years in *Memoirs of the Life, Writings and Correspondence of William Smellie*, 2 vols (Edinburgh, 1811; reprinted Bristol, 1996); and Alexander Smellie's manuscript account of his father's life in the archives of the Society of Antiquaries of Scotland, National Museums of Scotland Library.

2. Kerr, *Memoirs*, 1, 28–30; see also Brian Hillyard, 'The Edinburgh Society's Silver Medals for Printing', *Papers of the Bibliographical Society of America*, 78 (1984), 295–319.

3. 'Manuscript papers of William Smellie', edited by Stephen W Brown (National Museums of Scotland Library), Book-trade documents, 6 September 1795.

4. Smellie MSS, Familiar correspondence: Dr William Buchan.

5. Smellie MSS, Familiar correspondence: William Tod; Samuel Charteris. See also a list of works issued by Hamilton, Balfour, & Neill during the years of Smellie's apprenticeship in Warren McDougall, *Spreading the Word: the Distribution Networks of Print, 1559–1850*, edited by Robin Myers & Michael Harris (Winchester, 1990), 187–232.

6. Smellie MSS, Familiar correspondence: Maria Riddell, 16 October 1792.

7. Smellie MSS, Other writing: item 11.

8. William Smellie, 'Preface', *The History of Man: or, the Wonders of Human Nature*, 2 vols (Edinburgh, 1790).

9. Smellie MSS, Book-trade correspondence.

10. 'Letter-books', John Murray Archives, 1 December 1778. All subsequent quotations are taken from the letter-books for 1774–1779. Dates are given in the text.

11. 'Streetum Edinense', Kerr, *Memoirs*, 2, 230.

12. See *Edinburgh Advertiser*, 19 January and 17 April 1787.

13. Smellie MSS, Book-trade correspondence.

14. William Smellie, *Literary and Characteristical Lives* (Edinburgh, 1800; reprinted Bristol, 1997), 63.

15. Smellie MSS, Natural history.

16. Smellie, *Lives*, 65.

17. It is likely that *The Merry Muses* was printed by Alexander Smellie and distributed to the Fencibles, who disbanded after William Smellie's death, in memory of the ribald friendship shared by Burns and William Smellie.

18. William Zachs, *Without Regard to Good Manners: a Biography of Gilbert Stuart* (Edinburgh, 1992), 63–95.

19. *Edinburgh Magazine & Review*, 5 vols (Edinburgh, 1773–6; reprinted Bristol, 1998), 2 (October 1774), 722–8.

20. See article on James Harris in *Edinburgh Magazine & Review*, 4 (July 1775), 426–33.

21. Smellie MSS, General correspondence: Lord Dreghorn, November 1776.

22. Smellie MSS, Other writing: item 1.

23. Smellie MSS, Book-trade correspondence: William Strahan.

24. William Smellie, *An Address to the People of Scotland on the Nature, Powers, and Privileges of Juries by a Juryman* (Edinburgh, 1784); see also Smellie MSS, Other writing: item 12.

25. Smellie MSS, Other writing: items 8 & 9.

William Buchan's Domestic Medicine: *Laying Book History Open*

RICHARD B SHER

ETWEEN ITS ORIGINAL PUBLICATION in 1769 and the author's death in
B 1805, William Buchan's *Domestic Medicine* averaged a new authorized
edition every two years or so, all but the first in London, and all with large print
runs of two to six thousand copies. It was frequently reprinted in Dublin and
America, and by the turn of the century unauthorized editions were common
in London, too. Translated into French, Spanish, Russian, and other European languages, it continued to enjoy global popularity until well into the nineteenth century. As the preeminent medical advice book of its day, *Domestic
Medicine* gained Buchan a gold medallion from Catherine the Great and a
privileged burial in Westminster Abbey, and it earned a great deal of money for
its publishers.[1]

As it passed through eighteen authorized editions during Buchan's lifetime,
the book underwent considerable change. The first edition of 1769, printed in
Edinburgh by Buchan's friend William Smellie of the firm Balfour, Auld &
Smellie, was already a large octavo of more than six hundred pages. From the
second edition of 1772 onwards, *Domestic Medicine* was printed in London
with a new subtitle and a higher price (7s.6d neatly bound instead of 5s
stitched in blue covers) by a group of publishers in London (William Strahan
and Thomas Cadell sr, later succeeded by Andrew Strahan and the firm of
Thomas Cadell jr & William Davies, respectively) and Edinburgh (John
Balfour, and the firm of Alexander Kincaid & William Creech, giving way to
Creech alone after the second edition). It kept getting fatter as the author
added and revised various types of front matter, an appendix, a glossary, an index, new textual material on topics such as venereal disease, and completely
new chapters on sea-bathing and mineral waters (1786, expanded 1803), and
on the diet of the common people (1797). To the eighth edition of 1784
Buchan added some sixty-four new or substantially revised footnotes, and in
the eighteenth edition of 1803 he augmented most chapters with additional
text. In order to accommodate these changes, the publishers added five lines

to the page in 1790 and three more, along with more characters to the line, in 1803. Even so, the 1803 edition was well over 750 pages long, and strained the limits of the one-volume octavo format.

A perennial best-seller with such a rich bibliographical record of book editions and printing information is a book historian's delight, and this article might well have been devoted solely to that subject. Instead, I want to focus here on the importance of going beyond the bibliographical record whenever the sources permit. As much as bibliography, in the broadest sense of that term, can tell us about the making, selling, and collecting of books, and as vital as it is for that reason, it is constrained by its inability, except in rare instances, to humanize the study of book history. By this I mean showing how stories about books are also stories about authors, readers, and members of the book trade, seen as flesh-and-blood individuals with their own interests, aspirations, motives, strengths, and weaknesses. For an eighteenth–century book, rendering book stories as human stories almost always depends on a single type of source which is not always available, private correspondence. Fortunately, in the case of Buchan's *Domestic Medicine*, the epistolary record is as full and varied as the bibliographical one, and it enables us to transcend the bibliographical record in ways that I shall now attempt to explore.

There exist at least four contemporary varieties of private correspondence having to do with *Domestic Medicine*. First, there are the letters from the 1760s that William Buchan sent to his Edinburgh friend William Smellie, whose personality and career are skilfully analysed in the article by Stephen Brown elsewhere in this volume. As an experienced copy-editor and printer with a medical education, Smellie was an ideal person to prepare Buchan's manuscript for the press. Buchan paid him £100 to edit, and especially to cut down, a bulky text he had prepared in England, where he was employed at the Foundling Hospital in Ackworth, Yorkshire, and subsequently practised privately in Sheffield.[2] The Buchan-Smellie correspondence reveals much about Buchan's motives and tactics in the years leading up to the publication of *Domestic Medicine*. What comes through above all is Buchan's awareness of the commercial aspects of his endeavour. In the same letter (undated but probably written in 1765) in which he offers Smellie the job of editing his manuscript on an undisclosed topic, Buchan says he is about to open a subscription with a view to publishing the book in weekly numbers, first in Sheffield, and then perhaps in London and Edinburgh. Teasing his friend about his high expectations for his book, he observes 'You certainly think I am very vain of my performance; but you will find that I am not so vain a parent as you may imagine; *only I think I have hit upon something that will sell*' (Kerr, 1, 260; emphasis added). By 15 December 1765 Buchan had given up the scheme of publishing in weekly numbers on account of 'the vast Expence and Trouble that I saw would attend the distribution' of such an edition and decided instead upon a proper book edition, to be published by subscription, in Edinburgh or Sheffield rather than London because of lower printing costs in those towns. From this letter it is clear that Buchan had previously asked Smellie to calculate a comprehensive price for producing ten thousand copies stitched in blue paper covers – an extraordinarily high number which obviously caused Smellie to recoil and Buchan himself to back off by noting that he was only asking for an estimate (Kerr, 1, 266). The very fact that Buchan was enquiring about a printing of that magnitude, however, shows that from the outset he conceived of his book as a commercial best–seller, and this point is confirmed by a newspaper advertisement claiming that he actually printed, and quickly sold in Scotland alone, more than five thousand copies of the first edition.[3]

In this letter Buchan also says that he is sending Smellie a copy of his 'proposals' in order to launch the subscription campaign, meaning presumably *Proposals for Printing by Subscription an Original Work, Intitled, The Family Physician . . . by William Buchan, M.D.* (Sheffield, 1765).[4] And he discusses in some detail the availability and cost of paper (which he considers 'the grand article' in planning the work), and the size of the print and the layout of the book, remarking that if a pica letter is used 'the pages must be as full as possible', and wondering if Smellie thinks it right to have 'forty lines in the page, and fifty letters in the line' (Kerr, 1, 267–8; Smellie Papers). In a subsequent undated letter from the late 1760s, Buchan goes on at length about the marketing of the book, explaining how he manages the subscription campaign in order to create incentives among his selling agents, cajoling Smellie to try to persuade students in Edinburgh to commit to six copies for sale to others in order to get a seventh one free for themselves, requesting that Smellie 'take particular care to recommend it to the Clergy', and revealing that, although he generally tells people that the book 'will be out next Spring', he actually believes it will be advantageous to delay publication 'as long as we can' (Kerr, 1, 270–2).

Does all this attention to the making and marketing of *Domestic Medicine* in his pre-publication letters to Smellie signify that Buchan cared *only* about the commercial success of his book, and that the professions of concern for improving people's health that appear in his prefaces and introductions are mere window dressing? Not at all. The letter to Smellie of 15 December 1765 that is so largely devoted to delineating Buchan's technical and commercial plans for publishing his book also contains the following passage, in which Buchan finally reveals the nature of his book to Smellie:

> You seem to have a strong inclination to know my Subject and indeed I think it is hardly friendly to keep you in the dark about that, but there is not room now to say much about it, only in general, I shall tell you that it is a medical Performance calculated for general use and is something in the manner of Dr Tyssot's *advice to the People* but upon a more general Plan and will, I hope, be more extensively useful. I am so far come to the cool part of life as to begin to look upon Publications which are not calculated for the Benefit of mankind as a Prostitution of Talents, an abuse of Time, and a gross Imposition. (Kerr, 1, 267)

Similarly, in the undated letter that discusses various marketing ploys, Buchan observes that

> My Plan, in one word, pray God prosper it, is this – To put Mankind on their guard against diseases by pointing out their Causes and likewise to show them how far it is in their own power to remove slight Disorders by the use of simple Remedies. (Kerr, 1, 270)

Of course, this rhetoric about 'the Benefit of mankind' in Buchan's pre-publication letters to Smellie does not necessarily establish the truthfulness of similar pronouncements in the front matter of the various editions of *Domestic Medicine*. Authors can deceive their friends, or for that matter themselves, as easily as they can deceive their readers. But the fact that Buchan consistently expressed such enlightened motives in private correspondence with a friend strengthens the probability that he meant it when he published similar sentiments. Nor are these public and private professions of humanitarianism incompatible with his private expressions of ambition and anxiety about printing and marketing. Like many an author before and after him, Buchan seems to have been motivated by a mixture of lofty ideals about the value of his work and equally high hopes about achieving best-seller status.

Buchan's letters to Smellie also contain hints about why Buchan turned to professional publishers in London after privately printing the first edition in Edinburgh. Managing a large subscription publication was an exceedingly taxing operation for an author. Although in theory an edition of more than 5000 copies could have grossed at least £1250 from subscriptions and retail sales at five shillings each, that figure does not look so impressive when one considers the various expenses and difficulties that were involved in an edition of this kind. Buchan told Smellie that he was paying his subscription agents a shilling per copy, which is to say, twenty per cent of the subscription price, and that if he thought he could trust the agent he would pay him half that amount in advance, with the remaining 6d to be paid when the agent delivered the book (Kerr, 1, 271). Thus, if a subscriber (or an agent) failed to honour his commitment, Buchan could be out not only the expected five shillings but perhaps also the sixpence he had paid the agent in advance; a circumstance of this kind apparently strained relations with Smellie, who was required by Buchan to cover the cost of delinquent subscriptions he had procured (Kerr, 1, 263). Buchan also had to cover a host of other expenses, including all the printing costs and whatever profit the firm of Balfour, Auld & Smellie received for its trouble;[5] the enormous cost of the paper, which he had announced in his *Proposals* would be a 'fine Demy'; the cost of books given gratis to subscribers who purchased six copies; the cost of warehousing unsold or undelivered copies; the cost of the large number of advertisements that appeared in Scottish newspapers (I have located seven of them in the *Edinburgh Evening Courant* alone between 10 May and 20 September 1769); the £100 that Smellie received for editing the work; the cost of printing and distributing the sixteen-page *Proposals*; and the considerable amount of time and effort that he himself or a paid agent had to expend on managing the entire undertaking. It therefore seems unlikely that the author earned more than a few hundred pounds from the first edition of his book despite its extensive sales. Moreover, for all his effort and success, Buchan had not begun to tap the vast potential market for his book in England, for which London publication and distribution was practically a necessity.

A second group of letters, from Buchan to the London printer-publisher William Strahan, carries the story further. At present I have located five of Buchan's letters to Strahan, all written between 1771 and 1778, largely for the purpose of reporting on Buchan's progress on revisions for upcoming editions of *Domestic Medicine*. For example, from the earliest of these letters, dated 21 December 1771, we learn that Strahan was responsible for changing the subtitle of the second edition; that Buchan rejected Strahan's suggestion to dedicate the book to the king, 'especially as I intend to do that soon' in another work (more on this other work later), and decided to dedicate it to Sir John Pringle instead; that Buchan opposed the idea of packaging the book in two volumes; that Buchan was sending Strahan new material on venereal disease for the second edition; and that the rest of Buchan's revisions would soon be sent to London.[6] Information of this kind is useful for piecing together the revision process, with which Strahan seems to have been very much involved.

But the value of the Buchan-Strahan correspondence goes well beyond its usefulness for reconstructing textual revisions. In a letter of 11 February 1773, written after the success of the second edition of 1772 had called forth a third edition that the author was then preparing, Buchan goes on at length about his desire to reduce the size of the type from 'a large pica without scabbarding' (*ie* leading) to 'a small pica with a pretty thick scabbard'. If this were done, he tells Strahan, 'I should have an opportunity of improving the Book and you of reducing the price a little, which would both make the sale more general and likewise prevent pirating'. The retail cost of the book was a matter of special concern because Buchan believed that 'the price is rather too high for Scotland', especially in the current bad economic climate, and he begged Strahan to reduce it to seven shillings. He suggested that by using the same print size as the one Strahan had employed in the octavo edition of David Hume's *History of England*, the third edition of *Domestic Medicine* 'might be reduced to less than three fourths of its present size; and as it is not so much calculated for being read as consulted there would seem to be the less occasion for a large letter'.[7] Here we learn how the author conceptualized the use of his book by readers: less as a volume to be read from beginning to end than as a reference work to be consulted. We see that Buchan continued to take great interest in the printing, publishing, and marketing details of his book, and continued his concern with making the book available at a low price. There is more of the same in a letter to Strahan of 24 April 1773, where Buchan goes on for pages about the format ('I think it a matter of some importance'; 'I hate to see print crowded'), the desirability of lowering the price, the form of the 'Family Dispensatory' of medicines he is adding as an appendix, and his affirmative response to Strahan's suggestion that headings be introduced to the long opening chapters ('I think the more a book is broken into sections by such lines as you propose the better. Provided such divisions be not too frequent and affected they give a lightness to the Book, an ease to the Reader and have many good effects').[8]

In the second half of his letter of 11 February 1773, Buchan discusses the unexpected death of his friend Dr John Gregory, professor of medicine at the University of Edinburgh, who had passed away in his sleep two nights earlier. 'Our very souls seemed to have been cast in the same mould', he writes. He goes on to imply that Gregory had often told him that he was his choice as successor in the chair, as well as to report that 'in the very last conversation we had together he expressed a peculiar satisfaction in finding that we were both engaged in the same Plan, viz, rendering the medical art more generally useful'. Historians of medicine and medical ethics have noted the Gregory-Buchan connection on this issue, and particularly the fact that Buchan may have lifted from Gregory the phrase 'laying medicine open'.[9] Buchan's letter to Strahan reveals the private side of that connection. Not only does Buchan say that he was 'shocked' into speechlessness, and made 'quite stupid', by Gregory's death, but he also asserts that this event destroyed any chance he might have had for an academic chair in Edinburgh. 'Few very few of the Faculty view medicine in the same extensive light as he did', he observes, and with his passing 'I have lost almost the only true friend I had in the University'. Buchan's fears proved correct, for in May 1773 he lost his bid for the institutes or theory of medicine chair, and the following autumn he appears to have made an unsuccessful try for the natural philosophy chair.[10] By the time he writes to Strahan on 12 November 1774, Buchan is preparing to go to London, believing 'I have few temptations to stay here. All access to the College will be deny'd me as long as a certain Professor who wants to conceal Physick lives'.[11] The professor was undoubtedly William Cullen, who was not only Gregory's opponent on the issue of 'open' medicine, but also Buchan's bitter enemy for having publicly challenged the authenticity of some of the facts in *Domestic Medicine*.[12] It is interesting to note, at any rate, that for Buchan personal and ideological opposition are indistinguishable, and the whole medical profession is classifiable into those who want to reveal its truths and those who wish to conceal them.

While accepting that Gregory's death would have dire consequences for his academic aspirations, Buchan held out hope for securing another of Gregory's offices, as one of his majesty's physicians. Although the salary is 'small', he tells Strahan (it was actually £100 per annum), this position 'would be a great object to me as it is a feather in the cap of an Author and might be a step to further Preferment'. In the second edition of *Domestic Medicine*, Buchan identifies himself on the title page as 'William Buchan, M.D., Of the Royal College of Physicians, Edinburgh' instead of the simple 'William Buchan, M.D.' that adorns the title page of the first edition; the new affiliation derived from his having become a licentiate of the Royal College of Physicians on 6 August 1771. After his election as a fellow of the Royal College of Physicians on 3 November 1772, he inserted the word 'Fellow' after 'M.D.' in the third edition of 1774, and that is how the title page of every authorized edition identified him for the rest of his life, and beyond. No doubt he would have wished to enhance his status further with the additional title 'Physician to His Majesty', which appeared on the title pages of Gregory's books, and which might have increased the sales of *Domestic Medicine* by improving its author's personal stature as a physician.

Buchan's letter to Strahan of 11 February 1773 contains a remarkable offer concerning this office:

> I make no doubt but your interest joined to that of my worthy Patron Sir John Pringle would be sufficient to obtain that honour for me, in which case you will not only lay me under infinite obligations but I will and hereby do promise to make over to you and yours the sole property of my Domestic medicine without asking any Price for the same in Testimony of my gratitude and in return for your kindness and trouble. May I beg of you to consider seriously of this matter, and, if you think it can be done, not to lose a moment, as there will be numerous applications and very probably the first who applies will obtain it.

It is not known if Strahan refused this offer or simply could not deliver his part of the bargain (the office went to Cullen). On the basis of this passage, however, we may infer that Buchan had not signed over the whole copyright of *Domestic Medicine* to Strahan and his publishing partners in 1770, when they paid him £500 for the right to reprint a revised edition in London,[13] even though it is difficult to imagine their paying him that much money without some assurances in regard to later editions. The two men continued to negotiate about this matter in 1774, and finally reached an agreement, for in his letter to Strahan of 12 November Buchan writes 'I accept your offer of 100 copies of every edition, which indeed I would not have requested had it not been to oblige my friends, and, I speak my real sentiments when I say, to promote your interest'. As a gentleman-physician with a private practice, Buchan apparently felt the need to maintain a façade of aloofness about the compensation he was to receive for *Domestic Medicine*.

These letters to Strahan raise another major theme in regard to Buchan's future career as an author: his plans to write a new book (or another volume of *Domestic Medicine*) called at various times 'Political Medicine' or 'Preventive Medicine', which would be dedicated to the King. Since no such book ever appeared, it cannot be studied through the bibliographic record or the account books, catalogues, and advertisements of booksellers and printers. Even Buchan's known letters to Strahan contain little more than vague hints about it. Fortunately, we can learn more about Buchan's projected second volume – and much else, too – by examining a third major category of personal correspondence relating to Buchan and *Domestic Medicine*, the surviving letters of William Strahan to William Creech, who took over the business of his senior partner, Alexander Kincaid, in 1773.[14] In these letters Strahan, who was something of a father-figure to his younger associate in Edinburgh, discusses the various cooperative book projects that he and Cadell were pursuing with Creech during the 1770s and early 1780s. Some of Strahan's remarks about *Domestic Medicine* are interesting simply because they show how these publishing partners exchanged information about their authors and editions. For example, on 17 January 1774 Strahan writes 'Dr Buchan's 3d Edition is now published, of which a number shall be sent you by the first ship for Leith. He has been long in preparing it; but I hope it will be found much improved.'

Other references to Buchan in Strahan's letters to Creech are more reveal-ing. In a letter of 9 September 1774, written shortly after offering Buchan one hundred copies of each new edition, Strahan tries to soothe Creech's anxiety about giving the author so many books:

> Dr. Buchan we must not differ with for a few Books. His constant Correc-tions will merit such a Present, and tend much as well to the Preservation of the Property as to the Sale of it. As he asks them, in order to *price away*, I imagine he will think it beneath him to [take?] Money for any of them. This, however, you will give an Eye to. I think with you, the Size and Price should remain as it is.

Strahan's strategy is clear. He is willing to give Buchan one hundred copies of each new edition as payment for the author's revisions, not only in order to boost sales but, equally important, in order to enable the publishing partners to extend their copyright with each new edition. Buchan himself had pro-posed changing the type and lowering the price as a way of preventing pirat-ing, but Strahan rejects that option in favour of a plan based on continual revision. In February 1774 the House of Lords had finally struck down the principle of perpetual copyright that Strahan and Cadell had fought zealously to establish on common-law grounds, and in June the so-called 'booksellers bill' that was designed to bring some relief to London copyright owners like themselves had died in the Lords. Henceforth legal copyright was to last be-tween fourteen and twenty-eight years (depending on the duration of the au-thor's life), as set down in the Statute of Anne, or Copyright Act of 1710. Continual revision was one way to circumvent the copyright law, for by the time the copyright of the first edition expired, a book could be so completely transformed by revisions that it would become, in effect, a new entity.

The long-term success of Strahan's copyright strategy is evident from re-marks in the manuscript copy of the inventory of William Creech's copyrights sold to the Edinburgh trade after Creech's death in January 1815:

> Buchan's Domestic Medicine – The early editions have been common property for some years, but the author made additions to every successive edition to the time of his death in 1805 and since that time his Son (the present Dr. B.) has edited and improved the Proprietors' editions. The vari-ous additions possess considerable value as Copyright.[15]

A letter to Creech of 4 July 1776 leaves no doubt that the complimentary book arrangement with Buchan, which was retroactive to the second edition of 1772, was intended by Strahan as payment for revisions: 'I return you the Account of Books delivered to Dr. Buchan. You know the Dr. was to have 100 Books *out of every Impression which he revised*' (emphasis added). But our understanding of the agreement is complicated by the fact that on 12 March 1779 Strahan tells Creech that the publishing partners had agreed to give Buchan £50 'upon every Impression', implying later in the same letter that the agreement to provide him with one hundred books from each impression was in lieu of cash.

Creech had apparently expressed some concern about Buchan cutting into his own sales by selling his complimentary copies for profit in Edinburgh. At first Strahan doubted this would happen, since Buchan had told him he wanted the copies to oblige friends who would presumably receive them gratis, as well as (we later learn) patients, who were expected to buy them from him privately. But Creech continued to complain, first about the number of books Buchan was claiming as compensation, and then, more seriously, about Buchan wholesaling his copies to the trade in Edinburgh for less than Creech's own wholesale price. In a reply of 12 March 1779, Strahan observes that

> the Dr... I should imagine is rather pushed for Money, otherwise he would not act in regard to his Book as you tell me he does. It is his own Loss, not ours, if he undersells his Book, which I see not how we can prevent, unless by giving him the £50 in money; and even then he will get into our Debt, you see, by asking us for a Number of the Books which I do not see how we can prevent.

Two months later he adds:

> I must refer you to Mr Cadell in regard to Dr Buchan. He has had already from him more Books than he is entitled to; so the Books he has had from you cannot be charged either to his [Cadell's] Account or mine. As for myself, I have no Account whatever with him; and I heartily agree with you, that it is prejudicial to the Sale, to let him have any Books at all; unless for Ready Money, as you tell me he sells them to the Trade at an under-Price. This he must do for a little present Cash; tho' he led Mr Cadell and me to imagine he sold them among his patients. (14 May 1779)

It is uncertain if the publishers began to pay Buchan in cash rather than kind after the sixth edition of 1779, although a reference in another of Strahan's letters, quoted below, implies that they did just that. Strahan's suspicions about Buchan having financial problems are certainly correct. It is something of a mystery why Buchan was never able to capitalize on the great success of *Domestic Medicine* by building up a lucrative medical practice after emigrating to London. He seems to have conducted his practice, such as it was, in the Chapter Coffeehouse. A long obituary that appeared in the *Gentleman's Magazine* in March 1805 speculates that his sociability, and particularly his fame as a conversationalist and teller of anecdotes, 'probably prevented him from attaining that degree of eminence, as a practitioner of physick, which his address and manners, as well as his popular reputation, were, in other respects, well calculated to command'. A later account is more straightforward: 'His success might have been considerably greater but for his convivial habits'. A contemporary remarked that Buchan was known for prescribing a glass of punch, or else brandy and water, and then adding 'if one glass won't do, call for a second'.[16] Given his humanitarian values and convivial nature, it is not surprising that Buchan became a freemason in London, joining the Royal Somerset House and Inverness Lodge on 11 February 1782.[17]

In this way Buchan passed the closing decades of his life in London, more sociable than industrious. He did publish a work on venereal disease in 1796, but the description of it in his obituary is telling: 'Plain and practical axioms, for the amusement of some leisure hours at the Chapter coffee-house, wherein much of his time was spent, and containing a great deal of wholesome advice'.[18] In 1803 Buchan produced *Advice to Mothers on the Subject of their Own Health, and on the Means of Promoting the Health, Strength, and Beauty of their Offspring*, which Andrew Strahan and Cadell & Davies published as a large six-shilling octavo. Both these works were the size of books but had the character of long pamphlets, in that they focused on practical solutions to a narrow range of medical problems and were filled with anecdotes drawn from Buchan's personal experiences as a physician.

Another clue to Buchan's final days in London appears in a letter that his son Alexander, a physician in his own right, wrote to his cousin James Buchan on 20 March 1805, shortly after his father's death:

He was buried in Westminster Abbey on the 6th of March, where it is my intention to erect a small monument to his memory, as he was a man whose reputation will probably be greater now that he is gone, than it was ever during his life. He has left no property behind him, except some contingent profits on future editions of the domestic medicine. This to me is no disappointment as I did not expect any thing, tho' considering that my Mother brought him a decent fortune it is rather hard.[19]

Unable or unwilling to sustain a successful medical practice in London, William Buchan evidently lost his late wife's fortune and sank into something close to poverty. Perhaps that is why in 1790 he published a pamphlet endorsing a commercial product, *A Letter to the Patentee, Concerning the Medical Properties of the Fleecy Hosiery*, though Buchan himself defended that work on humanitarian grounds. Certainly the £50 that he continued to receive for each new edition of *Domestic Medicine* in cash or kind must have mattered a great deal to him. Towards the end of his life Buchan obtained another £300 when the copyright was renewed, as we learn from a letter from Andrew Strahan to Creech of 22 February 1803. In all, Buchan must have earned something of the order of £1500 from the Strahan publishing partnership for his famous book, counting the initial payment of £500, the 1803 renewal for £300, and the payments of either one hundred books or £50 that he received for every new edition.

Buchan's plan to write another book did not fare so well. We have seen that he had mentioned this scheme in a letter to Strahan as early as 21 December 1771, but nothing was done about it for some time. In 1776 he apparently contacted Creech about the project, for on 20 May of that year Strahan penned this reply to a letter from Creech (now apparently lost) of 13 May:

I know not what Idea Dr. Buchan may have of the Value of his new Work; but Mr Cadell and I have of late suffered so much by buying Gold too dear, that we shall, in future, be very cautious how we give large Sums for any Work whatever, the Merit of which is not well known, and the Subject popular. We shall, I suppose, soon hear of what the plan of it is, and what he demands for it.

By the latter part of 1778 Buchan was even more ambitious and enthusiastic about his projected book, as we learn from a letter he sent Strahan from Edinburgh, where he had gone to deliver scientific lectures:

I have desired my good friend Mr Cadell, whom I take to be an excellent
Judge of these matters, to write me his opinion concerning my intended
Publication. I have totally changed my Plan since I saw you. I intend to take
in every branch of the medical art, and to render my Book as extensively
useful and agreeable as the nature of the subject will admit.[20]

Imagining his new book as an expensive quarto, Buchan is now a long way
from the outspoken populist who had once tried to lower the retail price of *Domestic Medicine* below the already modest level of 7s. 6d. Interestingly, he now
phrases his ambition in highly personal terms: 'If you think my character will
support it, the Book ought certainly to be printed in two vol. quarto and sold at
two guineas. If not we must confine it to a smaller size'. Here a book's format
and price are viewed as reflections not merely of one's worth as an author but
of one's 'character' as a person; they are representations of the status of the
book's creator. Buchan appeals to Strahan and Cadell, as 'the best judges of
these matters', to make a determination about his true value.

There was only one problem, of course: Buchan's grandiose scheme could
only reach fruition if he actually wrote the great book he was planning and, as
Strahan and Cadell well knew, the chances of his ever doing so were growing
slimmer by the year. Why, then, did these shrewd publishers decide, in spite of
their reservations, to purchase Buchan's unwritten tome for £500? Their reasoning, as expressed in William Strahan's letter to Creech of 22 August 1781,
is worth quoting at length, because it constitutes the kind of cynical, behind-the-scenes account of a publication agreement that can only be acquired
from the letter of one bookseller to another:

As for Dr. Buchan I have hardly seen him since his Return here, nor do I
know in the least what he is doing. Mr Cadell and I agreed for his second
Volume [ie *Preventive Medicine*], and advanced him £100 of the
Copy-Money, purely to prevent him from disposing of it to any other of the
Trade, as in that Case he might have been tempted to insert in it the most
valuable Part of *our* Volume [ie *Domestic Medicine*], and by that means have
injured the Sale of it very naturally. Whereas now, should he never write a
Line of the second Vol. we can reimburse ourselves, in process of Time, by
withholding the £50 we give him on the Publication of every Edition. It has
been a good Copy to us, and is worth preserving, even at some extra
Expence.

Balfour has declined to go in on the deal, Strahan observes, but Creech is given the same opportunity, with this further explanation:

> £500 for an Octavo Volume is certainly a great Price, and I doubt whether he will ever write another that will deserve it; and yet I am perswaded that if ever he finishes a second Volume, the Success of the first has been so great, that I dare say the Sale will be more than sufficient to indemnify us even at that Price. I have stated the Matter precisely as it stands and as it appears to me; and, after all, you are at perfect Liberty, either to be concerned in it or not, as, after due Consideration, you shall think proper. I don't apprehend Dr. Cullens Work will much interfere with Buchan's, should the latter ever appear.

Note that Buchan's projected book is now being treated by the publishers as an octavo, not the two-volume quarto that the author had dreamed of writing.

As we learn from Strahan's next known letter, dated 4 October 1781, the contract for Buchan's new book stipulated that the author would receive £100 in advance, another £100 on publication of the book, and the remaining £300 a year after publication. The contract itself survives in the British Library and confirms these details; it also provides a better idea of Buchan's intention by showing the book's full title *Preventive Medicine, or the Means of Preserving Health to Extreme Old Age, adapted to the various situations of Mankind, with respect to Age, Sea, Climate, Constitution, Occupations, etc. To which are added, Observations on the Nature and Importance of a Proper Medical Police*.[21] Strahan repeats his assurances that 'if he never writes' the new book the publishers can recoup their investment on the advance from payments owed to Buchan for future editions of *Domestic Medicine*, all the while preventing the author 'from trafficking with any other Bookseller here about this 2nd Volume, which might have turned out greatly to our Prejudice'. Finally, on 18 October 1781 Strahan expresses himself even more bluntly: 'We never see Dr. Buchan, and I begin now to think he will never write this 2d Vol. And between ourselves I wish he never may'. To Strahan's horror, Buchan had used the £500 contract for his unwritten book as security against a £400 Scottish debt.[22]

If Strahan's letters to Creech give us the inside story from the publishers' standpoint, a fourth set of letters, from Buchan to his friend George Cumberland, provides the *author*'s private version of events. Cumberland was a man of the arts, and it expands our view of Buchan to find him regularly alluding to their mutual interests in painting and also in poetry, which Buchan apparently wrote for private circulation. Buchan's letters to Cumberland are also filled with allusions to business. 'One of the best pieces of news I can tell you is that 6000 copies of the domestic medicine have been sold in less than 12 months', he remarks in 1791, 'and that the book is sent to th[e] Press for a new edition today'.[23] Some parts of the correspondence discuss Buchan's involvement with marketing fleecy hosiery, which apparently irked some physicians, though Buchan himself justified his actions on humanitarian grounds that say a great deal about his own self-image:

From the Faculty I have nothing to fear. They have done their worst, and I hold them all in defiance. You have hit upon the only character which I would be proud to deserve viz, that of a true Philanthropist.[24]

Cumberland would have known that philanthropy was not the only thing on Buchan's mind, however. In an extraordinary letter of 1786, some five years after contracting with Strahan, Cadell, and Creech for *Preventive Medicine*, Buchan solicits Cumberland's aid in helping him to secure a loan of £50 (down from an initial request of £100) from a wealthy mutual friend, so that he will have the necessary resources for completing his new work. Incredibly, he claims to have already printed twelve sheets, or nearly 200 pages of the book. Of more interest for our purposes, he explains his request for a loan without ever mentioning that the book in question was already under contract, and he demonizes his booksellers in terms no less harsh than those they privately applied to him:

I could have the money I want from a Bookseller but not without giving him such a hold of the work as to deprive me of the future benefits arising from it; and I have every reason to believe that this work will not only free me from any little incumbrances, but enable me to pursue business in a manner very different from what I do at present. It is so calculated that every person who has the domestic medicine will buy it; in which case it will prove a little fortune to me.[25]

If not simply a scam, this passage means that Buchan knew the price of a loan from Strahan, Cadell, or Creech would be control over later editions of his projected second book, which he was unwilling to concede.

In 1796, at the conclusion of the Preliminary Observations prefixed to his *Observations Concerning Venereal Disease*, Buchan made his only public pronouncement about the book he had contracted to write fifteen years earlier. *Domestic Medicine* is now proclaimed 'a juvenile performance... in many things, defective', but 'as the book is now become too bulky to admit of any farther additions, they must appear in a separate volume' (xxxii). A footnote elaborates, although the details remain characteristically vague: the new book will be 'a second volume of the Domestic Medicine, by way of Appendix', which will contain 'many new articles' and 'the practical observations of above thirty years'. With a touch of melodrama, Buchan adds in the main text that completion of this projected work will ensure that his life has not been lived in vain. But the new book never appeared, as William Strahan had predicted, whereas *Domestic Medicine* remained a steady seller for some years to come.

Just as William Buchan sought to 'lay medicine open', so should our aim be to lay book history open by exposing its hidden dimensions. For in addition to being a text created by one or more authors and an artefact produced and marketed by various members of the book trade, every book contains a tale of contingent, complex, and often contested interactions among the people involved with it. In regard to eighteenth-century books, it is chiefly through the study of personal correspondence that we can learn about such things. The various letters discussed in this article show how an author who was both idealistic and ambitious achieved fame and substantial amounts of money from his popular book; how his publishers' strategy for maintaining control of the book's copyright in the face of stiff competition created financial incentives for the author to expand and revise successive editions; how the author failed to achieve his dreams of greater fame, glory, and wealth as a professor of medicine, as a royal physician, or as the author of a planned sequel that his publishers contracted for chiefly in order to keep him under their control; and how he spent his last years in London hard-pressed for money, socializing conspicuously at a coffeehouse, and perhaps also at his masonic lodge, while occasionally producing more practical medical advice literature. These letters shed new light not only on Buchan, Smellie, Strahan, Creech, and the publication history of *Domestic Medicine*, but also on relations among eighteenth-century British authors and members of the book trade in general. Such is the power of the epistle to transform the history of books into the history of books and people.

NOTES

This article is drawn from a larger study of the role of the book trade in the Enlightenment, supported by grants from the John Simon Guggenheim Memorial Foundation and the Spencer Foundation.

1. The popularity of *Domestic Medicine* is discussed in a number of studies by historians of medicine, including Charles E Rosenberg, 'Medical text and social context: explaining William Buchan's *Domestic Medicine*', originally published in 1983 but reprinted, with a new introduction, in Rosenberg, *Explaining Epidemics and Other Studies in the History of Medicine* (Cambridge, 1992), 32–56; C. J. Lawrence, 'William Buchan: medicine laid open', *Medical History* 19 (1975), 20–35; and several of the contributions to *The Popularization of Medicine 1650–1850*, [ed] Roy Porter (London and New York, 1992).

2. *Memoirs of the Life, Writings, and Correspondence of William Smellie*, [ed] Robert Kerr, 2 vols (1811; reprinted Bristol, 1996), 1, 263. I am grateful to Stephen Brown for providing me with copies of Buchan's letters to Smellie from the Smellie Papers in the Royal Scottish Museum, Edinburgh, which I have used to correct and augment the flawed transcriptions in Kerr's *Memoirs*. I have discovered no evidence, in the Buchan-Smellie letters published by Kerr or in those edited by Brown, for believing that Smellie was either the co-author or the ghostwriter of *Domestic Medicine*, as asserted by Lawrence ('William Buchan', 20–1) and Smellie's friend Gilbert Stuart (Kerr, 1, 97), respectively.

3. When the second edition of *Domestic Medicine* was about to be published in autumn 1772, a newspaper advertisement claimed that when the first edition appeared in 1769 'above FIVE THOUSAND copies of it were sold in Scotland in the course of a few months' (*Edinburgh Evening Courant*, 31 October 1772). See also *London Chronicle*, 29–31 October 1772.

4. The only copy of the *Proposals* seems to be in the Library of the Wellcome Institute for the History of Medicine, London.

5. Some idea of this expense may be gleaned from a sentence in his letter of 15 December 1765 that is not reproduced by Kerr, where Buchan informs Smellie that he has found a printer in Sheffield willing to print the work for 'a Shilling the Copy' in addition to 'a certain number of Copies for himself', and wonders if the job can be done as cheaply at Edinburgh.

6. Francis A Countway Library of Medicine, Boston, B/MS misc.

7. National Library of Medicine, Bethseda, Maryland, MSC1.

8. British Library, Add. MS 35,057, fols 38–40.

9. Lawrence, 'William Buchan', 23; Lisbeth Haakonssen, *Medicine and Morals in the Enlightenment: John Gregory, Thomas Percival and Benjamin Rush* (Amsterdam and Atlanta, 1997), chap. 2, especially 65–70. The phrase 'laying medicine open' appears twice in Gregory's posthumous *Lectures on the Duties and Qualifications of a Physician* (London, 1772), 230, 236. The second edition of *Domestic Medicine* had appeared earlier in 1772, with a new

introduction that speaks of 'laying Medicine more open to mankind' (xiii). It is not impossible that the phrase originated with Buchan, whom Gregory is alleged to have acknowledged as a major influence (*Edinburgh Evening Courant*, 19 May 1773).

10. *Edinburgh Evening Courant*, 5 May 1773; Alexander Bower, *The History of the University of Edinburgh*, 3 vols (Edinburgh, 1817–30), 3,148. Bower's claim that Buchan was a candidate for the natural philosophy chair vacated by the death of James Russel or Russell is based on 'private information' and therefore cannot be verified, but in light of Buchan's attacks on physicians for preserving their secrets and mysteries, instead of doing their utmost to promote good health, his explanation rings true: 'Some of his strictures [in *Domestic Medicine*] gave offence, and these formed an imperious barrier to his promotion on this occasion'.

11. Francis A Countway Library of Medicine, Boston, B/MS misc.

12. Kerr, *Memoirs of Smellie*, 1, 261–2; Laurence B McCullough, 'John Gregory's medical ethics and humean sympathy', in *The Codification of Medical Morality, vol 1: Medical Ethics and Etiquette in the Eighteenth Century*, ed. Robert Baker, Dorothy Porter, and Roy Porter (Dordrecht, 1993), 147; Rosalie Stott, 'Health and virtue: or, how to keep out of harm's way. Lectures on pathology and therapeutics by William Cullen, ca 1770', *Medical History* 31 (1987): 128.

13. Strahan's papers in the British Library record his paying £166.13s.4d. for a one-third share of *Domestic Medicine* on 25 October 1770, as noted in Richard Lutes, 'Andrew Strahan and the London sharebook system, 1785–1825: A Study of the Strahan Printing and Publishing Records' (PhD thesis, Wayne State University, 1979), 187. When the second edition was registered at Stationers' Hall on 6 November 1772, Thomas Cadell was recorded as also owning one-third, and the remaining third was divided equally between John Balfour and William Creech.

14. Creech Letter-books, National Archives of Scotland, RH4/26. All references to letters from the Strahans to Creech are cited by kind permission of Anderson Strathern WS, Edinburgh.

15. 'Inventory of the stock of books in quires and copyrights. Property of late Mr Wm Creech 14 January 1815', Creech Papers, Edinburgh Room, Edinburgh Central Library. The remarks do not appear in the printed version of this inventory that was apparently distributed among booksellers attending the sale.

16. Recollections of Alexander Stephens, quoted in John Timbs, *Clubs and Club Life in London* (London, 1898), 155.

17. Arnold Whitaker, *Oxford, No. 4: An Introduction to the History of the Royal Somerset House and Inverness Lodge* (London, 1928), 270.

18. *Gentleman's Magazine* for March 1805, 287. This account is similar to Buchan's own characterization of the work as 'the amusement of some leisure hours in a coffee-house', in *Observations Concerning the Prevention and Cure of the Venereal Disease. Intended to Guard the Ignorant and Unwary against the Baneful Effects of that Insidious Malady* (London, 1796), xix.

19. Royal College of Physicians, Edinburgh. Along with the £300 contract renewal in 1803 that is mentioned below, the 'contingent profits on future editions of the domestic medicine'

mentioned by Alexander Buchan caused concern to William Creech, who complained to Cadell & Davies on 22 December 1807 about the account for the impression of the twentieth edition that he had just received: 'I understood that the gratuity to the author ceased on our paying the £300 for his last improvements, & that there was no further obligations. By the two last Editions we have got nothing'. After hearing from his publishing partners, he replied on 18 February 1808 'You have explained the allowance to the authors family which I did not before know of' Creech Letter–book (copies), Edinburgh Central Library, Green Box 120.

20. Buchan to Strahan, 19 September 1778, New York Public Library, Cadell and Davies Correspondence.

21. British Library, Add. MS 48, 901, fol. 22.

22. British Library, Add. MS 48, 901, fols 25–6.

23. Buchan to Cumberland, 12 February 1791, British Library, Add. MS 36,496, fols 264–6. The reference is to the eleventh edition of 1790 selling out, and the twelfth edition of 1791 going to press. From the eighth edition of 1784 to the end of Buchan's lifetime at least, every edition of *Domestic Medicine* printed by the Strahans had a print run of six thousand copies – a total of 66 000 copies in less than twenty years. See the Strahan printing records in the British Library, Add. MS 48, 814A, fol 9, and 48, 815, fol 43.

24. Buchan to Cumberland, 16 December 1790, British Library, Add. MS 36, 496, fols 236–7.

25. Buchan to Cumberland, 18 November 1786, British Library, Add. MS 36, 495, fols 158–9.

Medical Secrets and the Book Trade:
Ownership of the Copy to the College of Physicians'
Pharmacopoeia (1618-50)

JONATHAN SANDERSON

A T THE TURN OF THE SEVENTEENTH CENTURY, the London medical profession was organised in a hierarchical system of authority at whose pinnacle stood the Fellows of the London College of Physicians. The College was founded in 1518 and two subsequent Acts of Parliament, in 1540 and 1553, granted it control over the working practices of the apothecaries who were then members of the Company of Grocers.[1] Fellows of the College had the power to examine apothecaries' stocks and their methods of preparing medicines, and it was this which led to the preparation and, eventually, the publication of a Latin pharmacopoeia in 1618. The College intended the *Pharmacopoeia Londinensis* to control and regulate the apothecaries' practices: it contains the official simple remedies and the preparations of compounded medicines, and constituted the only medicinal formulae licensed apothecaries could dispense. In 1649, Peter Cole (*d* 1665) published an English translation by Nicholas Culpeper (1616–54). A work, which had originally been meant to standardise, control, and regulate the craft of the apothecaries, now appeared in English and became, in the words of Charles Webster, 'a medium for the liberalisation of medicine'.[2] Culpeper's translation revealed the receipts of those medical professionals who had had an economic interest in maintaining their secrecy from a non-professional audience.[3]

George Urdang in his 'Introduction' to the facsimile of the first edition of the *Pharmacopoeia* looks at the events that surround the publication of two editions in 1618 and 1619.[4] He compares the texts of the two closely, but does not engage with the publishing history of this important book. More recently, in her review of Culpeper's books from the second half of the seventeenth century, Mary McCarl mentions the confusing exchange of the right to the title in the Stationers' Register, but does not relate this to internal events recorded in the College's 'Annals'.[5] Rather than looking separately at the arrangements for the original 1618 Latin edition, Culpeper's 1649 translation, and the publication of a revised Latin edition in 1650, this paper examines the interlinked publishing histories of all three books. The Charter of the Stationers' Company in 1557 required each new book, or 'copy', to be registered at Stationers' Hall in the Company's Register.[6] Although its official purpose was as an instrument to control seditious publication, members soon realised that the value of the system lay in establishing ownership of a literary property and the right to profit from its publication.[7] The exchanges of copy for the College's *Pharmacopoeia* recorded in the Register reveal how a series of astute London publishers were able to exploit the monopoly of the Stationers' Company to gain control over this profitable title. Supplemented by the evidence in the College's 'Annals', and the books themselves, the College emerges as an institution unable to control the publication of its text or prevent the attacks on its monopoly included in Culpeper's translation, who denounced it as a College of 'Dunces'.[8]

The ownership of the copy for both the College's original *Pharmacopoeia* and for Culpeper's English translation is complex and confusing. This confusion dates back to the publication of the two Latin editions in 1618 and 1619. The first reference to the production of a pharmacopoeia by the College, though, was made as early as 25 June 1585 when the College proposed the preparation of a pharmacopoeia to be followed by the country's apothecaries.[9] On 10 October 1589, it was 'proposed, discussed and resolved to compile and publish one uniform Pharmacopoeia or Dispensatory of prescriptions to be followed by shops', and a committee was formed to consider material for inclusion, and ordered to report back.[10] Later that year, on 23 December, the College charged six Fellows with the production of a pharmacopoeia. However, there is no mention of the project in the 'Annals' for the next five years, and it was not until December 1594 that a new committee was appointed.[11] There then followed a twenty-year lapse until June 1614 when the College again considered the proposal.[12]

During the second decade of the seventeenth-century, the apothecaries made moves to establish their own society independent of the Company of Grocers. It appears that the production of a pharmacopoeia was an important part of an agreement between the apothecaries and physicians, whereby the College would support the apothecaries' separation from the Grocers and the establishment of their own Society. Members of the Society of Apothecaries were required to take an oath which protected the physicians' monopoly: only prescriptions of Fellows were to be prepared and no apothecary was to visit the sick or administer his own medical advice.[13] The College, then, sought to control the apothecaries by stressing the importance of a pharmacopoeia produced by its Fellows. At the same time, an official pharmacopoeia would assert the apothecaries' monopoly over the preparation of medicines, as well as confirming the separateness of their new status from the Grocers.

At the June meeting of the College in 1614, the 'Annals' report that proposals were made with 'regard to the common dispensatory to be kept in the shops of the apothecaries', and a committee was duly appointed.[14] In September 1616, Doctors Mark Ridley (1560–1624), Edward Lister (*d* 1620), John Argent (*d* 1633) and Simon Fox (1568–1642) examined the material that the committee had collected. However, these papers were incomplete and the matter went unresolved.[15] Between September 1616 and June 1617, new members were appointed to assist the committee and medical receipts were collected, including one for a chemical oil from a Mr Hewet.[16] By September 1617, the 'Annals' reported that the manuscript of the pharmacopoeia was 'almost entirely prepared'.[17] On 20 February 1618, the College appointed Doctors John Argent, John Giffard, Matthew Gwinne (*d* 1627) and William Clement (*d* 1636) to see the pharmacopoeia through the press, and Doctors Clement and Fox were to supervise the press corrections.[18] Finally, on 30 March, the College made the final arrangements for its publication, when the 'Annals' record that Theodore Mayerne (1573–1665) 'was asked to write the dedicatory letter of the Pharmacopoeia to the King ... [t]he preface to be written by many ... was to be referred to the President'.[19] Following this, on 26 April 1618, a printed proclamation appeared which commanded all apothecaries to use the formulae of the *Pharmacopoeia Londinensis*.[20]

On the same day, James I granted John Marriot licence for the sole right to print and sell the *Pharmacopoeia* for the following twenty-one years.[21] Marriot was the son of Edward, a yeoman from Northampton. He was originally entered as an apprentice with the Stationers' Company in August 1607 by John Hodgettes, and although his term of apprenticeship was heavily disrupted, he was freed on 26 June 1615.[22] Marriot, then, was just beginning his career when he acquired the right to the *Pharmacopoeia*, and he went on to publish the works of Nicholas Breton, John Donne, Michael Drayton, Philip Massinger, Francis Quarles and George Wither. In order to receive a royal licence, though, the College must have initially supported him. Fellows may have thought that by selecting Marriot at the start of his career, they would be better able to control him than they could a more established publisher. If so, then as we shall see, Marriot showed little gratitude for their entrusting such a valuable monopoly to his hands. In 1649, the College endorsed another young stationer, Stephen Bowtell, to publish the 1650 revised edition of their *Pharmacopoeia*. Presumably by doing so the College hoped to be able to gain control over the publication of this book, and to steal the initiative from Peter Cole and Culpeper whose English translation had just been published. Nevertheless, in both cases it failed to do so.

The 1618 Proclamation created an instant market for the *Pharmacopoeia*, because it ordered that apothecaries could only make up those medicines listed in the College's official book. Marriot was keen to satisfy this demand. In May 1618, he published the *Pharmacopoeia Londinensis* as a folio printed by Edward Griffin.[23] Ten months after this edition appeared another, announced in Latin on its new engraved title-page as having been 'diligently revised, elaborately renewed, more correct and more comprehensive', was published.[24] On the face of it, this suggests there had been an immediate and eager demand for the *Pharmacopoeia* which had exhausted the print-run of the first edition. This, however, was not the case. The Latin 'Epilogus' to the second edition stated that the first had been hastily published, and consequently the President of the College had called for its withdrawal and the printing of a revised edition. In translation it reads:

> We now edit the *London Pharmacopoeia* in a second endeavour, with more fortunate result. We (I say) edit. For that previous unformed as well as deformed [book], may we say the hasty printer has edited it? On the contrary, he hurled it into the light. As a blaze flares up from a fire and in a greedy famine deprives the stomach of its still unprepared food, so the printer snatched away from our hands this little work not yet finished off, without consulting the president.[25]

On 25 September 1618, Marriot attended a meeting of the College in person, and undertook to reprint the *Pharmacopoeia*, with alterations required by the College, if the Fellows would contribute to his costs. According to the 'Annals':

There was some discussion with regard to the new printing of the London Pharmacopoeia entrusted to the Registrar at last, and the printer being present stated that he would refuse to proceed unless whatever the Fellows contributed was handed over to him and that as soon as possible. Then the President and many others promised to him twenty pounds, failing that twenty marks, when the corrected book appeared.[26]

Although the 'Candido Lectori' in the second edition is dated 7 December 1618, the book could not have been published until after 13 January 1619, for on that date the 'Annals' record that 'there was considerable discussion regarding the epilogue to be included in the Pharmacopoeia now sent back'.[27] Neither edition contains anything about the medical attributes of any of the medicinal compositions. These consist only of a catalogue of the simple ingredients used in the preparation of medicines, followed by the receipts for the compounded remedies. The first edition lists 680 simple ingredients, but by the second edition this had increased to 1190, together with an additional 251 compound preparations.[28] The move was towards completeness, and the second edition, according to Urdang, 'represents the more pretentious pharmacopoeial combination of formulary and textbook, with the purpose of giving general information, [and] also a survey of the entire materia medica, *simplicia* and *composita*'.[29] Despite the College's dissatisfaction with Marriot's premature publication, he secured payment to go ahead with the revised edition. Urdang suggests that the explanation offered by the College in the new epilogue was an excuse to mask internal disputes within the College about what information the *Pharmacopoeia* should contain, but the subsequent publishing history of the title over the next thirty years reveals that Marriot had secured a powerful position as copy-holder of the title, while the College struggled to regain the initiative.

Following the 1618 and 1619 editions, Marriot published the *Pharmacopoeia* a further three times, in 1627, 1632 and 1639, with the same engraved title-page that had been first used for the 1619 edition. These editions, though, were criticised by the College for being falsely printed. In his 'Printer's Address', Marriot had claimed:

[T]his Worke,… is now free from all errors… by the great labour, pains, care and industry of that Honourable Society… and by them… diligently and truely corrected and amended, as also newly amplified, and enlarged and adorned with such additions as unto them seemed most needfull.[30]

Although this suggests that the College had approved each new edition, this was not the case. On 1 March 1633 the College charged Marriot with having 'printed our dispensatorye agayne without shewing itt to the Colledge; which hee pretendeth hee maye lawfullye doe'.[31] Marriot's legal rights are not clear from the 'Annals', but, as will be seen, had good basis: nevertheless, he promised that in future he would provide the College with a copy prior to publication for inspection. He failed to keep his promise, and on 8 April 1639 the 'Annals' again report that:

John Mariot printer of the pharmacopoea Londinensis apered and was accused, to haue abused the Colledge fowly, in makinge them the authorees of the last edition, wherin hee saith, that they had enlarged and corrected the same; ther beeinge indeed nether amendment nor any woord added.[32]

This episode demonstrates that the College was dissatisfied with Marriot and his production and publication of the College's *Pharmacopoeia*, not only with the original edition in 1618, but also with the subsequent editions he published.

The original publishing arrangements for the *Pharmacopoeia* taken together with what happened in 1649 between Marriot, Stephen Bowtell, the Stationers' Company and the College of Physicians, examined below, suggest that there was some difficulty over the ownership of the copy of the *Pharmacopoeia*. Despite the long gestation period, from 1585 to 1618, the first entry in the Stationers' Register is by Marriot on 16 January 1618, when he had entered for his copy 'vnder the hands of master TAUERNOR and both the wardens A booke Called *Dispensatorium Collegij Londinensis*'.[33] Significantly, this is a month before the College appointed the committee to see the *Pharmacopoeia* through the press. It is striking that Marriot's original entry for the *Pharmacopoeia* in the Register appears to have been for a book that was never published under this title. It was because of this entry, together with James I's proclamation on 26 April 1618, that Marriot was able to continue to publish the College's *Pharmacopoeia* during the 1630s against the Fellows' wishes. Throughout its production the College referred to its *Pharmacopoeia* also as a

'Dispensatory', and it is therefore not surprising that Marriot entered this title with the Company in the expectation that a book would be prepared with the same title. Given the College's dissatisfaction with Marriot's first edition in 1618, and then with the later editions, it is significant that on 8 April 1639 it was complaining of Marriot's dishonesty.[34] The College's meeting on this date was less than three weeks before Marriot's monopoly, awarded for twenty-one years in 1618, was due to expire. If the College was so dissatisfied with Marriot at the end of his tenure, why was he allowed to retain his monopoly, while the College itself did not determine to rewrite its *Pharmacopoeia* until 1647?

The most probable answer is that by entering the title 'Dispensatorium' in January 1618, Marriot anticipated the proclamation giving him the sole right to publish the *Pharmacopoeia*. By pre-registering a potential 'Dispensatory' with the Stationers' Company, Marriot had the rights in a future text based on the College's knowledge; the King's proclamation made him the official publisher of the official pharmacopoeia. The College could not register the *Pharmacopoeia* in its own right, and Marriot's pre-emptive entry gave him a legal basis to claim ownership of the title. That is, Marriot had the protection of both the King's licence and his Stationers' rights as a copy-holder. Following his entry in 1618 there are no further changes in the right to the copy until 1649 and 1650, when the College was preparing a revised edition published by Stephen Bowtell, and after Culpeper's translation had appeared.

Originally from Shalford in Essex, Bowtell was the son of James Bowtell, a yeoman, and his wife Sara Wright, and on 2 January 1620 he was christened at the local parish church.[35] In July 1635 John Bellamy took on Bowtell, then about fifteen or sixteen years of age, as an apprentice; he served the usual seven years and was freed in July 1642.[36] Although Bowtell was quick to register an apprentice only five months after his freedom, he only ever had two apprentices and after 1652 he had none.[37] Bowtell set up business at the sign of the Bible in Pope's Head Alley and began to publish pamphlets in 1642. He was in business until 1655, although he published most of his output between 1644 and 1650. Much of this consisted of sermons, and before 1650 the bulk of his entries in the Stationers' Register are of sermons delivered before Parliament by Stephen Marshall (1594–1655), the Presbyterian divine. He is perhaps best remembered, though, as the publisher of *The Tenth Muse Latley Sprung Up* (1650), which contained the work of the first woman to write English verse in America, Anne Bradstreet.[38]

On 27 November 1649, Bowtell gained the copy to the mysterious and perhaps bogus 'Dispensatorium', first registered by Marriot.[39] On the following day he registered the right to the Latin *Pharmacopoeia* and two weeks later, on 12 December, he was granted the right to an English translation.[40] The reasons Bowtell acquired these titles one by one lie in who previously owned the rights to them. On 27 November, Marriot sold Bowtell the copy of the 'Dispensatorium'.[41] The Latin *Pharmacopoeia* was entered on 28 November for Bowtell's 'copie under the hands of the PRESIDENT and censors of the Colledge of Phisitions of London', and in 1650 Bowtell did indeed publish an edition of this work.[42] A translation, entitled *Pharmacopoeia Londinensis or the London Dispensatory Further Adorned*, was entered on 12 December, 'under the hand of Doctor CLARKE pr[e]sident of the Colledge of Phisitions and Master FLESHER.[43] On 18 October 1650, the publisher Peter Cole gained the rights to the copy of the College's Latin *Pharmacopoeia* and of the English translation. According to the Register, Bowtell 'by vertue of a bill of sale... subscribed by Master STEPHENS warden' passed on the rights to Peter Cole of

> these three books or copies... [1] *Dispensatoriu[m] Collegii Londinensis...* [2] *Pharmacopeia Londiniensis ...* [in Latin], and [3] *Pharmacopoeia Londinensis, or the London dispensatorie further adorned ... in English.*[44]

The problem here is that only two books, the Latin *Pharmacopoeia* and Culpeper's translation seem ever to have been published, and yet the payment of 1*s*. 6*d* for the entry establishes that Bowtell sold the rights to three titles at 6*d* each. This unique episode goes back to events surrounding the publication of the original Latin edition, and Marriot's entry in the Stationers' Register in January 1618. It prompts three questions. Why did Bowtell need rights to the apparently non-existent 'Dispensatorium'? Why did he fail to publish an English translation? Why in less than a year did he sell on the three, presumably lucrative, titles which he had recently acquired to Peter Cole?

Bowtell's acquisition of the copy of the mysterious 'Dispensatorium' from Marriot on 27 November 1649, the first sign in the Stationers' Register of his interest in the *Pharmacopoeia*, can, when taken together with the evidence in the 'Annals', offer a hypothesis which might account for both the third title and the order of registry. On 13 December 1649, the day after John Clarke (1582–1653), the College's President from 1645 to 1650, had witnessed Bowtell's entry of a translation of the *Pharmacopoeia*, the College voted that '[h]alfe of the mony due for the dispensatory was by the Colledge [to be] geven to Mrs. Grent in regard of hir husband Dr. Grent['s], ... great poverty at his death'.[45] Thomas Grent had been one of the Queen's physicians but had turned to inventing. His most famous project involved making artificial baths, for which he received a patent in 1627. Although a Fellow of the College since 1623, Grent's attempts at inventing presumably failed and when he died on 11 December 1649 he did so in poverty.[46]

The College's President had been present in Stationers' Hall on 28 November and 12 December 1649, when Bowtell gained the right to publish both the Latin and the English versions of the *Pharmacopoeia*. When members of the College gave support on 13 December for Dr Grent's widow, they did so with a secure knowledge of exactly how much Bowtell had paid for the privilege of a publishing monopoly in the College's Latin and English versions of its book. The 'Annals' suggest that the College's President was working with Bowtell to exclude Marriot. In September 1647, plans were made to revise the *Pharmacopoeia*, and the business of revising the text was entrusted to the President and the College's four Censors, Francis Prujean (1593–1666), William Rant, George Ent (1604–89), and John Micklethwaite (1612–82).[47] In June 1649, the revised text was scrutinised by the Fellows who voted that the book 'so corrected shalbe imprinted'.[48] At a meeting of the College on 27 July, Fellows were concerned 'whither the printing of the dispensatory should be permitted to Mr. Marriot or no[t]'.[49] The College was keen to prevent Marriot from printing the newly revised *Pharmacopoeia* and voted for Stephen Bowtell to publish this edition. Everything recorded in the Stationers' Register follows on from this decision, clearly one reached in response to Marriot's abuse, in the College's view, of his privilege to the *Pharmacopoeia*.

The decision by the College in June 1649 to prevent Marriot from printing the newly revised edition later that year reflects a long campaign on the College's part to get rid of him. The entries in the Register show that the College and Bowtell were working together to exclude Marriot from publishing any further editions. Despite the Licensing Order of 20 September 1649, which cancelled all previous licences and required all books to be licensed anew, it was necessary that Bowtell first secured Marriot's rights in the non-existent 'Dispensatorium'.[50] Whether Bowtell did this on his own, or with the knowledge of the College, the intention must have been to ensure that Marriot gave up any claim to the 'dispensatory' through the Stationers' Register. Bowtell must have paid Marriot in November to acquire his rights, and the fact that the President of the College signed Bowtell's entry in the Register on 28 November, when he would have seen the entry from the previous day, makes it likely that Bowtell and the College were working together.

In 1647, while the College began to plan a revised Latin version of its *Pharmacopoeia*, Nicholas Culpeper began to prepare his translation of the 1619 Latin edition, which took him, according to one anonymous critic, 'two yeres drunken Labour'.[51] Culpeper must have known that the College was preparing a new edition, which made it essential that his translation appear before the new revised Latin *Pharmacopoeia*. It did so at the end of August 1649, when Cole published Culpeper's work with the unexpected title *A Physicall Directory*.[52] Only after the appearance of an English version of their *Pharmacopoeia* did the College act as its President, John Clarke, tried to regain the initiative. In December Clarke intervened and allowed Bowtell the rights to publish an English version of the revised *Pharmacopoeia*.[53] However, Cole had already stolen the initiative and the episode was a *fait accompli*. Clarke intervened only after Cole had published, and his action was ineffective.

Presumably, Bowtell had persuaded the College to trust him, so they may have thought that by allowing Bowtell the rights to an English translation he could kill the already published Culpeper version. Although he did publish the revised Latin *Pharmacopoeia* in 1650, Bowtell never published an English translation. There are at least two possible explanations for this failure. Firstly, to publish the 1650 Latin *Pharmacopoeia* would have meant considerable additional financial outlay. If we look at the quantity and size of the books Bowtell published between 1648 and 1651, it is apparent that he was only a minor publisher. Along with the money paid to secure the rights to the copy from Marriot and the College production costs will also have been high.[54] This failure to publish the English translation suggests that Bowtell lacked access to sufficient capital in order to profit from his investment in the title. He may then have misjudged his own finances or thought he had made a poor bargain when he acquired the rights to a translation of the *Pharmacopoeia*. By November 1649, Culpeper's translation had already stolen the market. Bowtell went ahead with the Latin version and made a profit on that. Faced with the expense of a new translation and its publication, it was easier to sell the whole thing to Cole rather than invest more and fight him over the right to copy.

Another explanation is that Bowtell was working in collaboration with Cole all along to exclude the College from a controlling stake in any English versions of its *Pharmacopoeia*. Although only circumstantial evidence exists, the available facts seem to support this as a reasonable hypothesis. Bowtell and Cole had known each other since at least 1637 when they were both apprenticed to John Bellamy.[55] As well as serving their apprenticeships with the same master, their business addresses were very close. Bowtell's shop was at the sign of the Bible in Pope's Head Alley, while Cole's business was around the corner in Cornhill near the Royal Exchange. Having gained the rights to the spurious title of the 'Dispensatorium', along with the Latin and English titles of the *Pharmacopoeia*, Bowtell sold the rights to all three titles to Cole in October 1650. After publishing Culpeper's translation, Cole made a financial deal with Bowtell whereby he secured the rights to publish a translation of the new *Pharmacopoeia*. It took Culpeper two years to finish this new translation, which Cole published in 1653, entitled *Pharmacopoeia Londinensis: or the London Dispensatory Further Adorned*, the exact title originally registered by Bowtell and President Clarke in November 1649.

Events surrounding the publication of the first edition of the *Pharmacopoeia* in 1618 to Culpeper's translation show how a succession of London stationers exploited the monopoly offered by the Stationers' Company over their trade to challenge the professional monopoly of the College of Physicians. Although the College had been authorised as medical-book licensers in the Printing Act of 1643, it is only from 1649 that the College began to license such books, apparently as a way of raising capital.[56] It is money, then, that lies at the heart of these transactions, as might be expected of two monopolistic institutions. The willingness of President Clarke to register an English version of the revised *Pharmacopoeia* suggests that it was an attempt to gain some measure of control over an English version of the College's book, and silence Culpeper's attacks on its monopoly. However, the College failed once Bowtell had sold his rights to Cole in 1650. Cole now had established trade rights to the copy for the Latin and English versions of the Pharmacopoeia. The College was unable to take any further action and thereby lost control of the production of their Pharmacopoeia, their sacred text, with which Fellows had intended to assert their authority over London medical practice.

NOTES

Jonathan Sanderson was awarded the first British Book Trade Seminar Fellowship for this paper – *Editors*.

1. On the histories of the Royal College of Physicians, the Society of Apothecaries, and the practice of medicine during this period, see George Clark, *A History of the Royal College of Physicians of London*, 2 vols (Oxford: Clarendon Press for the Royal College of Physicians, 1964–66); E Ashworth Underwood and others, *A History of the Worshipful Society of Apothecaries of London: Volume I, 1617–1815* (London: Oxford University Press, 1963); Harold J Cook, *The Decline of the Old Medical Regime in Stuart London* (Ithaca and London: Cornell University Press, 1986); Lucinda M Beier, *Sufferers and Healers: The Experience of Illness in Seventeenth-Century England* (London: Routledge & Kegan Paul, 1987).

2. Charles Webster, *The Great Instauration: Science, Medicine and Reform 1626–1660* (London: Duckworth, 1975), 253.

3. The cost of seeing a physician in London will have usually been between 6s.6d and 10s, which meant professional medical care was beyond the reach of all but the wealthy (Doreen Evenden Nagy, *Popular Medicine in Seventeenth-Century England* (Bowling Green: Bowling Green State University Popular Press, 1988), 21).

4. George Urdang, 'Introduction', in *Pharmacopoeia Londinensis of 1618: Reproduced in Facsimile with a Historical Introduction*, Hallister Pharmaceutical Library, 2 (Madison: State Historical Society of Wisconsin, 1944), 1–81.

5. Mary R McCarl, 'Publishing the works of Nicholas Culpeper, astrological herbalist and translator of Latin medical works in seventeenth-century London', *Canadian Bulletin of Medical History*, 13 (1996), 225–76.

6. Mark Rose, *Authors and Owners: The Invention of Copyright* (Cambridge, Mass.: Harvard University Press, 1993); and John Feather, *Publishing, Piracy and Politics: An Historical Study of Copyright in Britain* (London: Mansell, 1994).

Chronology for the Production of a Latin and English *Pharmacopoeia*

Date	Event
1614 Jun. 25	College appoints committee to prepare a Pharmacopoeia.
1617 Sep. 17	Manuscript of the Pharmacopoeia 'almost entirely prepared'
1618 Jan. 16	John Marriot enters a 'booke Called *Dispensatorium Collegij Londinensis*' in the Stationers' Register.
Feb. 20	College appoints a final committee to see the manuscript through the press.
Mar. 30	College plans for publication.
Apr. 26	Proclamation commanding all apothecaries to use the formulae in the forthcoming *Pharmacopoeia Londinensis*. Marriot granted sole right to print and sell *Pharmacopoeia* for the next twenty-one years.
May	Marriot publishes *Pharmacopoeia Londinensis*.
Sep. 25	College unhappy with edition.
1619 Jan.	Marriot publishes revised and enlarged second edition of *Pharmacopoeia Londinensis*.
1626	Marriot publishes third edition of the *Pharmacopoeia*.
1632	Marriot publishes fourth edition of the *Pharmacopoeia*.
Mar. 1	College accuses Marriot of publishing the *Pharmacopoeia* without approval.
1639	Marriot publishes fifth edition of the *Pharmacopoeia*.
Apr. 8	College accuses Marriot of publishing another edition of the *Pharmacopoeia* without approval.
1647	Culpeper begins to work on his translation of the College's *Pharmacopoeia*.
Sep. 30	College plans to revise the *Pharmacopoeia*.
1649 Jun. 4	College approves revised text for the *Pharmacopoeia*.
Jul. 27	College votes in Stephen Bowtell as publisher of the new *Pharmacopoeia*.
Aug./Sep.	Peter Cole publishes Culpeper's translation of the College's *Pharmacopoeia*, entitled *A Physicall Directory*.
Nov. 27	Stephen Bowtell enters his rights to *Dispensatorium Collegii Londinensis* in the Stationers' Register, 'by vertue of a note under the hand & seale of Master MARRIOTT'.
Nov. 28	Bowtell enters *Pharmacopoeia Londinensis*, the official title of the College's book, 'under the hands of the PRESIDENT and censors of the Colledge'.
Dec. 12	Bowtell returns to Stationers' Hall to enter *Pharmacopoeia Londinensis, or the London Dispensatory Further Adorned*, 'under the hand of Doctor CLARKE president of the Colledge of Phisitions'.
Dec. 13	The College votes half of the money 'due for the dispensatory ... to Mrs. Grent'.
1650	Stephen Bowtell publishes the College's revised *Pharmacopoeia*. Peter Cole publishes a second enlarged edition of Culpeper's translation of the College's original *Pharmacopoeia*. Culpeper begins to translate College's new *Pharmacopoeia*.
Oct. 18	Peter Cole enters the following three titles in the Stationers' Register, which he purchased from Bowtell: 1) *Dispensatorii Collegii Londinensis*, 2) *Pharmacopoeia Londinensis*, and 3) *Pharmacopoeia Londinensis, or the London Dispensatory Further Adorned*.
1651	Cole publishes third enlarged edition of Culpeper's *A Physicall Directory*.
1653	Cole publishes Culpeper's translation of the College's recently revised *Pharmacopoeia*, entitled *Pharmacopoeia Londinensis: or the London Dispensatory*.

7. Feather, *Publishing, Piracy and Politics*, 35.

8. Nicholas Culpeper, *A Physicall Directory* (1649), sig A2^v.

9. Annals of the Royal College of Physicians, II, f 44a. Entries from this period were usually, although not exclusively, made in Latin. English as well as Latin typescripts exist for the first five volumes, and I am grateful to the College for permission to quote from the English typescripts.

10. Annals, II, f 75b.

11. Annals, II, ff 78b, 108b.

12. Annals, III, f 17a.

13. On the establishment of the Society, see Underwood and others, *History of the Society of Apothecaries*, I, 1–40.

14. Annals, III, f 17a.

15. On 14 September 1616, the College examined papers for the Pharmacopoeia and found many to be missing (Annals, III, f 25b).

16. Annals, III, ff 25b, 26a, 27a, 28b.

17. Annals, III, f 31 a.

18. Annals, III, f 32b.

19 .Annals, III, f 33a.

20. *A Proclamation Commanding All Apothecaries of this Realme, to Follow the Dispensatory Lately Compiled by the College of Physitians of London* ([26 April 1618]). The publication of the Proclamation is noted in the *Calendar of State Papers, Domestic 1619–62*, 40 vols (London: HMSO, 1858–93), *1611–1618*, 536.

21. *CSPD 1611–1618*, 536. Walter W Greg gives a fuller transcript of the licence in his *A Companion to Arber: being a Calendar of Documents in Edward Arber's 'Transcript of the Registers of the Company of Stationers of London, 1554–1640'* (Oxford: Clarendon Press, 1967), 162–3.

22. Marriot was turned over by John Hodgettes to Eleazer Edgar on 3 October 1608; to John Stepneth on 1 April 1611; and to Roger Jackson on 28 January 1613 (Donald F McKenzie, [ed] *Stationers' Company Apprentices 1605–1640* (Charlottesville, Virginia: Bibliographical Society of the University of Virginia, 1961), 65, 83, 88, 122; Henry R Plomer, *A Dictionary of the Printers and Booksellers who were at work in England, Scotland, and Ireland from 1641 to 1667* (London: Bibliographical Society, 1907), 122.

23. *Pharmacopoeia Londinensis, in qua medicamenta*, 1st edn (1618). The 'Candido Lectori' to this edition is dated 7 May 1618 (sig A2^r). On Griffin, see Plomer, *Dictionary of the Printers and Booksellers ... from 1641 to 1667*, 86.

24. *Pharmacopoeia Londinensis, in qua medicamenta*, 2nd edn (1618 [1619]). The title-page was engraved by Renold Elstrack *(b* 1571) and is described in Alfred F Johnson, *A Catalogue of Engraved and Etched English Title-Pages Down to the Death of William Faithorne, 1691* (Oxford: Bibliographical Society, 1934), 16.

25. Translated by Urdang in his 'Introduction', 23–24, from the second edition of the *Pharmacopoeia Londinensis* ([1619]), sig 2E2^v.

26. Annals, III, f 34b.

27. Annals, III, f 36a.

28. On the contents of the two editions, see Urdang, 'Introduction'; Allen G Debus, *The English Paracelsians* (London: Oldboume, 1965), 145–56; William Brockbank, 'Sovereign remedies. A critical depreciation of the 17th-century London Pharmacopoeia', *Medical History*, 8 (1964), 1–14; and W R Munk, *The Roll of the Royal College of Physicians*, 3 vols (London: Longman, 1861), III, 371–7.

29. Urdang, 'Introduction', 78.

30. *Pharmacopoeia Londinensis, in qua medicamenta*, 5th edn (1639), sig V7^v.

31. Annals, III, f 129a.

32. Annals, III, f 198a.

33. Edward Arber, *Transcript of the Registers of the Company of Stationers of London (1554–1640)*, 5 vols (London and Birmingham: Privately Printed, 1875–94), III, 618.

34. Annals, III, f 198a.

35. *International Genealogical Index*, microfiche edition (The Genealogical Department of The Church of Jesus Christ of the Latter-day Saints, 1988).

36. McKenzie, *Apprentices 1605–1640*, 41.

37. Donald F McKenzie, *Stationers' Company Apprentices 1641–1700* (Oxford: Oxford Bibliographical Society, 1974), [18].

38. On Bradstreet, see Emory Elliott, 'New England Puritan Literature', in *The Cambridge History of American Literature: Vol I, 1590–1820*, ed Sacvan Bercovitch (Cambridge: Cambridge University Press, 1994), 169–306 (236–43).

39. G E B Eyre, H R Plomer, and C R Rivington, *A Transcript of the Registers of the Worshipful Company of Stationers from 1640 to 1708*, 3 vols (London: Privately Printed, 1913 and 1914), I, 331.

40. Eyre, Plomer & Rivington, I, 331, 333.

41. Eyre, Plomer & Rivington, I, 331.

42. Eyre, Plomer & Rivington, I, 331.

43. Eyre, Plomer & Rivington,. I, 333.

44. Eyre, Plomer & Rivington, I, 353.

45. Annals, IV, f 25b. Clarke was educated at Christ's College, Cambridge, and admitted a Fellow of the College in November 1622; he also served the College as Censor (1639–44), Consiliarius (1642–44 and 1650–2), and Treasurer (1643–4) *(DNB;* Munk, *Roll of the Royal College,* I, 180–1; and Cyril Hart, 'John Clarke, M.D.', *St Bartholomew's Journal*, 55 (1951), 34–40).

46. On Grent, see R R James, 'Dr Thomas Grent, Sen. and Jun.', *Janus*, 43 (1939), 131–6; and William J Birkin, 'The Fellows of the Royal College of Physicians of London, 1603–1643: A Social Study', (doctoral thesis, University of North Carolina at Chapel Hill, 1977), 164–6.

47. Annals, IV, f 10a.

48. Annals, IV, ff 21 a and 22b.

49. Annals, IV, f 23a.

50. C H Firth and R S Rait, *Acts and Ordinances of the Interregnum*, 3 vols (London: HMSO, 1911), II, 245–54.

51. *Mercurius Pragmaticus*, 21 [4–11 Sept 1649], sig X3ᵛ.

52. *A Physicall Directory* was described as an 'excellent translation' in Henry Walker's *Perfect Occurrences of Every Dayes Journall in Parliament, 139* [*sic*] (31 Aug–7 Sep 1649), sig 7F4ᵛ

53. Arber, *Transcript... from 1640 to 1708*, I, 333.

54. If we accept the approximate production cost for printing a sheet at a farthing (0.25*d*), and we allow for approximately a thousand copies in an edition, then this will have meant an outlay in excess of £60 (Philip Gaskell, *A New Introduction to Bibliography*, (Oxford: Oxford University Press, 1972; repr. 1985), 178).

55. McKenzie, *Apprentices 1605–1641*, 41.

56. *Acts and Ordinances of the Interregnum*, I, 184–7. Between 1649 and 1654, the College's two Presidents, John Clarke and Francis Prujean, along with George Ent, made nineteen trips to Stationers' Hall where they witnessed the entry of over twenty titles, half of which were English translations or originals (Arber, *Transcript... from 1640 to 1708*, I, 313, 327, 331, 333, 343, 345, 348, 363, 372, 375, 380, 396, 405, 406, 410, 419, 425, 435, 446). The evidence is only circumstantial and relates to the *Pharmacopoeia*, but it appears that publishers, such as Bowtell, paid the College for such endorsements. I shall examine this further in my doctoral thesis.

Charles Elliot and the London Booksellers in the Early Years

WARREN McDOUGALL

CHARLES ELLIOT started his book business in Parliament Close, Edinburgh, in May 1771, with the stock of the late bookseller William Sands. Three years later, Elliot's expanding enterprises led him to commence Letter-Books to keep copies of his outgoing correspondence, including those to many, diverse members of the London trade. In the autumn of 1775, aged 28, with a long list of booksellers to see, Elliot rode to London. An anticipated short jaunt turned into a stay of around seven weeks as he poked around the London bookshops and conversed with their owners. There were new books to buy and exchange, older ones of a Scottish interest to find, and his own publishing schemes to float. There were one or two feathers to smooth, and friendships to be renewed or made, although not in every case: not much could be done with a sour James Dodsley, who was biding his time before turning the screws in a copyright case.

This study is from work in progress on the Elliot Papers in the John Murray Archive. In it, I explore Elliot's relationships and trade with the London booksellers around the time of the London trip, drawing mainly on his first Letter-Book, 1774–1776.

The eight Elliot Letter-Books, which run to his death in January 1790, contain around 4500 entries – copies and memoranda of outgoing correspondence – and I cite them in the text below according to recipient and date. The copies were made by various hands, including Elliot's, carelessly at times, with idiosyncracies of the individual, and often without full stops. Since they do not reflect the standard of correctness of two extant originals by Elliot (to John Murray, at the Murray Archives, and to Dr William Cullen, at the Royal College of Physicians, Edinburgh), I regularise the punctuation and sometimes the spelling.[1]

INTRODUCTION

Elliot's business – This was a period when Elliot's bookselling and publishing preoccupations were being formed: acquiring the latest books from London, reprinting established titles, specialising in medical books and publishing new medical titles, buying literary property for himself, building up a large stock in sheets, getting outlets for his books beyond Scotland. Copyright was a theme of these years. While the Scots had been busy reprinting since 1750, the House of Lords decision on literary property of 1774 saved the Scots industry that had built up, and brought, on a British scale, opportunities for reprinting and selling work whose copyright time had expired.[2] The importance of registering literary property was seen by Elliot; he made more than forty entries at Stationers' Hall.

Piracy – Like many others in the trade, Elliot also sold clandestine books. Pirated books were common in Scotland in the 1770s and into the 1780s. Illegal, cheap imports of reprinted English titles were shipped in from Ireland at first openly, and then smuggled. In the early years, Elliot commissioned their import from William Anderson, a smuggling bookseller from Stirling. By the late 1770s, he was also getting reprints directly from Irish booksellers in exchange for his own books. Sometimes he expressed disquiet over the fairness of selling someone else's literary property, the troublesome business of getting them, and the danger of discovery, yet at first he was willing to oblige the Irish, and would also ask for particular titles of interest. At home in Edinburgh, a number of books were reprinted illegally, and various members of the trade, Elliot included, were prosecuted by London copyright holders.[3]

At the time of this study, Elliot was being pursued in two actions. He was one of the fringe booksellers in the case brought in 1775 by Thomas Becket, William Strahan and Thomas Cadell against David Willison for printing Laurence Sterne's *Works* and *A Sentimental Journey*. The court would rule in 1778 that the three Londoners were to be paid damages by Willison and had the right to damask the copies ('Smugglers' 175–6). More seriously for Elliot, James Dodsley would cast Elliot as one of the culprits in a relentless prosecution over the piracy of Chesterfield's *Letters*. When Colin Macfarquhar openly reprinted a four-volume 12mo edition, Dodsley, in December 1774, took out an interdict against thirteen Edinburgh booksellers and six printers, including the virtuous Creech and John Balfour. In July 1775, Dodsley won an injunction against Irish and Edinburgh editions during the term of his copyright. He had the option of going further, which he evidently pondered in the latter half of 1775, including the time Elliot saw him in London, and in December he had the Edinburgh attorney who specialised in copyright prosecution, James Walker, pursue Elliot, Macfarquhar and the paper merchant George Douglas as the publishers of the edition. The case, during which Macfarquhar was made to admit that he had sent 1000 of the 1500 copies to England, lasted two years, and ended with Dodsley being allowed to damask the remainder of the edition ('Smugglers' 174–5).

Elliot and William Creech – The shops were very close to each other – Elliot's on the east side of Parliament Close, next to John's Coffee House, William Creech's in the Luckenbooths on the High Street – and they became the leading booksellers in town, but the two men were different. Archibald Constable, who saw them both as an apprentice, contrasted an Elliot who had an independent Edinburgh publishing spirit with a Creech who was content to play second fiddle to London.[4] Richard Sher has described Creech's personality as contradictory – he had manners, wit and knowledge, but he was also 'vain, egotistical, miserly, puritanical, and self-righteous'.[5] The Letter-Books show Elliot's dislike of Creech. It seems to me reasonable to link this to their trade rivalry, and to the function that Creech took on.

Creech was an informer for London copyright holders. One can understand why he kept an eye out for illegal books in Edinburgh – he owned shares in literary property along with William Strahan and Thomas Cadell, and their titles were a favourite target. Creech was in a position to spy out other transgressions. In 1772 one of the Dillys had written to Creech and his then partner Alexander Kincaid ('Smugglers' 173)

Gentlemen… if you can possibly hear of any bookseller in Edinr that has taken from Irish booksellers Entick Dict. Spelling, Langhorne's Plutarch, or any other of our London property please to inform me directly and I will give orders to the Attorney to Prosecute immediately. Shall be glad to hear how he goes on with [William] Anderson for selling Nugents Dict – Mr Cadell will be glad to be informed if anything belonging to him is offered by the Irish Booksellers.

Creech played an active role against his neighbours; he encouraged Strahan not to come to an accommodation with Willison, the pirate of Sterne in 1775, but to prosecute him to the utmost. When Excise officers seized Irish reprints from a wagon at Glasgow in 1781, Creech proposed to Strahan that Anderson of Stirling be prosecuted and then liaised with the Board of Customs and the Londoner's attorney, James Walker. Creech wanted to keep quiet about his involvement, and Strahan agreed. One wonders how secret this was around Parliament Square. Another Creech role, that of the expert called on by Customs after book seizures, would have been known about, since his opinions were circulated between the Customs Board and the ports and then recorded. As Customs Expert, Creech commented shrewdly on the illegal Irish trade when a shipment for Elliot, from Luke White of Dublin, was taken up in 1786 ('Smugglers', 152–76). Cadell knew quickly that his titles were included. It was always Elliot's contention that information on him fed to London was inaccurate, and that everybody had piracies in their shop, more so than he, and now he wrote to Cadell (Cadell, 23 Dec 1786)

> I do believe the Person that has given you much wrong information, as well as some true, whatever he say or write, deals more in such books than I do.

Elliot, in his Letter-Books, tried to put Creech in a bad light. He complained to London booksellers about Creech's lack of cooperation in trade, or, as in the letter to Cadell, implied Creech was hypocritical over piracies and gave wrong information. Yet, even if information from Creech did lead to questions being raised against him, Elliot readily provided answers to excuse and justify, and he went on to do thousands of pounds' worth of trade with Cadell, and business with Thomas Becket, and Edward & Charles Dilly.

LONDON BOOKSELLERS

Elliot traded with dozens of London booksellers, across the spectrum from traditional copyright holders to those like John Murray, John Bell and Thomas Carnan, who were opposed to the old monopoly. His general suppliers were Hawes, Clarke & Collins, Paternoster Row, who sent him books and magazines once or twice a month; Richardson & Urquhart also sent large amounts of books regularly. He bought paper in quantity from Bayles & Staples, and from Bloxham & Fourdrinier. George Robinson, who sent him *The Town and Country Magazine* and *The Lady's Magazine* in 1772 with orders to advertise in the *Caledonian Mercury* and the *Edinburgh Evening Courant*, would become one of Elliot's main London associates in the 1780s. Among the publications he took from Carnan & Newbery was the *Dictionary of the World*. Francis Newbery supplied Elliot with children's books, titles such as

The Brother's Gift, or Naughty Girl Reformed, 1*d*, *The Fortune Teller*, 2*d*, *The Bag of Nuts Ready Cracked*, 3*d* (*Edinburgh Advertiser* 14 January 1774). Elliot developed a light touch with editions for the young; his advertisement for a new edition of *Mother Goose's Tales*, a shilling bound and gilt, was 'For the instruction and entertainment of all good little Masters and Misses' (*Edinburgh Evening Courant* 8 July 1775).

Elliot, in buying books from London, wanted good terms. He told John Knox, a Scotsman located in the Strand, to charge his order as low as possible: 'I flatter myself I am as well entitled to that as many on this side of the Tweed' (Knox, 12 May 1774). He asked Ben White of Fleet Street, that he be on an equal footing with White's other Edinburgh customers, John Balfour and William Creech. Elliot asked for twelve copies each of Thomas Pennant's *A Tour of Scotland and Voyage to the Hebrides* (White, 21 May 1774)

> but I think the allowances not very great, after we do them in boards and pay other expenses. I will and can safely venture on 25 of each if you give any additional encouragement such as the Quarter copy, but dare say you'll make me no worse than my neighbours... Beg the books may be shipped on board the very first vessel, that I may have them at least as soon as any here.

Elliot was disappointed when Balfour and Creech received the books sooner than he did 'many of my customers are carried from me', and annoyed by a report that Creech had got the books a shilling a copy cheaper.

> I hope you'll make it up in some shape or other. I don't chuse to be troublesome, but one naturally thinks he has a right to every advantage another has for his money. (White, 14 June 1774)

White said there had been no difference in price. Elliot half-apologised, admitting he had not heard this from Creech, but from another bookseller in Parliament Close, William Gordon (White, 5 July 1774).

Elliot sent a large quantity of reprints to the London bookseller John Scott, some of which were his own or from Edinburgh, but others of which were probably Irish. He wrote out a long list giving the charges followed by the retail prices, showing he was offering a good margin of profit. They included Pope's *Homer*, 2 vols 12mo, 3*s*.6*d* (retail 7*s*.6*d*); *Tom Jones*, 3 vols, 3*s*.6*d* (7*s*.6*d*); Fielding's *Works*, 12 vols, 18*s* (36*s*); *Clarissa*, 8 vols 12mo, 8*s*.6*d* (24*s*); Thomson's *Works*, 4 vols 12mo fine, 4*s*.6*d*. (12*s*); Plutarch's *Lives*, 6 vols 12mo, 9*s* (18*s*); Langley's *Builder's Jewel with supplement*, 2*s*.6*d* (5*s*). Those that were Elliot's own included Rousseau's *Works*, 10 vols 12mo fine paper, 15*s* (*30s*) (Scott, June 1774).

Thomas Cadell had a long association with Elliot. The first entry in Elliot's account ledgers records £23 of books received from Cadell at the start of his business in 1771, and he bought and exchanged books with Cadell about every two months thereafter. Books he offered to Cadell included the school texts of Thomas Ruddiman, which he had bought up. Some shipments from Cadell were eagerly awaited. Elliot ordered fifty copies of Dr Johnson's *A Journey to the Western Isles of Scotland* and was sorry when only twenty-five came on the ship to Leith.

> Mr. Balfour's son was present at the opening of the small parcel as he brought it out of the ship, we having agreed to divide the no. whatever parcel came first to hand (as some days intervene before the ship is full cleared) and were both disappointed in finding these no. so small. I fancy a new edit. will soon be ready, if so could wish to have my other 25... shipped immediately.

Elliot had another complaint about Creech (Cadell, 14 Feb 1775).

> When anything such as Dr Johnson's comes out, & I have a no. sent as well as Mr. Balfour & Creech, beg you'll give order to Creech & insert my name in the advertisement here. Mr. Balfour & I are upon & have always been on the best footing. The other I say nothing of, only altho Mr. Balfour desired my name to be inserted, the other would not, as he said he had no order for doing so.

With Cadell, Elliot started his practice of putting in his imprints the names of Londoners who agreed to take a substantial number of copies. This was for Thomas Ewing's *A Synopsis of Practical Mathematics*, Edinburgh: printed by William Smellie, and Co. for C. Elliot; and T. Cadell, London, 1771. Cadell took 200 copies. Elliot assumed Cadell would take other good titles. 'I shall finish a translation of Dr. Simson's Conic Sections in a few days & I intend putting your name together with Mr. John Murray as venders in London', he told Cadell. He sent 250 copies.

> I have given order to advertise it in your name to Mr. Murray, to whom only I send so many. I will be obliged to you to promote the sale. It was generally read and much esteemed in Latin. It certainly is more useful now. (Cadell, 14 Feb & 7 March 1775)

The imprint of *Conic Sections* read 'Edinburgh: printed for Charles Elliot. Sold, in London, by T. Cadell, and J. Murray'.

John Bell sold *Bell's edition of Shakespeare's Plays*, 1774, to Elliot, as well as books on sale or return, popular titles such as *The Economist*, Henry Bracken's *Ten Minutes Advice to Every Gentleman Going to Purchase a Horse*, Chesterfield's *Principles of Politeness*, and *The Gentleman's Pocket Farrier*. Elliot complained that Bell did not allow enough profit.

I have been often in the way of receiving books from publishers on Return, but must confess I was never charged in the manner you have done, viz for every 1 sh. pamphlet you charge 10d, for 1/6d ditto 1/3d, & 2s. at 1/8d. Your larger books that retail for 3s. per vol. in calf you charge 1/10d, for 3/6d ditto 2/4d, for 6s. 8vo ditto 4/2d, 7s. ditto 4/7d, & so on... Pray add the bindings in calf to the articles above mentioned & see what profit remains... I see you have given Mr Creech very liberal orders for advertising your articles in the different papers of this place, without his as much as mentioning one single person besides himself. If this is by your orders it is wrong. If contrary I leave you to challenge it, but I think I had as good a title to be advertised as a seller as him and might have turned out equally well. (John Bell, 4 April 1775)

Thomas Becket, of the 1774 *Donaldson v Becket* case in the House of Lords, who also prosecuted in Edinburgh over Sterne, was interested nevertheless in buying the poetry collections being printed in Scotland, made possible because of lapsed copyright. Elliot wrote him out the titles of forty-four volumes printed by Foulis of Glasgow, but cautioned that it was difficult to get a complete set, and the Foulis's practice of printing on two kinds of paper, meant that Becket might get several volumes in coarse paper. Elliot joked about attitudes when he described the great British poets venture by his two neighbours:

There is a more uniform although much longer Edit. of the British Poets been publishing here two years by these great patriots for Literary Property Balfour & Creech, but there is only 20 vol. finished and they are a pott 8vo. (Becket, 30 August 1774)

Creech's letter supporting Strahan and other London booksellers in their opposition to the 1774 decision had been used in the House of Lords; as Alexander Donaldson had already pointed out to the public, had they won the day, there would have been no British poets.[6] Elliot bought a considerable amount of books from Becket, although he returned quantities of two of his plays,

Burgoyne's *The Maid of the Oaks*, and Cumberland's *The Choleric Man*, when they arrived damaged. 'Shall be glad to have a few of any thing new you publish', Elliot told him. He promoted his own stock: 'Pray, do you never want any of Ruddiman's Grammar or Rudiments? I have now purchased all the copies' (Becket, 14 April 1775).

Elliot bought books from Edward & Charles Dilly, including fifty copies of Ash's *Easy Introduction to Dr. Lowth's English Grammar*, and twenty-five of Hester Chapone's *Letters on the Improvement of the Mind, Addressed to a Young Lady*, asking for a free quarter copy of the Chapone, since he was paying ready money (E & C Dilly, 5 July 1774). Elliot was on the imprint of *The Decisions of the Court of Session, From its Institution to 1764*, 5 vols 12mo, the imprint of one of its issues reading 'London: printed for the editor, and sold by E. & C. Dilly, London and Charles Elliot, Edinburgh, 1774'. Elliot advertised the publication for Dilly in the Edinburgh papers (*Edinburgh Evening Courant* 18 January 1775). He informed the Dillys which of their books were not selling. The run on *Letters of Lady Rachel Russell* had stopped before the third edition came out and he had ten left. Falck's *The Seaman's Medical Instructor* 'won't answer our refined students', and there were sixteen unsold. He had expected to sell many of Langhorne's *Plutarch's Lives*, 'but we have so many cheap editions of Dryden prevents it' (E & C Dilly, 13 January 1775). Elliot ordered twelve copies of Entick's *Latin Dictionary*; 'I am beginning to sell them now. I have prevailed on a teacher here to introduce it, but am obliged to give him an allowance, so hope you'll give as much as possible on them' (E & C Dilly, 13 April 1775).

Particular books Elliot wanted from James Dodsley in 1774 were the *Annual Register* and Lord Chesterfield's *Letters*. Elliot first sent for the Chesterfield in June; in August alone, he had four more orders. It was the rage in Edinburgh; an Irish edition was being sold, and in December 1774 came Macfarquhar's version with his name openly on the imprint 'Edinburgh printed for C. Macfarquhar, and sold by the booksellers, 1775'. Dodsley had paid around £1500 for the copyright, and on 21 December 1774, he took out his interdict at the Court of Session. He meant business, and agreed to take out a £500 security to pursue the case.

A few weeks later, Elliot brought the case up during a business letter to the Dillys.

There is a curious affair just happened here, which I dare say you have heard of. I mean the printing of Lord Chesterfield's Letters. I wish my name is not taken in vain in the matter as I have reason to think some of my neighbours here bear me no great will, and would be very busy at a time like this. You must know, I did sell some of them, but it was owing to particular circumstances that I did.

He said the publishers (Macfarquhar and the paper-merchant Douglas) had made the edition after consulting two lawyers, who told them the title was not protected. Elliot said he was not in on the planning, and only took copies because there was a creditable printer's name on the title.

I would have been better pleased (between you and I), whatever the issue is, for many reasons, that I had not sold any. Therefore I expect of you that you won't allow any thing to be said worse of me than I deserve amongst the Trade. (E & C Dilly, 13 January 1775)

After the interdict was made permanent in July, Elliot sent Becket a book order and then talked about the case:

It has made a great noise here & I am led to understand that some of my good <u>Neighbours</u> here have, in London, represented me as a party concerned in the affair. I think it my duty to Vindicate myself in that particular, and it is entirely false, at least so far that I was not directly concerned. I indeed engaged with the publisher, for it was done openly... From these two or three copies my <u>Rivals</u> in <u>trade</u> I am sorry to say have turned into many shapes to my disadvantage, & this is only meant as a Vindication to those false aspersions, in case they may have reached you to my prejudice... I aver it is a fact that I deal as little in that kind of Contraband Trade, as any in Scotland, not even <u>Creech</u> excepted. (Becket, 28 July 1775)

THE LONDON JAUNT

Elliot planned his trip to London for early autumn. In the last few weeks before he went, he was in the shop in Parliament Close writing to correspondents and clearing up business. He was promoting his first great publishing venture, which would soon start going to press, a new edition of Van Swieten's *Commentaries upon Boerhaave's Aphorisms Concerning Knowledge and Cure of Diseases*, 18 vols 12mo, 1776. The renowned Edinburgh medical professor

COMMENTARIES

UPON

B O E R H A A V E's

A P H O R I S M S

CONCERNING THE

KNOWLEDGE and CURE of DISEASES.

BY

BARON van SWIETEN,

Counsellor and First Physician

To their Majesties the Emperor and Empress of Germany;

Perpetual President of the College of Physicians in Vienna;

Member of the Royal Academy of Sciences and Surgery at Paris;

H. Fellow of the Royal College of Physicians at Edinburgh;

&c. &c. &c.

Translated from the LATIN.

V O L. I.

E D I N B U R G H:

Printed for CHARLES ELLIOT, Parliament Square.

Sold by J. MURRAY, Fleet Street, *London.*

M. DCC. LXXVI.

Dr William Cullen had given Elliot crucial support by approving the plan and agreeing to accept the book's dedication. The subscription price was £2.3s sewed, or £2.14s bound in calf, half the price of the London edition. Elliot wrote to one of his medical customers in the West Indies, Dr Daniel Macfarlane, Serge Island, Jamaica 'Inclosed you have a proposal for Van Swieten, which from its elegance & cheapness you'll encourage, and beg you may show to any of your medical acquaintances' (Macfarlane, 25 August 1775). More proposals went to James Magee of Belfast (Magee, 4 Sept 1755).

Elliot set off for London on 7 September, leaving his clerk, James Sutherland, in charge. A few days later, Sutherland sent him a package care of John Murray, Fleet Street, with the routine business of the shop: Elliot should send up vol 1 of an edition of Pope, the *Annual Register* for 1773, Wilson's Newspaper, and a *Copperplate Magazine*; there was a letter from the lawyer Cornelius Elliot, his cousin, and a letter and a poem from the author Miss Edwards; the clerk had written to Jonathan Kidd of Newcastle about quills (see pp 108–9), and was paying bills (Elliot, 11 Sept 1775).

In London, Elliot went around the bookshops. He fulfilled tasks for customers – sending word back for James Meek, schoolmaster in Falkirk, about the price of Adams's 18-inch globes (Meek, 2 Oct 1775). He found by chance some new copies of William Maitland's folio *History of Edinburgh*, printed by Hamilton, Balfour & Neill in 1753, and sent them back for sale (*Edinburgh Evening Courant*, 23 Dec 1775). The first exchange he completed was with William Watts, near the Foundry, Upper Moorfields. One reason Elliot had gone to see the engraver and printseller was to pick up the *Copperplate Magazine*. Sutherland received Elliot's letter and shipped Watts two bales from Leith, including forty copies fine and twelve coarse of Elliot's edition of Rollin's *Ancient History*, 10 vols 12mo, 1775; 'Beg you'll be so kind as ship Mr. Elliot's articles immediately' (Watts, 19 Oct 1775).

The Londoners Elliot did business with included Cadell, Murray, the Dillys, Becket, John Wilkie, John Nourse, Francis Wingrave, Mileston Hingeston, James Mathews, David Steel, Thomas Evans, Richardson &

(*Opposite*) Title-page of vol 1 of van Swieten's *Commentaries upon Boerhaave's Aphorisms* – reduced slightly from 177x101 mm
(Reproduced by permission of the Wellcome Institute Library, London)

Urquhart, James Buckland, Hawes & Company, Thomas Bell and Edward Johnston. When he returned to Edinburgh, Elliot wrote friendly letters. To Joseph Johnson 'We arrived safe… and I hope all the good people round St. Paul's do well. Complts. to Mr. F. Newbery whom I know you see now and then' (Johnson, 24 Nov 1775). To George Keith, Grace Church Street 'I intended myself the pleasure of calling again upon you while in London but your distance from my part of the town prevented it' (Keith, 19 Jan 1776).

James Dodsley traded books but was suspicious about money. Elliot gave him two notes payable at Cadell's house, telling Cadell that Dodsley thought 'Edinr too distant a part for payment' (Cadell, 11 Nov 1775). There were some payment problems with John Bell, too. Back in Edinburgh, Elliot would wait impatiently for Bell's books, then wrote 'I did business with many people in London, but must confess you are the only person that has not at least sent me part of the transaction' (Bell, 29 Dec 1775). Bell was not budging until he received £40 he said Elliot owed him. Although he spoke sharply, Elliot continued to have a considerable trade with Bell, and bought the rights for the sale of Bell's *British Theatre* in Edinburgh (Bell, 17 Sept 1776).

As well as making book exchanges, Elliot was arranging to act as an agent in Edinburgh, and for cooperation in publications. John Murray, on a subsequent visit to Edinburgh, agreed to take 100 copies of the Van Swieten. Thomas Cadell proposed that one of his copyrights, Raynal's *History*, be published in Edinburgh. Becket arranged for Elliot to advertise and sell in Edinburgh Sterne's *Works, Letters, Tristram Shandy, Sentimental Journey* and *Sermons* – despite having named him in the current prosecution against Willison – and it was an assignment that Elliot carried out well (Becket, 11 Nov 1775).

EDINBURGH 1775-76

Elliot rode back to Edinburgh in eight days, arriving at the end of October. He would like to have lingered in his home town of Selkirk for a half-hour to speak to friends, but his two companions – one of whom appears to have been the Edinburgh bookseller John Bell – wanted to reach town before nightfall, and they pressed on (William Huggan, Edward Johnston, Nov 1775). Elliot told Cadell, whom he had been meeting right up to his departure, that it was 'a safe altho not altogether an agreeable journey' (Cadell, 11 Nov 1775). For the first week Elliot was busy collecting book orders for London and writing to his correspondents there. The *Abercorn*, Capt William Beatson junior, had a lot of books on it when it sailed out of Leith. After organising his London trade, Elliot turned to his friend William Anderson of Stirling:

> As you expect to be very soon in Edinr, Mr. Bell thinks that will be the best time to settle Smellie, which I think also. You must keep it very quiet as those affairs will be resented to the utmost by the London booksellers. I am safely arrived but confoundedly hurried & will tell you all my news at meeting. Till then, adieu. (Elliot to Anderson, 8 November 1775)

What Elliot appears to be urging caution over was an illicit edition of William Smellie's *Midwifery* in three volumes.

At the beginning of December 1775, it became apparent to Elliot that Dodsley was preparing to prosecute him and the two others further over Chesterfield's *Letters*, and he tried to head him off:

> I declare upon my honour, I knew nothing of the undertaking until it was finished... My concerns in such undertakings has been less perhaps than any in this country without exception. Altho your counsel threw out some illiberal things during this pleading on every person of the Trade in this Country – paying only some gross compliments to Balfour and Creech – I beg you'll order my name to be struck out. (Dodsley, 7 Dec 1775)

Elliot received Dodsley's negative reply and wrote angrily:

> I do not give one farthing how it goes. If you do not believe what I say to be true, act as you please... I look upon the word of an honest man to be sufficient. If that is not relied upon, he ought to be d – – d.

Elliot calmed down and talked about an order: 'NB. The Articles I formerly commissioned will make up a tolerable parcel. If you chuse to send them on ye terms you would another, let it be immediately' (Dodsley, 16 Dec 1775). Elliot offered a concession – to pay Dodsley profits on copies sold and to give up copies still in his possession (Dodsley, 28 Dec 1775). Dodsley kept up the prosecution. However, they continued doing business, and Elliot even offered Dodsley 500 copies of his edition of James Gregory's Latin treatise on diseases caused by changes in climate: 'It is to be printed by Mr Smellie... who is perhaps ye best Latin scholar of this country, so that the execution will be in every respect neat' (Dodsley, 13 Feb 1776). Dodsley continued to sell Elliot books such as the *Annual Register*.

The London trip had an effect on Elliot's publishing. In 1774 and 1775, he was connected with eleven titles a year. In 1776 he had thirty-six publications, fourteen of which had London involvement. The editions included Cadell's commission, the J O Justamond translation of Raynal's *A Philosophical and Political History of...,* *the Europeans in the East and West Indies*, Edinburgh: printed for T. Cadell, London; and J. Balfour and C. Elliot, London, 1776, 3 vols 12mo with plates and maps. Elliot appears to have been protecting Cadell against piracy; he gave news of the progress of printing and urged Cadell to get the plates up from London quickly to forestall an edition which, he said, John Robertson might print. Creech was not far away. Although Cadell wanted Creech's name on the title, Elliot said the request arrived too late, and all he could do was to insert Creech in the advertisements along with their own. Later, he passed on news:

There has been a good deal of altercation between Mr Balfour and Mr Creech (and very foolishly in my opinion by the latter) respecting Abbe Raynal's History published here. Mr Balfour showed me his letters, which were perfectly right and agreeable to the facts therein set forth.

Elliot and Balfour set the price of the edition at a higher level, 16s bound or 14s in boards, to suit Cadell's London profit (Cadell, 5 March, 11 July, 5 Aug 1776).

John Murray had a significant role in selling Elliot publications and appears on many of his imprints.[7] Elliot promised to give Murray first offer of buying copies of his original medical publications from Edinburgh. Editions that Murray took included those of Dr John Innes, Professor Monro's dissector at Edinburgh University: *Eight Anatomical Tables of the Human Body*, and *A Short Description of the Human Muscles, Chiefly as they Appear on Dissection*, 1776. Elliot paid Innes £100 for the copyright of the *Anatomy* plates; the price of the book stitched was planned at 6s in Edinburgh, but Elliot suggested Murray sell it at 7s in London to defray the cost of advertising. The imprint of Van Swieten's *Commentaries* read 'Edinburgh: printed for Charles Elliot. Sold by J. Murray, London', 1776. The book was a statement by Elliot of what he could do in medical publishing, and he made a mark. When it was published, Dr Cullen called at the shop to ask if Elliot and Murray would be interested in selling copies of *First Lines of the Practice of Physic*, which he intended to print soon, and he also talked about his other work, *Materia Medica* and the

Synopsis. 'It is of infinite advantage to one in my situation to be concerned in such publications', Elliot told Murray (11 May 1776). Cullen was actually interested in Murray, but the acquaintance with Cullen eventually led to success; some years later Elliot bought the copyright of *First Lines* for £1200 and paid a large sum also for the property of *Materia Medica.*

Following his jaunt, Elliot settled into a solid trade with London and was co-operating with many booksellers there. One sign of his access to London books at good rates from their suppliers was his reply to John Irvine of Greenock, who asked about a library fit for a lady. Elliot drew up a list 'chiefly historical & entertaining' containing only a 'very few novels of late date, most of them being trash'. He told Irvine he did not have them on hand, but could get them at cheap London prices, saving the buyer carriage and risk (Irvine, Greenock, 18 Dec 1775).

The business was expanding considerably. For the first five years the shop was a single room. In May 1776 he acquired more space for the shop, turning it into two rooms with a lower or laigh storey below. There was a legal problem over the conveyancing, and a lot of alteration and enlarging to do, but after a year he told Murray 'I think I can say now I have as good a shop as any in Fleet Street' (Murray, 24 July 1777).

Some piracy continued, although this became more difficult with the formation of the Edinburgh Booksellers' Society in 1776. Creech was the driving force, and Elliot was also a member. An early proposal banned members purchasing any book in violation of the 1710 Copyright Act.[8] Around this time, Elliot was hearing from his Stirling supplier about the scheme hatched on his return from London. Anderson sent him 300 sets of the Smellie's *Midwifery*. There were also small numbers of sets of Hume's *History* and other illegal reprints, with fake London titles, that Elliot had ordered. 'After considering the affair of Smellie, I am seriously afraid of it', Elliot told Anderson. '... I am constantly in danger of prosecution, which from my particular circumstances are much more liable than you' (Anderson, 5 October 1776). Elliot reckoned it would take him seven or eight years to clear the Smellie, but he would take them, if Anderson lowered the asking price from 4*s* to 3*s*.6*d*, to make them more saleable to medical students. Cheaper books were what students wanted.

And despite all his worry about the risk, surely there was some satisfaction for Elliot in the trade, as when he took sets of books from William Sleater of Dublin in 1778. 'I should be very well pleased to to have the Annual Register London Titles, as I frequently export books. It is in this way I get clear of Irish copies' ('Smugglers', 168). This was one lot of *Annual Registers* he did not have to buy from their literary proprietor, James Dodsley.

NOTES

1. The Elliot papers also include four account ledgers, 1771–1790, and a Trustees' minute book 1790–1805. I am working on a catalogue of the papers and a longer study of Elliot, and to this end, I have microfilmed around 7000 frames of the papers; these reels will be put on access at the National Library of Scotland when the research is concluded. I thank Virginia Murray for her support of the project and her encouragement. I am grateful to Champlain College, Trent University, and Master Stephen W Brown for a residency in March and April 1999 which allowed me to research the Elliot papers.

2. For reprinting and the copyright issues around 1774 see Richard B Sher, 'Corporatism and consensus in the late eighteenth-century book trade: the Edinburgh Booksellers' Society in comparative perspective', *Book History*, 1 (1998), 32–93. For the earlier period see Warren McDougall, 'Copyright litigation in the Court of Session, 1738–1749, and the rise of the Scottish book trade', *Edinburgh Bibliographical Society Transactions*, 5 pt 5 (1998), 2–31.

3. Warren McDougall, 'Smugglers, reprinters, and hot pursuers: the Irish-Scottish book trade, and copyright prosecutions in the late eighteenth century', in *The Stationers' Company and the Book 1550–1990*, [ed] Robin Myers & Michael Harris (Winchester, 1997), 151–83, hereafter cited in the text as 'Smugglers'.

4. Thomas Constable, *Archibald Constable and his Literary Corrrepondents* (Edinburgh, 1873) 1, 533–6.

5. Sher, 'The Edinburgh Booksellers' Society', 74.

6. *Edinburgh Advertiser*, 20 May 1774.

7. For Murray's trade and relationships with Elliot, the Edinburgh booksellers, and Edinburgh authors, see William Zachs, *The First John Murray and the Late Eighteenth-Century Book Trade* (Oxford, 1998).

8. Sher, 'The Edinburgh Booksellers' Society', 55–6.

Charles Elliot and the English Provincial Book Trade

PETER ISAAC

A S WARREN McDOUGALL has shown, Charles Elliot was a considerable publisher and bookseller in Edinburgh. The *English Short-Title Catalogue* lists 476[1] titles with his name in the imprint as publisher or bookseller between 1766 and his death in 1790; of these he was the sole publisher of 143 and joint publisher of 197. His co-publishers were mainly London booksellers and publishers, but thirty imprints combine his name with English provincial booksellers, publishers or printers. These imprints, which date from 1773 to 1789, are a first source of information about Elliot's association with the English provincial book trade, dealing only with published work. An even more diverse and illuminating source is his collection of eight letter-books in the Archives of John Murray (Publishers) Ltd,[2] which demonstrate his dealings – on matters altogether more widespread than books alone – with the English provincial trade. This paper is a first glance at these business dealings, as one example of the cross-border book trade in the late eighteenth century. These dealings are illustrated by a few examples, which caught my eye on first reading and which may not give a truly balanced picture.

It may help to set the following discussion in context to give the results of a crude analysis[1] of the 476 books given by the *ESTC*. The fourteen subjects covered were medicine 117, religion 92, literature 79, science and mathematics 35, education 28, politics 23, the law 22, agriculture, brewing, the home etc 20, reference (including the *Encyclopædia Britannica*) 14, history 13, geography and travel 12, the classics 9, philosophy 8, and miscellaneous 4. It will immediately be seen that like John Murray I, with whom he had strong contacts, Elliot specialized in medical books. This specialization is emphasized in a three-page advertisement headed 'Medical Books printed for and sold by Charles Elliot, Parliament Square' at the end of vol 16 of van Swieten's *Commentaries*, listing sixty-eight items, and goes on 'And every book now in print on the subject of Physic, Surgery, &c. &c. these being branches in which C. Elliot studies to be more generally assorted than any other whatever'.[3]

THE SHARED IMPRINTS

Nineteen towns are listed sixty-two times in the thirty 'shared' imprints: Bath (5 times, with 3 traders), Berwick(1,1), Birmingham (2,2), Bristol (2,1), Cambridge (6,2), Canterbury (4,4), Chester (1,1), Eton (1,1), Gainsborough (2,1), Gloucester (1,1), Hull (1,1), Marlborough (1,1), Newcastle (10,4), Nottingham (1,1), Oxford (7,4), Rochester (1,1), Warrington (1,1), Worcester (1,1) and York (13,6). The names of thirty-seven members of the English provincial book trade occur in these imprints. It will readily be seen that though these nineteen towns range from Bath in the Southwest to Berwick on the Border, the Northeast preponderates with York and Newcastle – as might be expected, and as is strongly demonstrated in the correspondence.

In at least fourteen cases the provincial trader was the printer of the work, the earliest being Matthew Dobson's *A Medical Commentary on Fixed Air* (1779), printed by John Monk of Chester. Printing in provincial centres suggests that the book was the work of a local author, and the inclusion of Elliot's name as the Edinburgh outlet for the work clearly shows that he had quickly acquired a national reputation as a bookseller and publisher.

The subjects dealt with in the thirty shared imprints are religion and science each 7, medicine 5, education and politics each 3, reference and literature each 2, and brewing 1. Although this small-scale analysis differs from the earlier one, it will be seen that medicine, religion and science again predominate.

The first of these thirty books was *A Clear Display of the Trinity* (1773) by a Newcastle schoolmaster, Alexander Murray. Several books by William Perry, lecturer in the Academy at Edinburgh, were among the shared imprints, including *The Royal Standard English Dictionary* (1775), *The Only Sure Guide to the English Tongue* (1776) and *The Man of Business, and Gentleman's Assistant* (1777 & 1780); all were published for the author. Another connexion of interest was with Henry Mozley (1720–1790), printer, bookseller, publisher and stationer of Gainsborough, who had wide dealings with other members of the provincial trade. Henry Mozley printed two works by Edward Peart (1756?–1824), a physician: *The Generation of Animal Heat, Investigated* (1788) and *On the Elementary Principles of Nature* (1789).

A connexion which particularly caught my eye was Francis Spilsbury's *Free Observations on the Scurvy, Gout, Diet, and Remedy*, printed in Rochester in

1783 by T Fisher. Elliot's name appears in the imprint of this quite substantial book because at that time he was acting as the wholesaler in Edinburgh for Spilsbury's Antiscorbutic Drops, an antimonial nostrum that I have discussed elsewhere.[4] This was, no doubt, intended to popularize the Drops, but Spilsbury wrote widely, being the author of one of the earliest manuals for household medicine chests, *The Friendly Physician* (1773). He also wrote an attack on some of Pitt's tax-raising efforts, *Discursory Thoughts, &c. Disputing the Constructions of His Majesty's Hon. Commissioners and Crown Lawyers, relative to the Medicine and Horse Acts* (2nd edn, 1785).

THE LETTER-BOOKS

The eight letter-books of Charles Elliot in the Murray Archives contain some 4500 copies of letters, bills or abbreviated contents of letters, as numbered and indexed by Dr Warren McDougall. The earliest letter dates from May 1774 and the series continues to Elliot's death in January 1790. A very approximate 'guestimate' suggests that just under one in ten of these were to members of the English provincial book trade. In all more than 150 English provincial correspondents are represented in this collection, including a few 'self-publishing' authors, with whom the Edinburgh bookseller was dealing. The copies are made in several hands, not all of which are now very legible, and by no means always grammatical and correctly spelt; however, a letter of 24 August 1789 to John Murray I, for example, suggests that the letters proper were more carefully written. Some of the later letters were signed by the assistants who wrote them. The letters usually give the date of that to which they are the reply, and it is often surprising how swift the post could be – not seldom as prompt as present-day First-Class mail![5] In reading through the letter-books it is noticeable that often the letters are grouped by destination, presumably for the post; this is particularly the case for letters to north America or Jamaica, but is also true for inland addresses.

The correspondents are listed in Table 2, which gives locations and dates. The first letter-book begins in May 1774, and it will be seen from the Table that the earliest date is 1775, although the majority are a good deal later. Elliot's ledgers in the Murray Archive begin 1771, at the start of the bookseller's career. A check of the first ledger yields no more than a few earlier mentions of members of the English provincial book trade: Robert Taylor of

Berwick (1771), Richard Batty of Ripon (1771), Jonathan Kidd of Newcastle (1772), and Thomas Saint also of Newcastle (1773).

Several topics come to light in the correspondence, such as the difficulty of transferring payments before the days of cheques and the clearing banks, and the consequent occasional need for payment by exchange of books or materials. It is clear that booksellers, in common with many other traders, had to wait long to be paid, with the result that there are times when Elliot was strapped for cash. Occasionally he felt compelled to threaten legal action.

Of such well-selling items as Thomas Slack's *Newcastle Memorandum Book*, which started in 1755 and survived as an annual publication until 1893, Elliot bought annual batches of 100 copies, often with the condition that he was the only seller in Edinburgh. At times when he was pushing his own publications Elliot wrote to his more important provincial correspondents to insert advertisements in their own newspapers or in the 'best' local papers,[6] these being timed to appear just before the publication concerned came out. On more than one occasion Elliot issued catalogues of new and secondhand books, at least one of which was widely distributed.

This necessarily one-sided correspondence shows that his relationship with the provincial trade was generally cordial, and he was particularly friendly with several booksellers. On occasion, however, he could be appropriately acerbic.

While it is not germane to this paper, it is interesting to note how widely spread in England, as well as in Scotland, were Elliot's individual retail customers, often but by no means always surgeons or physicians. Amongst the latter was Dr John Pigot, of Southwell, father of Byron's friends Elizabeth and John, the latter of whom studied medicine at Edinburgh University.[7]

VAN SWIETEN'S *COMMENTARIES*

Perhaps Charles Elliot's most considerable sole publication was his edition in eighteen duodecimo volumes of Baron van Swieten's *Commentaries upon Boerhaave's Aphorisms concerning the Knowledge and Cure of Diseases* (1776), an important medical work, which also carries in the imprint the name of John Murray I as selling the book (see p 90).

In his correspondence with the more substantial provincial booksellers about this work Elliot often mentions 'subscriptions', but it seems likely that by this he meant advance orders and not what we now understand by the word. For example in a letter of 13 June 1776 to Nathaniel Thorne, a Durham bookseller, he writes 'You only commission 1 copy of Van Swieten', but sends two copies, adding 'but must Observe they are and must be absolutely sold at £3.3 bound and £2.14 sewed'.[8] In the same letter he reports that John Murray I paid him £1.13s per set for 100 copies, and in a letter of 1 June 1776 to Wilson & Son, booksellers of York and one of Elliot's more substantial provincial correspondents, he quotes the same prices adding 'Mr Murray wont sell Copies under 40 or 42s in quires and 25 at £1.16 [each]'.[9] On the other hand, in writing on the same date to William Tesseyman, another York bookseller and another of Elliot's more substantial correspondents, he refers to copies 'not subscribed', giving the same prices as to Thorne or 2s.2d per volume (which seems to be only £1.19s for eighteen volumes – is this, perhaps, the price for advance orders?).[10] A careful examination of all eighteen volumes of the work in the Library of the Wellcome Institute for the History of Medicine yielded no list of subscribers.[3]

The first six volumes were ready in January 1776, as may be seen from a letter of 18 January to John Ware, proprietor of the *Cumberland Pacquet* of Whitehaven, in which Elliot had advertised van Swieten.[11] In this letter, too, he mentions subscriptions. Although the majority was sold in London,[12] quite substantial numbers were sold to the English provincial trade, as the correspondence shows; several letters mention the dispatch of six copies, as, for example, his letter of 2 October 1776 to Christopher Etherington of York.[13] The price was to increase after completion in March 1776.[12]

BULK PURCHASES

Although Charles Elliot, as a bookseller on a large scale, made many substantial purchases from, and sales to, London publishers, he also made several from the English provincial trade, the purchases sometimes, it would seem, on his own initiative and sometimes prompted by requests from academic institutions in Edinburgh.

As an example of the former we may note the edition of the Revd Charles Cordell's translation of *Letters of Pope Clement XIV, with Anecdotes of his Life*, an octavo in two volumes printed in 1777 by Thomas Saint for William Charnley, of Newcastle, both important correspondents of Elliot. Cordell, born 5 October 1720, was ordained priest at Douay, which he left in 1748 to become chaplain to the Duke of Norfolk at Arundel Castle. In June 1765 he came to the house and room-chapel in Newgate Street, Newcastle. He spent most of his time writing, editing and translating,[14] and by October 1776 was in touch with the Edinburgh bookseller about the publication in parts of the letters of Giovanni Vincenzo Antonio Ganganelli, who reigned as Pope Clement XIV 1769-1774. Although of humble birth Ganganelli was an excellent and accomplished pope, much calumniated, perhaps because, in 1773, he had suppressed the Jesuits; Charles Cordell felt it his duty to defend him, and translated his life as well as these letters.[14]

The earliest letter to Cordell is dated 24 October 1776.[15] It may be that either Saint or Charnley had suggested this contact to the author. Elliot acknowledges a letter of 15 October, and writes that he has

advertised Ganganellis Letters only once in the Mercury[16] by way of Putting the Publick on their Guard against any other Edition[.] You desire me to advertise by hand bills, this will do very well about three weeks hence when our Court of Session down and our Town grows throng; I wish the work was fully Printed of[f], Buyers of such books here are very averse to Su[b]scriptions. Therefore I wou[l]d recommend it to you to have it printed of[f] as fast as possible: that need not hinder your Delivering the week[l]y numbers in Terms of the proposals a Quantity cou[l]d with propriety be Sent heare and if you are determined to raise the price I can advertise the N° and at the Same time the Book Complete mentioning the raise to Commence when the weekly numbers are finished[.]

Elliot is undecided how many weekly numbers to order, since 'all the Subscribers I have got with it complete... most of which have been procured by the Influence of your Friend Mr Drummond'.[17] In the meanwhile Elliot ordered '2 Dozen in Sheets', and had no doubt that, if the book were ready, '100^d might be Sold'. He had received six copies 'of the London Tra[n]slation which must sell at 5/-'. He finishes 'Send another Dozen of the popes Life[18] I have 2 or 3 Left but the one will Certainly Sett of[f] the other'.

There is an abstract of a letter of 11 January 1777, recording that 'Mr Gordon[19] & I wou[l]d give him 3/ pr Copy for 100^d & Expected he will allow 7/ or 10/6 for advertising'.[20] Elliot also records that he had received five subscriptions for complete copies of the work from 'Gent^n that did not Chuse them in N^c. Elliot and Gordon were to share this order equally, and the former took it for granted that Gordon would also take fifty copies of the second volume when it came out, but the latter seems to have gone back on this agreement, as we may see from a letter of 2 March 1778,[21] with its statement of account, Elliot owing Cordell £55.4s (less the cost of twenty-four copies apparently not delivered) and charging £2.10s.9d for advertising. Cordell's account had come to Elliot through George Hay,[22] whom he promised to write quickly to the author. Elliot excuses his delayed letter by

The Difference with a Neighbour Mr Gordon about ordering the last 100 Gang he had ½ of vol 1 at 3/ which he have also of vol 2^d but it not Selling So well has Certainly Put it out of his head as he now insists he did not give an order altho I am Certain the Same order was given for vol 2^d as for vol 1

Elliot says in this letter, and in later letters,[23] that he cannot find the copy of his order to confirm Gordon's commitment to the second volume, but 'Perhaps the order was given to Mr Drummond or Mr Hay from me to transmit you'. Some accommodation was evidently achieved, for, on 27 March 1780,[24] Elliot wrote to Cordell, returning eleven copies of Clement's *Life*, and remitting a balance of £15.12s.9d, adding

Mr Gordon has some vols imperfect I have also two in the same manner; these he says he is to return if so they must be deducted from the Calc Mr Leake [through whom this account was being transmitted] will Explain any other matter more fully

Cordell seems to have taken offence; Elliot explained, in a letter of 24 April,[25] that he had ordered the last batch of 120 copies of the *Life* on 'sale or return'. In spite of the slight friction Cordell's books, including a work that Elliot calls 'Bergier', sold well in Edinburgh. It was listed as item 1100 in one of his catalogues, possibly that for 1779 to be mentioned later. It was one of the books ordered by Mr W Hunter, of Berwick, and was charged at 9s in quires.[26]

Many letters make it clear that the retailer's margin depended on the quantity ordered. For example, Elliot writes to Robert Taylor, bookseller of Berwick upon Tweed, on 29 August 1776[27]

must Confess was not a Little Astonished to read of the [*illegible*] All returned Except 12 never was any transaction in my opinion more Conclusive I expressly said unless 50 copies was taken they Could nor would not be put at 9/ and marked the N° 50 Accordingly

Again in a letter to Thomas Slack of 12 September 1776[28] Elliot complains about the Newcastle bookseller's poor terms

> I Dare say I sold 50 of your lady Maud[s29] but you allow no more than my Miscellaneous Correspondent at London it is much more for my Interest to get them from him who furnishes with every kind and must have every[?] besides when I get them... it cost me I may say nothing, in Comparison of the Expence from you,[30] so that if you do not let me have them at 9/... I'll not depend on you for them

In writing to Mrs Slack (Anne Fisher, the author of educational books) on 8 October of the same year[31] for 50 copies of her *Ladies' Own Memorandum Book* for 1777, Elliot suggests that he should advertise it and be the sole outlet in Edinburgh; he has no doubt that, in these circumstances he would sell 100 or 200 copies. The account at the head of this letter reads '50 Ladies own mem: Books for 1777 with Quarter Copies @ 9/ £1.16'; Below this is a later interpolation '12 N Castle Mem Books'.[31] Something, however, seems to have gone wrong, because on 5 December 1776 Elliot wrote to Thomas Slack

> I wrote Mrs Slack on the 8[t] Oct[r] last in ans[r] to hers to me of 14[t] Sept in Which I desired 50 of the Pocket book be sent to me and to which I Refer — I am very much surprised you have not sent them long er[e] this since the Article I then mentioned were advertised the first of Nov at London on the Cover of the Mag.[32]

He continues in a sharp vein to say that he has ordered a similar work from London.

We have noted that Elliot specialized in medical books, but he was a bookseller with a considerable stock, as may be seen from one of his secondhand catalogues, now in the Murray Archives.[33] Although, therefore, only nine of his 476 imprints were works of classics (Latin & Greek), he occasionally bought such texts in bulk from publishers and booksellers in Eton, Oxford and Cambridge. In 1776 Elliot was in touch with James Fletcher in Oxford,[34] and, in 1779, with John Nicholson in Cambridge,[35] but his longest-lasting correspondence was with Joseph Pote in Eton. For example, on 26 October 1776 he wrote[36]

> Our Professor of Greek here / Mr Dalzel / has some thoughts of Introducing some of your Eton Books Particularly he wishes to try this Season the Collection Intitled Poetis Graecae Minor[?][37] 1771 8[o] Provided it does

not come too high in price, youll therefore be so good as tell me pr mail[?] what you can let me have 50 copies for by which means we shall be enabled to Determine whether it will answer or not

Elliot then goes on to suggest that the Eton bookseller might accept books in exchange, and gives possible titles.

Andrew Dalzel (1742–1806) was Professor of Greek in the University of Edinburgh from the end of 1772 until ill-health forced him to retire in 1805; he was also Librarian of the University from 1785. He found 'the studies of his chair at the lowest possible ebb', following his infirm and inefficient predecessor Robert Hunter.[38] He set about raising standards; Elliot was ready to develop the market opened up in this way, as is clear from a letter to Joseph Pote in the next month,[39] when he confirms his order for sixty copies of Pote's edition of the minor Greek poets and lists several classical texts that Pote might take in exchange. In a postscript Elliot writes 'you may have it in your power to serve me in future and perhaps I may [tell] you this is a very flourishing university'; in later letters to Eton Elliot identifies himself with 'our' university.

This two-way supply of books went on for several years; for example, on 26 May 1780, Elliot wrote to Pote[40]

Yours of 5 last I duely received and on 12 I ship[p]ed on board the Ship Tartan... the Livy's[41] charged in exact proportion to your books to me which were considerably below the usual Charge I have sent you 2 Virgil & Sallust[41] as a Specimen I have cheap copies of each same impressions the former at 9[d] and the Sallust at 6[d] the ordinary school copies may be supplied

This active correspondence continued until at least 1786, the year before Joseph Pote died.

SELLING BY CATALOGUE

Charles Elliot's catalogue of 1778 has already been mentioned in passing.[33] The cover title tells us several things about the bookseller's methods. The catalogue contained details not only of 'several libraries and parcels of books lately purchased' but also 'the stock of the seller', suggesting that, as well as the secondhand books indicated by the first phrase, Elliot was using the sale to clear some of his 'remainders'. This particular sale started on Whit-Sunday 1778 and the books were 'Sold for Ready Money', being at prices 'much lower than the usual stated Prices'. There was a charge of sixpence for 'this very extensive Catalogue', which would be repaid on the return of the catalogue after perusal or deducted from 'the first purchase of five shillings from the Sale'. Elliot mentions one of these libraries, in a letter of 17 April 1778 to William Charnley,[42] bookseller and publisher of Newcastle, 'the property of Mr Carneston[?] Late of the English Chapel here but originally from your Neighbourhood', suggesting, therefore, that 'the Sale will be great with you'.

The letter-books contain lists of those booksellers to whom several later catalogues were sent, and letters contain mention of earlier catalogues, for example one of September 1777 to Nathaniel Thorne, a Durham bookseller.[43] Unfortunately, the 1778 catalogue is the only one that I have seen, and so it is impossible to know how extensive the others were. In October 1779 there is a three-page 'Note of Booksellers who got Catalogues';[44] seventy-seven provincial booksellers were recipients out of a total of 151 – a substantial proportion. Their locations range from Chelmsford in the South to Berwick on the Border; there seems to have been none in the Southwest.

Elliot also used his catalogues to open correspondence with English provincial booksellers. On 24 July 1777 he noted that he had written to Nathaniel Frobisher of York that 'Mr Wm Fettes of Glasgow who was lately in York insinuate[*sic*] to me that a mutual correspondence might be of great service to both should be happy if any thing in the catalogue sent Mr Frobisher would answer him'.[45]

The works advertised in these catalogues were available in his shop in Parliament Square, and the low prices were attractive to private buyers as well as to the trade. A long letter of 12 June 1780 to Mr W Hunter, at Mrs Cowles, Silver Street, Berwick,[46] sets out the catalogue numbers (ranging from 474 to 3698), titles and prices of 32 items ordered by Hunter. Two are indicated as 'none left', and there is a note on the price of Johnson's & Steven[s]'s Shakespear[e]

New edit much enlarged in London and raised to £3..10- in Lond. bd can give one qrs printed 78 by title although not finished till end of 79 for £2..12..6 in sheets this is Cheaper than your bookseller can get it from London

This is interesting as showing the extent of the purchases from such a catalogue of a provincial book-buyer. The covering letter to Hunter not only discusses the differences in price between books bound and in sheets, but also indicates that Elliot had received further stocks of some of the new items, including the Shakespeare mentioned at the higher price.

> am certain the articles are low priced it is in fact giving you an advantage by deducting the binding of many articles and giving copies in Sheets many of the prices in the Catalogue which must be something below Current Shop prices took their low price perhaps from the copy then bound and perhaps sullied w^h years Standing in the Shop

Booksellers also did not always get all the 'articles' that they ordered from Elliot's sale catalogues, as is clear from a letter of 26 November 1779[47] to John Nicholson, a Cambridge bookseller who must have been slow off the mark; Elliot begins his letter

> Your favours in October concerning an order from my sale came duely to hand but really the prices of the good books was so very low you could not expect many of them I only with some difficulty got for you the above to which I added 6 copies of Livy at your own price merely that you may see the book it cost $^1/_4$ more of paper & print with Correction but I hope these may be a means of increasing the demand in your place... [*Verb sap*]

The letter-books contain several later lists of booksellers to whom catalogues had been sent, that of August 1787 being as long as that of 1779.[48] These lists and the many letters dealing with, and soliciting orders from, them make one regret that similar catalogues are uncommon, and even more rarely accompanied by supporting correspondence. How frequently were they used? And how widely distributed to the trade? More information on this topic is needed. The booksellers' and publishers' lists more commonly found are of 'recent' publications, often intended for binding at the end of one of the works concerned.[49]

STATIONERY

Elliot was also a stationer and, in partnership with Colin Macfarquhar, a printer, he bought paper in quantity mainly from such London stationers and paper merchants as Bloxham & Fourdrinier. He bought other stationery from English provincial merchants and booksellers, but letters about this are much less common than those about the sales and exchanges of books.

There is, for example, a series of letters to Jonathan Kidd, of Newcastle, about the supply of quills. Kidd seems to have been 'trying it on', and Elliot's letter of 25 February 1775[50] starts

I must confess I was Truley surprised when I this moment Received your Draught on me for £35.6. – youll easily remember it was with some difficulty I agreed to take in the qui[l]ls on Commission as they have Really proved as said very Troublesome I indeed agreed to keep some of the finest ones providing they turned out well but I can assure you at the price of £1..10 per 1000ˢ but have not drawn what I expected in Retail

He also points out that Kidd had charged 14 000 of the best quills at 30*s* and 17 000 of the second quality at 18*s*, while the figures should have been 13 000 and 18 000 respectively. He goes on

I shall account for what is sold, I believe there is about 3000 or a few Dos more and after opening out a Bunch I really upon my honour think them very dear for the other I will not meddle with others but as I need them which I dont think will be the case these several months what I have sold of your best kind has turned poorly out they look Tolerably in Bunch's of 200 but in Single Quil[l]s or even quarter look very ill and are very ill dressed

Kidd was pertinacious and drew on Elliot again in the autumn. At that time the bookseller was away from Edinburgh, and one of his clerks, James Sutherland, wrote on 9 September 1775[51] that he had no authority to accept the draft, adding

Besides there is very few of your best Quills sold and mostly some of the other kind The 5000 you mention shall be taken care of when they come to hand, but if they are not very good of the kind Im afraid they will not answer Mr Etlliot…

A few days later Sutherland again had to write to Kidd, reiterating the position in the most polite terms, and adding a postscript 'You can very well stop the Draᵗ with this Excuse of your being advised of Mr Elliots being at London'.[52] (For Sutherland's report of this correspondence see p 91.)

It seems that Kidd visited Elliot in Edinburgh, when the latter made it clear that he would not pay the whole of Kidd's draft 'when I had not sold one half of your goods', adding 'I have Repeatedly said I would take the largest which are however too high by a great many shillings I am off[e]red Quills this moment by the person who used to dress yours 7/- cheaper'. He ended 'The whole of the 2nd Quills I cannot upon any account take and I will send them all back Rather than you should be Drawing every month for what you cannot expect to be paid'.[53]

Kidd immediately returned to the fray, driving Elliot to reply a week later, on 22 December 1775[54]

I Recd yours on Wednesday but not being a post night Could not write you in Course I told you in my last that a former had surpris'd me, but must confess the latest surpassed it in both Instance and Indescretion [*sic*] and I may add Impudence

He goes on to repeat the conditions on which he had accepted the quills, concluding 'you shall pay me Warehouse Room and all postages you put me to... you need not Expect I will pay your Draught'. Some thirty pages later there is an undated reconcilation, which corrects the numbers of quills supplied by Kidd and indicates that 17 000 of the original 18 300 second-quality still remain unsold. The Edinburgh bookseller offers to pay 28*s* per thousand for the first quality and 15*s* for the second, making a total of £31.18*s*.6*d* in place of Kidd's figure of £36.9*s*.6*d*. The copy invoice is endorsed 'Copy of this given to Mr Ferguson'; was this the end of the matter?[55]

A letter of 6 February 1777[56] to John Soulby, merchant and bookseller of Penrith, shows Elliot writing in a more complaisant tone. After starting 'wish [you] cou[l]d make it Convenient as soon as possible to pay the Money as I am Real[l]y in need of it', he promises 'I shall do everything in my power to sell [for] you some thousand of Undress'd Quil[l]s but has very little prospect I dar[e] say I Have 40 Thousand Dressed Quil[l]s of one kind and another by me w[h]ich will last me Retailing some years'.

Another Penrith bookseller, Anthony Soulby, also appears to have been 'trying it on', and Elliot wrote to him about his debt on 10 February 1782[57]

I received Several Letters from you and 3 Rms of Vile Coarse paper which you charge 6/ for pr Ream it is No Earthly use to me and not worth 3/6 it is only indeed fitt a little House it cost besides 2/ some odd of Carriage... Advise what I must do with your paper as I can make no Earthly use of it unless sold for waste – It was very odd of thinking of Sending me Such paper here, or that I would be foolish enough to accept of Such as a Just debt, if you mean to have any future commissions executed by me you will pay up the Old Balance & be more regular in future

Elliot obtained sealing wax from John Procter, printer and stationer of Darlington. He found the quality satisfactory, but complained about the unpunctual delivery.[58] The last items of stationery to be mentioned are ink stands, indiarubbers, powder flasks and boxes, and spectacle cases ordered from Marham & Potts, of Leeds, on 29 or 30 August 1786.[59] The last item makes one wonder if, as well as the nostrums that we know Elliot sold, he also dealt in spectacles.

RECRUITING STAFF

On at least two occasions Charles Elliot helped to recruit trained journeymen binders for his correspondents in Northumberland. In April 1777 he recommended to Alexander Graham, bookseller, stationer and bookbinder of Alnwick, one named Ranken.[60] After commenting that 'hands in the Binding way are very Scarce' he goes on to say of him

I have very good accounts both as to Character & abieletes [sic] he promises to Sett of[f] once this week... I Cou[l]d make no wage with him but told him & Indeed assured him he Should have better wages than he had here which I believe from 7/6 to 8/6 and at any Rate engaged in Case of the worse that if you Did not agree which I hope wont be the Case that you must bear his Traveling Charges upon foot this I thought but reasonable

Three months later he wrote to William Cay, bookbinder and printer of Newcastle upon Tyne, that he had[61]

Engaged a man of the name of John Lightbody a bookbinder of whom I have an Excel[l]ent Character for Sobriety & a Tolerable good hand his master tells me I assured him 4/- p'Week & bed & board I find he Thinks it Little enough he cannot Set out Sooner than monday Se[n]night I Sup[p]ose you may expect him on Tewsday or Wedansday following

These two letters give us an insight to the poverty even of the skilled journeyman bookbinder in the late eighteenth century – and of the manner in which some provincial master binders recruited staff.

CONCLUSION

These selections from Elliot's letter-books give some idea of the riches of this archive. Several other topics could be quarried from this source, including, for example, the often vexed problem of transport by land or sea (and that in a time of war in the North Sea), and the provision of specialist works such as atlases and botanical diagrams. And much more could be worked out about the exchange of stock between booksellers. I hope that these few morsels may whet the appetite of other investigators.

NOTES

1. These numbers must be treated with some caution. *ESTC* includes what appear to be identical titles; the numbers given do not always include apparent duplicates.

2. John Murray II (1778-1843) married Charles Elliot's daughter Anne on 6 March 1807, seventeen years after her father's death; probably she brought the eight letter-books and four ledgers to Murray. Once more I express my warmest thanks to Mrs Virginia Murray, Archivist to John Murray (Publishers) Ltd, for her kindness in allowing me to work on these archives and to quote from them. The Elliot archives have been microfilmed by Dr Warren McDougall, who has deposited copies of the microfilms with Murrays and at the National Library of Scotland; they are not at present generally available. I am grateful to Dr McDougall for originally drawing my attention to these fascinating records, which he is indexing.

3. Baron van Swieten, *Commentaries upon Boerhaave's Aphorisms concerning the Knowledge and Cure of Diseases* (1776); the copy examined is in the Library of the Wellcome Institute for the History of Medicine (shelfmark 50404/A). This set was formerly in the library of the Manchester Medical Society.

4. See Peter Isaac, 'Charles Elliot and Spilsbury's Antiscorbutic Drops' in Peter Isaac & Barry McKay [ed], *The Reach of Print* (Winchester: St Paul's Bibliographies, 1998), 157-74.

5. See, for example, the letter of 24 August 1779, replying to one of 22 [August] from William Charnley, of Newcastle upon Tyne (Murray Archives, Letter-book [hereafter MAlb] 3, folio 469).

6. For example, on 20 January 1776 Elliot asked William Charnley, of Newcastle, to advertise his edition of van Swieten to the amount of 15 or 20s in your 'best papers' (MAlb 1, folio 318). Similarly, on the same day he wrote to Wilson & Son, of York, to insert three or four advertisements for the same work (MAlb1, folio 316). This is, indeed, a recurring theme, and on 27 April he requested Charnley to advertise it 'with Slack', ie in *The Newcastle Chronicle*, which Thomas Slack had launched in 1764 (MAlb1, folio 387).

7. One such letter is dated 29 October 1781 (MAlb 5, folio 155). For details of the friendship of Byron and the Pigots see, for example, Thomas Moore, *The Life of Lord Byron* (London: John Murray, 1844), 33-7.

8. MAlb 1, folio 419.

9. MAlb 1, folio 416. Not many of the copy letters contain detailed accounts, but Elliot's letter of 12 September 1776 (MAlb 1, folio 479) to Thomas Bell, bookseller of Temple Bar, London, has such details; Bell bought twenty-five copies of van Swieten at £1.13s each. Since this is less than the price quoted to Wilson & Son, it might have been part of a larger order.

10. MAlb 1, folio 415.

11. MAlb 1, folio 312.

12. Letter of 20 January 1776 to Wilson & Son (MAlb 1, folio 317).

13. MAlb 2, folio 58.

14. Richard Welford, *Men of Mark 'Twixt Tyne and Tweed* (Newcastle: Walter Scott, 1895), 1, 625–9. Some information about Clement XIV from *Chambers Biographical Dictionary* (Edinburgh, 1974).

15. MAlb 2, folios 48 & 49.

16. *The Caledonian Mercury*. Clement XIV's death must have created considerable interest in his life and work; there were ten editions of the *Interesting Letters* in 1777, although the *British Library Catalogue* lists only three, one from London and one from Dublin in addition to the Newcastle edition.

17. Possibly R Drummond, an Edinburgh bookseller of Ossian's Head first stair below the Exchange. (Information from the *Scottish Book Trade Index*, prepared by John Morris at the National Library of Scotland [hereafter *SBTI*].) Drummond was also making a selection of these letters.

18. Charles Cordell's *The Life of Pope Clement XIV*. From the French of Caraccioli, 8vo (London, 1776).

19. *SBTI* lists three possible Gordons, but this is almost certainly William Gordon, bookseller who was in Parliament Close 1753–1779. Robert and another William Gordon, possibly sons, are also shown at the same address at similar and later dates.

20. MAlb 2, folio 92.

21. MAlb 2, folios 441 & 442.

22. *SBTI* gives an Edinburgh printer who married in 1750, but this may not be the man concerned in this increasingly difficult matter.

23. Letters of 17 August 1778, 12 September 1778, and 29 June 1779 (MAlb 2, folios 525 & 526, and MAlb 3, folios 14 and 407 & 408).

24. MAlb 4, folio 129.

25. MAlb 4, folios 158 & 159.

26. Letter to Mr W Hunter, at Mrs Cowles, Silver Street, Berwick (MAlb 4, folios 205–7).

27. MAlb 1, folios 465 & 466.

28. MAlb 1, folios 480 & 481.

29. I have not been able to trace this in an *ESTC* printout of Slack's imprints.

30. The implication of this comment, if it was true, is that carriage by sea from London to Leith was less costly than carriage by wagon from Newcastle to Edinburgh.

31. MAlb 2, folio 30. Presumably each *Ladies' Memorandum Book* was charged at 9*d*, with an extra book for each 'quire' of 24; 'Quarter' in this annotation is half of the quire of 25.

32. MAlb 2, folio 77.

33. *Charles Elliot's Catalogue of Books for 1778... the Whole Forming about Fifteen Thousand Volumes in Various Languages, Arts and Sciences* (Edinburgh, 1778). This extensive octavo catalogue runs to 216 pages; it contains 5700 items numbered every five. It is divided into sections by the format of the books, the more extensive groups being subdivided by subject. It is noticeable that medicine is not one of the subjects listed.

34. Letters of 4 January, 6 February & 26 March 1776 (MAlb 1, folios 310, 328–9 & 367).

35. Letter of 26 November 1779 (MAlb 3, folios 569–71).

36. MAlb 2, folios 54 & 55. The British Book Trade Index records Joseph Pote (1703–1787) as carrying on business in London as well as Eton.

37. *ESTC* gives this as *Poetæ Græci: sive, Selecta ex Homeri Odyss. Hesiodo, Theocrito,… Cum Vulgata Versione Emendata, ac Variis Partim Scholiatarum Græcorum, Partim Doctorum Recentiorum Notis. In usum scholæ Etonensis.* Editio altera. Etonæ: apud Jos. Pote, 1771. It is an octavo with separate pagination for the Greek and Latin texts.

38. For more details of his productive life see the *DNB*.

39. MAlb 2, folios 70 & 71.

40. MAlb 4, folio 191.

41. These are not in the *ESTC* printout of Elliot's imprints, but must have been from a stock of sheets of another publisher's work held by the Edinburgh bookseller.

42. MAlb 2, folios 450 & 451.

43. MAlb 2, folios 277 & 278.

44. MAlb 3, folios 508–10.

45. MAlb 2, folio 228.

46. MAlb 4, folios 205–207.

47. MAlb 3, folios 569–571.

48. MAlb 7, folios 655–658 & 660. See also MAlb 7, folios 352 & 354 for list of June 1786.

49. The lists of publications of John Murray I & II in that company's archives, for example, are mainly of their own publications.

50. MAlb 1, folio 157.

51. MAlb 1, folio 241.

52. Letter undated but bewteen 11 September and 2 October 1775 (MAlb 1, folio 242).

53. Letter of 15 December 1775 (MAlb 1, folio 290).

54. MAlb 1, folio 298.

55. Date between 6 & 8 February 1776 (MAlb 1, folio 330).

56. MAlb 2, folio 111.

57. MAlb 6, folio 34.

58. Letter of 14 April 1777 (MAlb 2, folio 150).

59. MAlb 7, folio 432.

60. MAlb 2, folio 147.

61. Letter dated 19 July 1777 (MAlb 2, folios 224 & 225).

TABLE 1

Charles Elliot & the Provincial Book Trade - 'Shared' Imprints

Bath
  C[?] Cruttwell
  William Frederick
  William Taylor
Berwick
  Robert Taylor
Birmingham
  Piercy & Jones
  Myles Swinney
Bristol
  James [or John] Norton
Cambridge
  J & J Merrill
  T & J Merrill
Canterbury
  Flackton & Marrable
  James Simmons
  Simmons & Kirby
  Thomas Smith
Chester
  John Monk
Eton
  Joseph Pote
Gainsborough
  Henry Mozley
Gloucester
  Robert Raikes
Hull
  Thomas Browne

Marlborough
  Edward Harold
Newcastle
  William Charnley
  Solomon Hodgson
  Thomas Robson
  Thomas Slack
Nottingham
  Samuel Cresswell
Oxford
  James Fletcher
  Fletcher & Prince
  David Prince
  C[?] Rann
Rochester
  Thomas Fisher
Warrington
  William Eyres
Worcester
  William Smart
York
  Christopher Etherington
  Nathaniel Frobisher
  William Tesseyman
  John Todd
  Anne Ward
  Thomas Wilson

TABLE 2

Correspondents by Locations (with first & last dates)

Alnwick
Graham, Alexander 1777 1777
Barnsley
Bent, John 1779 1779
Berwick upon Tweed
Phorson, William 1780 1789
Taylor, Henry 1777 1777
‡Taylor, Robert 1776 1777
Birmingham
Jones, Edward 1786 1789
*Pearson & Rollason 1779 1779
Pearson, Thomas 1789 1789
‡Piercy & Jones 1785 1786
Piercy, Edward 1786 1789
‡Swinney, Myles 1776 1789
Boston
*Preston, Caleb 1779 1779
Bristol
Gayner, W 1785 1785
Burlington
Woodcock, Thomas 1779 1779
Cambridge
Nicholson, John 1779 1779
Carlisle
Barton, John 1779 1782
Holmes, Isaac 1778 1779
Hyslop, John 1784 1784
Jollie, Francis 1780 1789
Milliken, J 1783 1789
Chelmsford *Gray, Samuel 1779 1779
*Strait, Charles 1779 1779
Chester
Poole, John 1788 1788
Coventry
*Bird, Richard(?) 1779 1779
*Bowen, Richard 1779 1779
Darlington
Procter, John 1777 1777
Derby
Drewry, John 1786 1786
*Roome, Francis 1779 1779
Doncaster
*Plummer, Charles 1779 1786
*Smith, Joseph 1779 1779
Durham
Eubank, Thomas 1778 1778
Sanderson, Patrick 1777 1777
*Thorne, Nathaniel 1776 1783
Eton
‡Pote, Joseph 1776 1786
Gainsborough
‡Mozley, Henry 1785 1789
*Mozley, John 1779 1788
Halesworth
*Miller, Thomas 1779 1779
Halifax
*Binns, Nathaniel 1779 1779

Edwards, [William] 1786 1789
*Smith, Alexander 1779 1779 *Hawes*
Metcalf, James 1777 1777
Huddersfield
*Brooke, Colin 1779 1779
Brooks[?], James 1786 1786
Hull
*‡Brown, Thomas 1779 1787
*Millson, Richard 1779 1787
Millson, Thomas 1786 1789
Ipswich
*Punchard, John 1779 1779
*Shave & Jackson 1779 1779
Kendal
*Ashburner, James 1779 1779
*Penington, William 1779 1779
King's Lynn
*Hollingsworth & Son 1779 1779
*Withingham, William 1779 1779
Knutsford *Leech, Mary Mrs 1779 1779
Lancaster
*Ashburner, Anthony 1779 1779
*Heth, James 1779 1779
Randal, Charles 1785 1789
*Walmsley, Henry 1779 1789
Langholm
Hyslop, John 1776 1776
Leeds
*Binns, John I or II 1779 1789
*Copperthwaite, George 1779 1779
Marham & Potts 1786 1786
*Ogle & Smith 1779 1779
Leicester
*Gregory, John 1779 1779
*Ireland, John 1779 1779
*Jackson, John 1779 1779
Lichfield
*Morgan, Major 1779 1779
Lincoln
*Wood, William 1779 1779
Liverpool
Crane, Samuel 1783 1789
Hodgson, Henry 1786 1789
Lennox, J 1785 1785
Rogers, Edward 1782 1785
*Sibbald, John 1776 1789
Loughborough
Clark, John 1784 1784
Malton
*Sagg, George 1779 1779
Manchester
Clark, John 1786 1786
Clarke & Co, J 1789 1789
*Clarke, James 1779 1787
*Falkner, Matthew 1779 1779
*Falkner, Samuel 1779 1779

*Harrop, James 1779 1779
*Haslingden, John 1782 1782
*Prescott, John 1779 1779
Nantwich
*Taylor & Snelson 1779 1779 *Newark*
*Cullen, William 1779 1779
Halliday, John 1780 1780
*Tomlinson, James 1779 1779
Wood, William II (prob) 1779 1779
Newcastle upon Tyne
*Akenhead, Richard 1779 1779
Atkinson, Joseph 1783 1785
*Barber, Joseph or Martin 1779 1779
Cay, William 1777 1785
*‡Charnley, William 1776 1789
Cordell, Charles Rev 1776 1780
*Gray, Gilbert 1779 1779
‡Hodgson, Solomon 1784 1789
*Humble, Edward 1779 1779
Kay, Robert 1782 1782
Kidd, Jonathan 1775 1776
*Roddam, Cuthbert 1779 1779
Saint, Thomas 1778 1787
Slack, Ann Mrs 1776 1776
*‡Slack, Thomas 1774 1780
Whitefield, Joseph 1782 1789
North Shields
Kelly, William 1782 1787
Roddam, Cuthbert 1782 1786
Thomson, W 1786 1788
Northampton
*Lacy, John 1779 1779
Norwich
*Beatniffe, Richard 1779 1779
*Berry, Christopher II 1779 1779 W'9
*Booth, Martin 1779 1779
Nottingham
Burbage & Son 1786 1789
*Burbage, George I 1779 1779
*‡Creswell, Samuel 1779 1779
Tussiman[?], Samuel 1779 1779
Oxford
*Bliss, David 1779 1779
Fletcher, J & J 1776 1776
‡Fletcher, James 1776 1776
Nourse, Charles 1782 1782
Prince & Cook 1779 1779
Penrith
Roper, Adam 1778 1778
Soulby, Anthony 1778 1786
Soulby, John 1775 1784
Preston
*Stuart & Walton 1779 1779

Ripon
Batty, Richard 1776 1776
Rotherham
*Wilson, William 1779 1779
Sheffield
*Ridgard, Ezra 1779 1779
Smith, John 1786 1789
Stewart, Duncan 1782 1782
Southampton
Skelton, Thomas 1785 1785
Stockton[?], Thomas 1785 1785
Stockton
*Christopher, Robert 1779 1789
*Pickering, John 1779 1779
Sunderland
*Craighton, Henry ? d 1776 1779 1779
*Graham, James 1779 1789
Tewksbury
*Harwood, Samuel 1779 1779
Warrington
Banks, Mrs 1779 1779
Whitby
*Clark, George 1779 1789
Whitehaven
Benn, John 1782 1782
Steel, John 1776 1776
*Ware & Sons 1778 1785
Ware, 1776 1776
Wigton
Blair, John 1780 1781
Wisbech
*Nicholson, William 1779 1779
Woodbridge
*Ridley, John 1779 1779
Wooler
Trotter, J 1788 1788
Worcester
*Lewis, L Mrs 1779 1779
*‡Smart, William 1779 1779
Workington
Eckford, William 1785 1789
York
‡Etherington, Christopher 1776 1776
*‡Frobisher, Nathaniel 1777 1790
Frobisher, William 1779 1779
*Sotheran, Henry 1779 1779
*‡Tesseyman, William 1776 1789
*‡Todd, John 1779 1789
Wilson & Son 1776 1776
*‡Wilson, Thomas 1779 1789

* Recipients of 1779 catalogue
‡ With 'shared' imprints

Scotland and the Welsh-Language Book Trade during the Second Half of the Nineteenth Century

PHILIP HENRY JONES

REFERENCES TO Wales in discussions of the Scottish book trade during the second half of the nineteenth century are few in number and, at best, of a general nature. J A H Dempster's valuable study of T & T Clark, for example, remarks that several of Clark's titles were translated into Welsh and lists the titles of Welsh periodicals which carried advertisements for the firm's publications.[1] The brief history commemorating Blackie's hundred and fiftieth anniversary merely notes that the firm published several Welsh-language titles in the 1860s and 1870s.[2] On the other hand, the enthusiastic participation of Scottish and English publishers in the Welsh-language book trade during these decades formed an important element in G J Williams's depiction of the period as the golden age of Welsh-language publishing:

> *English and Scottish publishers were responsible for many of these expensive books [published] between about 1850 and 1890... It was not a desire to promote the cultural life of Wales that led them to pay Welsh authors to write the books and organize the work of selling them in every part of the country. They were businessmen, not philanthropists... They could make a substantial profit...*[3]

I have maintained elsewhere that the idea of a golden age of Welsh-language publishing is a myth which needs to be reconsidered.[4] This paper is intended to advance that process by suggesting that the involvement of Scottish and English number publishers in Wales may well have weakened the indigenous Welsh-language book trade by draining away money that would otherwise have gone to Welsh publishers and booksellers. The first part of this paper examines the nature and extent of this involvement and attempts to assess its effects on the Welsh-language book trade. The second part explores more briefly a topic which has been ignored by both Scottish and Welsh historians of the book trade, namely that at least one major Welsh publisher had a number of substantial Welsh books produced in Scotland during this period, which may well have been more beneficial to Welsh-language publishing than the better-known activities of Scottish number publishers.

During the nineteenth century, substantial Welsh-language books were almost invariably published in parts or numbers. The effectiveness of this method was first revealed when sales of the first edition of Peter Williams's Bible with notes and comments, published in shilling parts between 1767/8 and 1770, achieved the hitherto unparalleled figure of 8600 copies.[5] The relative poverty of most purchasers of Welsh-language books and the limited resources of Welsh publishers meant that part publication was particularly well suited to conditions in Wales. Religious titles predominated, but the growing interest in self-improvement led to the publication of an increasing number of substantial secular titles from the later 1840s onwards, a process which culminated in the publication of Thomas Gee's ten-volume Welsh encyclopaedia, *Y Gwyddoniadur Cymreig*, between 1854 and 1879.[6] From the later 1850s the profitability of the Welsh-language market attracted both English and Scottish specialists in number publishing who flooded it with large, illustrated, and (by Welsh standards) expensive books. Excluding those firms (such as J G Murdoch) which confined themselves to providing family Bibles, six non-Welsh publishers were involved in the number trade. Two were English, Virtue (apparently the first in the field in 1856 with a translation of John Fleetwood, *The Life of... Christ*) and the London Printing and Publishing Company. The others, Blackie, Mackenzie, Fullarton, and T C Jack, were Scottish[7] firms with a long-standing interest in number publishing.[8]

Despite its intensity, Scottish exploitation of the Welsh-language market was comparatively short-lived, extending from the early 1860s to 1881, and resulted in the publication of no more than sixteen titles (including rival editions of family Bibles but excluding reprints). It came to an end partly because of external factors, notably the onset of the great depression which, as the Wrexham publisher Charles Hughes told the Aberdare Commission, greatly reduced the demand for more expensive Welsh books from the mid-1870s onwards.[9] At the same time, educational and demographic changes also began to erode the monoglot Welsh readership which had provided a captive market for translations. Factors peculiar to the number trade also hastened its end. The publishers may well have saturated the market for their products, the novelty of large-format illustrated works wore off, and press exposure of the aggressive sales tactics of canvassers brought the trade into disrepute.

Tracing which titles were issued and when they appeared is complicated by the lack of a bibliography of Welsh publications between 1821 and 1908 and by the fact that the title-pages of number publications rarely bore a date. Sales through canvassers meant that few advertisements appeared in the Welsh-language press. Fortunately, reviews in Welsh periodicals of individual numbers of several publications enable us to trace their progress and form the basis of the provisional listing of titles provided in the appendix. Of the sixteen titles listed there, three were family Bibles containing the perennially popular notes and commentary by Peter Williams, and three were translations of Bunyan's works. Two translations, those of works by Brown and Goldsmith, were of hopelessly outdated material. Although old-fashioned, Keith's *Evidence* was arguably worth translating. *Credoau y Byd* was an adaptation of James Gardner's *Faiths of the World* for a Welsh readership and thus served a useful function. Law's veterinary work was up-to-date but, judging from the rarity of second-hand copies, probably did not enjoy extensive sales. All three historical compilations, *Cymru, Hanes y Brytaniaid a'r Cymry*, and *Enwogion y Ffydd*, were original works specifically designed for a Welsh readership and presented material that was otherwise largely unavailable. Though defective in its execution, *Holl Weithiau... William Williams* was a praiseworthy attempt to produce the first complete edition of the works of the Methodist hymn-writer who can be regarded as one of the most important Welsh writers. *Ceinion Llenyddiaeth Gymreig*, an anthology of the beauties of Welsh literature, was generally regarded by contemporary critics as being a lost opportunity.[10] Apart from the veterinary text, all were safe, popular titles which exemplified a contemporary observation that number publishers 'generally publish only books of ready sale'.[11]

Although compilations such as *Cymru* and *Enwogion y Ffydd* of necessity drew upon a wide range of contributors (if only to demonstrate their denominational impartiality), six writers were primarily responsible for all these titles. All but one were ministers of religion.

James Rhys Kilsby Jones (1813–1889) was an Independent minister who was too eccentric and plain-spoken to be a success as a pastor. He worked for

Mackenzie from the early 1860s to 1870, probably to pay for a large house he had built for himself. According to his (infuriatingly vague) biographer he earned some £1400 from his lectures and writings.[12] How he was first brought to Mackenzie's notice is not known, but he claimed that he himself had persuaded Mackenzie to publish at least one title, *Holl Weithiau... William Williams.*[13]

The Calvinistic Methodist minister Owen Jones 'Meudwy Môn' (1806–89), a versatile and prolific author from the early 1830s onwards, began working for Blackie in the early 1860s and was responsible for preparing all the firm's Welsh titles. In 1867/8 he retired from the ministry to concentrate on his literary work. His advice was sufficiently valued for W G Blackie to visit him in Llandudno to discuss proposed publications.[14] On the other hand, the firm was prepared to over-rule his objections and insist that translations of English 'elegant excerpts' were included in *Ceinion.*[15] His account-books detailing his dealings with Blackie have survived and I hope to discuss them in the near future.

Robert Edward Williams (1825–79), an Independent minister, was an unsuccessful pastor, possibly because he preferred to concentrate on his literary work.[16] Brought to Fullarton's notice by William Rees 'Gwilym Hiraethog', a fellow minister and prominent author and journalist, he was responsible for the two Welsh titles published by that firm.[17]

R J Pryse 'Gweirydd ap Rhys' (1807–89) was a self-educated scholar, employed by the Welsh publisher Thomas Gee as a literary factotum from 1849 to 1863. After leaving Gee's office he scraped a living by writing, journalism, competing for eisteddfod prizes, and translating works such as Kitto's *Llyfr Darluniadol y Sabboth*, a part-work published by the London Printing and Publishing Company in the mid-1860s. Drawn into the service of Scottish publishers when R E Williams invited him to translate the introductory essay to the translation of Goldsmith,[18] he subsequently contributed 381 articles to *Credoau.*[19] When *Credoau* was almost completed (probably in the spring of 1870), Harrison, Fullarton's agent, asked Gweirydd to compile a history of Wales.[20] R E Williams, fearing that this would deprive him of an important source of income, travelled to Edinburgh in an attempt to persuade Fullarton that Gweirydd did not possess the requisite historical abilities. After Fullarton had decided in 1870 to abandon Welsh-language publishing, Harrison approached Gweirydd once again, this time with an offer of £360 from Mackenzie for the *Hanes y Brytaniaid a'r Cymry*.[21] Work on this title provided most (if not all) of Gweirydd's income during the early 1870s but by 1876 he was once again financially *in extremis*.[22]

An Independent minister and notable scholar, John Peter 'Ioan Pedr' (1833–77) was the original editor of *Enwogion y Ffydd*. Mackenzie himself visited Peter in September 1876 and accompanied him to Llanwrin vicarage in order to persuade the scholarly clergyman Silvan Evans to assist with early parts of the work.[23] Following Peter's death Gweirydd ap Rhys became editor.

R Thomas Howell 'Carfanawg' was minister at Lady Huntingdon's Chapel, Swansea, from 1871 to 1882. According to the scanty biographical sources (like other failed ministers he was largely written out of the historical record) Howell overworked, took to drink, and had to leave the ministry. His fate is perhaps understandable given the amount of work translators and editors had to undertake. The text of Goldsmith's *Animated Nature*, for instance, amounted to about one and a quarter million words.[24] Since publication commenced well before copy was complete, writing was a hand-to-mouth process.[25] In February 1867 Owen Jones claimed that he had to work ten to twelve hours a day in order to prepare a 2/6 number each month and correct proofs of an *esboniad* (exposition) for Blackie.[26] In April 1870 he complained that proofs were arriving '*by every post*' and that all his time was taken up in reading and writing.[27] The crushing burden of work could lead to ill-health: in the preface to *Credoau*, R E Williams apologised for misprints which he had failed to detect because of his eye problems. It also led to carelessness: reviewers complained, for example, of the excessive number of errors in *Holl Weithiau... William Williams*.[28] Payment for this drudgery was scarcely generous. In April 1871 Owen Jones offered a friend 4/- per printed page for a contribution to *Cymru*[29] and it has been suggested that Gweirydd received about 3/- per printed page for his work on *Enwogion y Ffydd*.[30]

Since these books had to be set in Scotland from manuscript copy, several Welsh compositors were employed by Scottish printers. It is known, for example, that Gwenlyn Evans,[31] Owen R Owen,[32] and two other compositors from Caernarfon spent some years in Edinburgh at Ballantyne's setting the Welsh Bible published by T C Jack in 1874.

No reliable sales figures for the various Scottish number publications appear to have survived, but references in the Welsh-language press provide a rough indication of the scale of the trade. It was claimed in 1867 that more than 20 000 copies of one number publication had been sold in north Wales.[33] In 1870, about 1800 copies of *Hanes y Brytaniaid a'r Cymry* were being sold in north Wales.[34] T C Jack's 1874 Bible reputedly 'returned a good profit'.[35]

Several methods were used to promote the sale of these publications. Publishers clearly believed in the efficacy of testimonials from prominent Welshmen.[36] Fullarton, for example, sent Gwilym Hiraethog proofs of part of the translation of Goldsmith so that he could vouch in print for its accuracy.[37] Such testimonials and excerpts from favourable reviews were widely reproduced in handbills, prospectuses, and sometimes even in the book itself. 'Free' gifts were an even more important promotional device. In exchange for the tokens included with the last eight parts, subscribers to *Holl Weithiau... William Williams* were 'presented' with a large portrait of Williams suitable for framing.[38] Unfortunately for the publishers a dispute arose about the authenticity of the portrait.[39] Subscribers to *Ceinion Llenyddiaeth Gymreig* were offered a large portrait of Gwilym Hiraethog in exchange for vouchers, purchasers of *Credoau* were presented with a 'Coloured Tree of Religious Denominations' measuring 40 by 27 inches, and those who took *Enwogion y Ffydd* received a portrait of Henry Richard, suitable for framing.

Numbers normally appeared regularly, at short intervals, and on time.[40] Punctuality was such an important selling-point that publishers often guaranteed it in their prospectuses, Fullarton stating that each part of *Credoau* was to be published 'as nearly as possible monthly'. Even the largest indigenous Welsh-language publishers lacked the resources to match such promptitude. Thus publication of the parts of several works in progress which Thomas Gee had announced on 1 December 1869 would appear 'by the end of the month'[41] was repeatedly postponed to mid-February 1870.[42] Not surprisingly, reviewers of the Scottish-produced works were quick to point out that such '*speed and punctuality... will soon either reform or close Welsh printing offices*.[43] The attractive appearance of books produced in Scotland was another major selling-point. *Y Beirniad* claimed that '*The format, paper, type and presswork of Credoau y Byd is such as is commonly seen on the tables of the best Englishmen*'.[44] A later *Beirniad* review stated that '*The Scotchmen have developed a taste for publishing Welsh books... The tasteful manner in which they are produced is an example worthy of imitation by Welsh publishers*'.[45] The steel engravings, sometimes hand-coloured, were particularly acclaimed as being '*far beyond*' what had hitherto appeared in any Welsh book,[46] and it was claimed that no Welsh publisher could have ventured to spend so much on them.[47] No one pointed out that, since these engravings were recycled from English-language publications, their cost had already been written off by the publishers. Ornate bindings were another mark of the drawing-room book, even though Welsh firms could attempt to match these by buying in cases from specialist suppliers.[48] The books were so lavishly produced that a few reviews even expressed concern that publishers would not cover the costs of producing them;[49] one reviewer, however, consoled himself with the thought that since Fullarton was a Scottish firm, it had doubtless examined this question very carefully.[50]

Large-format family Bibles with steel engravings, coloured plates, bindings in morocco with brass clasps, and blank pages for recording family details, were frequently criticized by reviewers who complained that they were too large for practical use and served merely as decoration.[51] As *Y Traethodydd* pointed out, money spent on these expensive Bibles could have been better used: '*It is not uncommon to see in many houses a Family Bible which sometimes has cost many pounds lying amongst the ornaments, while there is scarcely another book of any value in the whole house*'.[52]

Although reviews in the Welsh-language press recognised that Scottish and English number publishers presented a serious threat to indigenous publishers, free-trade arguments initially prevailed:

> *We ourselves are not overfond of seeing Scotsmen undertaking the publication of books in Welsh... But the good of the majority comes first, the interest of a particular class second. Unless the printers of Wales look lively, their work will soon be stolen out of their hands by foreigners*.[53]

Since Welsh publishers could no longer hope to enjoy a monopoly, '*The only legitimate way they can drive the English from the market is by publishing better and cheaper books*'.[54] From the later 1860s onwards, *Y Traethodydd* regularly urged Welsh publishers to produce good Welsh books which would be much cheaper, and far better suited to the '*taste, spirit, and circumstances*' of the Welsh than translations of works originally written for a very different readership.[55]

The initial belief in free trade was challenged by the aggressive manner in which number publications were sold, which appeared to go beyond fair competition. In Wales, as elsewhere, number publishers relied on intensive house-to-house canvassing rather than the normal channels of the book trade: '*Would one in a hundred have bought Credoau y Byd, and similar books had this method of trading not existed?*'[56] The canvassers' zeal was sharpened by their being wholly dependent for their income on commission, unlike the deliverers (those who distributed the parts) who received a weekly wage.

Advertisements for canvassers in the Welsh-language press called for respectable and intelligent Welsh-speakers with business experience. Preference was allegedly given to members of religious denominations[57] and at least one advertisement maintained that the work was suited to '*lay-preachers of every denomination*'.[58] A few Welsh canvassers can be identified. The mediocre poet Edward Davies 'Iolo Trefaldwyn' (1819–87) suffered various business failures before settling in Wrexham and travelling about Wales '*for many years*' soliciting orders for Scottish publishers.[59] Griffith Jones 'Glan Menai' (1836–1906), initially a schoolmaster, became an itinerant bookseller, author, and journalist. While at Caernarfon (from about 1870 onwards) he was appointed agent for Mackenzie and Blackie, and in the course of ten years gained them '*thousands and thousands*' of orders. According to his biographer this was the most prosperous period of his life.[60]

Although knowledge of the language was desirable, the inability of many canvassers to speak Welsh was no impediment to their success:

> ... *recently one of Mackenzie's men visited a rural Welsh area with the splendid edition of the Works of Williams Pantycelyn... and although the man did not know a word of Welsh he still succeeded in persuading almost every family in the district to take the book.*[61]

Irrespective of whether they were of Welsh origin or *'foreigners'* ('estroniaid'), by the later 1860s canvassers had come to be viewed with suspicion. Some of them were undoubtedly dubious characters. James Jamieson Wilson, an 'educated man' turned 'book hawker' sentenced to twelve months' hard labour for theft in July 1869,[62] was the brother (and probably the accomplice) of A G Wilson, perpetrator of the great Bangor jewellery robbery of March 1869. But the main reason why canvassers came to be disliked was their ruthless and unscrupulous pursuit of sales, memories of which lie behind Caradoc Evans's short story 'Be This Her Memorial'. The aged and religious Nanni, surviving on poor relief of three shillings and ninepence a week, wished to give her minister a gift on his departure to a wealthier church. The arrival of the 'Seller of Bibles' provided her with a welcome opportunity:

> He unstrapped his pack, and showed Nanni a gaudy volume with a clasp of brass, and containing many coloured prints; the pictures he explained at hazard: here was a tall-hatted John baptising, here a Roman-featured Christ praying in the Garden of Gethsemane, here a frock-coated Moses and the Tablets.
>
> 'A Book,' said he, 'which ought to be on the table of every Christian home.'
>
> 'Truth you speak, little man,' remarked Nanni. 'What shall I say to you you are asking for it?'
>
> 'It has a price far above rubies,' answered the Seller of Bibles. He turned over the leaves and read: '"The labourer is worthy of his hire." Thus it is written. I will let you have a copy – one copy only – at cost price.'
>
> 'How good you are, dear me!' exclaimed Nanni.
>
> 'This I can do,' said the Seller of Bibles, 'because my Master is the Big Man.'
>
> 'Speak you now what the cost price is.'
>
> 'A little sovereign, that is all.'
>
> 'Dear, dear; the Word of the little Big Man for a sovereign!'
>
> 'Keep you the Book on your parlour table for a week. Maybe others who are thirsty will see it.'
>
> Then the Seller of Bibles sang a prayer; and he departed.[63]

Although Caradoc Evans is frequently accused of gross exaggeration, complaints published in the Welsh press from the later 1860s onwards suggest that if anything he understated the wiles and stratagems of canvassers. In the autumn of 1867 Robert Ll Roberts of Carneddi accused Mackenzie of sharp

practice in issuing posters which quoted his approval of *Holl Weithiau...
William Williams*. Although, he maintained, Mackenzie's representative had
requested him to puff the book he had refused to do so because it was too expensive.[64] The following week Roberts (clearly under threat of legal action)
was compelled to 'explain' that he had not intended to attack Mackenzie's personal character and had been assured by him that, although he had no recol-
lection of so doing, he had in fact praised the book some three years earlier.[65]

The following week, a letter which the *Baner*'s editor significantly stated had
been purged of references to individual publishers to avoid legal complications, deplored the readiness of prominent Welshmen to promote the sale of
expensive illustrated books, and asked why they were so relentlessly puffed:
'*paid servants*' of English publishers had even been allowed to break the Sab-
bath by soliciting orders in Sunday schools.[66]

According to another writer:

*A few years ago, a two-footed beast happened to pay a visit to my little cottage
with the first part of Peter Williams's Bible in an enormously large format,
and attempted to make me subscribe to it... The price would be no more than
a guinea complete, with a picture worth five shillings as a reward at the end.*

Rather than providing printed terms, the canvasser gave his word that the
work would not cost more than a guinea and within a few days '*many hundreds*' in the county, including ministers and educated men, had ordered the
book. The canvasser then departed and no more was ever heard of him. When
the deliverer turned up with the parts, people discovered that the book would
cost four pounds, far more than the 'honest' canvasser had stated. They began
to complain and threatened to refuse to receive the work. The deliverer
claimed that he had no way of knowing what the canvasser might have said.
Customers had ordered the book in writing, they were bound to take it, and
could be compelled to do so.[67]

According to 'Gomerydd', the overseer of a Ffestiniog quarry had allowed a
canvasser to solicit orders there. The canvasser persuaded a poor old man to
subscribe and, on the pretext of ascertaining how his name was spelled, asked
him to write it in his notebook. Little did the old man realise that this constituted a legally binding order for the book. When the deliverer brought him the
first part the old man attempted to cancel the order because of his poverty, age,

and the lengthy time the volume would take to appear. The deliverer's oral warnings were followed by a letter from the publisher stating that the quarry-man would be prosecuted should he refuse to receive the book. After the quarry overseer had interceded on his behalf the publishers agreed that they would not insist on their rights as long as they were reimbursed for the com-mission (six shillings for a £2 book) which they had already paid to the can-vasser. The old man had to send them six shillingsworth of stamps.[68]

A widely reported trial indicates that such incidents were not the invention of mischief-makers sheltering behind pseudonyms. In June 1869 Blackie brought three subscribers before the County Court at Caernarfon for refusing to pay for *Y Beibl Teuluaidd Cynnwysfawr*.[69] One defendant, Pierce Griffith of Llanberis, claimed that Thomas Phillips, Blackie's canvasser, had led him to believe that the Bible would not cost more than £2.5s. Although the deliverer was told that the book would not be accepted because it was too expensive (it cost £4), he insisted on leaving the parts on Griffiths's table. Phillips then wrote to Griffiths informing him that he had to receive the book. The judge found for the defendant since 'the agreement was drawn up in the English lan-guage, which a Welshman could not understand': in his view it might as well have been in Chinese. Since the order had not been read over but simply filled in by the canvasser it was not binding. The judge pointedly added that 'to a man in a humble rank in life, £4 was a large sum to invest in a book, and al-though done in the name of religion, he could not for a moment disguise from himself that much is done for the sake of making money, and not for the pur-pose of spreading religion'.

A final assessment of the effects of the activities of Scottish and English num-ber publishers on the Welsh book trade must wait until much more is known about the economics of Welsh-language publishing. In particular, we need to investigate the nature of the demand for Welsh books in order to decide whether the extensive sales of expensive books by outsiders reduced the mar-ket share of indigenous publishers. Contemporary English discussions of the number trade stressed that house-to-house canvassing reached what Curwen described as 'a substratum of the public... which is entirely out of the stretch of the regular bookselling arm'.[70] Whether the activities of Scottish and Eng-lish number publishers similarly extended the market in Wales remains un-clear. What is known is that the total pool of money at stake was not large:

Charles Hughes estimated that £100 000 was spent in 1875 on 'Welsh literature of all kinds'.[71]

Whatever the effects of the number trade on producers of Welsh books, its reliance on canvassers and deliverers rather than on booksellers probably inhibited the growth of the retail book trade – a significant consideration since the scarcity of specialist Welsh-language booksellers was often deplored in the later nineteenth century.[72]

Although Scottish number publishers undoubtedly kept a few Welsh-language authors afloat during the 1860s and 1870s, most of them were established figures and, apart from John Peter and (to a lesser extent) Gweirydd ap Rhys, they were literary journeymen rather than scholars. Since serious scholars who chose to write in Welsh (such as Lewis Edwards and Owen Thomas) were published by the major Welsh publishers, it might be argued that the number publishers merely fostered the development of a geographically dispersed Welsh Grub Street.

A final criticism of Scottish and English number publishers is that although they were ready enough to exploit the Welsh market when conditions were favourable, their interest evaporated as soon as demand began to slacken. Welsh publishers, weakened by the creaming off of substantial sales during the 1860s and 1870s by 'foreign' publishers, were left to face deteriorating conditions.

Links between Welsh printer-publishers and Scotland took several forms. Welsh firms purchased equipment and type from Scottish manufacturers. In 1869, for example, Hughes & Son of Wrexham bought a Double Demy platen machine and a six-inch-ram hydraulic press for £325 from Davies & Primrose of Leith[73] and, later in the same year, a considerable quantity of type from Miller & Richard.[74]

A far more important development was that from 1868 onwards Hughes had many of its most substantial books produced in Edinburgh. Since its publishing activities during the 1850s had outgrown its own productive capacity, the firm had Welsh books set and printed in London, mainly by Clay, Son & Taylor. As London costs increased, Hughes began to consider transferring work to Scotland where both labour costs and overheads were significantly lower. The firm first approached Ballantyne in March 1865, 'believing that you can do for us on better terms',[75] and quoting as reference James Nichol of Edinburgh, the publisher of a series of Standard Divines printed by

Ballantyne.[76] Although nothing came of this, nor of a second approach in October 1867,[77] in April 1868[78] a link was formed which was to last until 1916.[79]

The first two books Ballantyne printed for Hughes were *Traethodau Duwinyddol* by Lewis Edwards (over 700 pages in length) and *Llyfr Emynau*, a hymn-book for the Welsh Independents. Ballantyne charged £27.15s.6d for setting and machining Part 3 of the *Traethodau* (probably in an impression of 5000 copies), and £90.12s.6d for printing 10 000 copies of the hymn-book, both sums being exclusive of paper costs.[80] The elaborate arrangements for producing *Llyfr Emynau* illustrate the extent to which Hughes was integrated into the larger British book trade: the book was printed in Edinburgh by Ballantyne on paper supplied by McCorquodale of Liverpool,[81] the sheets were bound in London by Straker and Son,[82] who then sent the finished book to Wrexham for distribution to the trade. As well as printing from stereotype plates prepared at Wrexham, Ballantyne set and stereotyped Welsh copy (both manuscript and reprint copy) for Hughes.[83]

Precisely how many titles were produced by Ballantyne for Hughes remains unclear. The books themselves are an unreliable guide since they were intended to mislead patriotic Welsh purchasers: titles which archival evidence proves were printed in Edinburgh usually claim to have been printed in Wrexham. Unfortunately the archival evidence is fragmentary, the only relevant material to have survived First World War salvage drives being two letter-books (one for 1862–73, the other for February to September 1887) and two volumes of Machine Room Records of Printing from 1870 onwards. References to books printed by Ballantyne were inserted into the second Machine Room book (probably in the 1930s), from a source now presumably lost. To complicate matters, not all Ballantyne-produced books were correctly identified in this source. Even so, sufficient evidence has survived to prove that many of the largest works published by Hughes over a period of forty years or more were produced by Ballantyne, often in what were (by Welsh standards) large impressions. A print order of 3500 copies of the first edition of a 448-page biblical dictionary, *Geiriadur Ysgrythyrol Newydd*, in 1887[84] was immediately followed by a second edition of some 3000[85] and a third edition of 1498 copies in 1891.[86]

Perhaps the most important examples of false imprints are the novels of the best-selling Welsh novelist, Daniel Owen. 3000 copies of his *Rhys Lewis* were printed by Ballantyne in November 1890 and a further 3000 in October 1895.[87] In 1893 Ballantyne printed 4125 copies of the second edition of the 384-page *Enoc Huws*[88] and in 1894 3000 copies of the 352-page *Gwen Tomos*.[89] All these claimed to have been printed in Wrexham.

I have attempted to demonstrate that Scottish involvement in the Welsh-language book trade was not necessarily as benign a development as was claimed by G J Williams. It may well have weakened the indigenous trade in Welsh-language books and did little to foster Welsh-language authorship. On the other hand, the hitherto unremarked production of Welsh books by Ballantyne undoubtedly permitted a major Welsh publisher, Hughes a'i Fab, to publish a wider range of substantial Welsh books than would otherwise have been possible.

APPENDIX

Short-Title List of Welsh Books Published by Scottish Firms

Blackie

1861–4

Cyfansoddiadau Allegol, Cyffelybiaethol, ac Arwyddluniol John Bunyan. Wedi eu cyfieithu i'r Gymraeg... gan... Owen Jones.

lxxvi, 840 pp. Plates, facsimiles, additional engraved title page.

A translation of the third volume of Offor's edition of Bunyan's works published by Blackie in 1861–2.[90]

1866–70

Y Beibl Teuluaidd Cynnwysfawr... gan... Owen Jones... At yr hwn y chwanegwyd, Sylwadau... Peter Williams...

xvi, 8, 1472 pp. Numerous steel engravings.

Published in thirty-two 2/6 parts, or in 7/6 *BIW* divisions.293.[91]

1866–7

Y Prawf o Wirionedd y Grefydd Gristionogol, wedi ei gasglu o gyflawniad llythyrenol Prophwydoliaeth... gan Alexander Keith... Wedi ei gyfieithu a'i gasglu gan... Owen Jones...

xvi, 656 pp. Plates.

Translation of Keith's *Evidence of the Truth of the Christian Religion.*

1870–2

Y Beibl Teuluaidd Cynnwysfawr...

xvi, 1472 pp.

Slightly rearranged reprint of *BIW* 293 with minor omissions.
BIW 300.

1871–5
Cymru: yn Hanesyddol, Parthedegol, a Bywgraphyddol. Dan olygiad... Owen Jones...
2 vols, viii, 728, 672 pp. 13 Maps, 9 plates.
Issued in twenty-two 2s parts, or four half-volumes, cloth, 13/- each, or 2 vols, cloth, 50/-.

1875–6
Ceinion Llenyddiaeth Gymreig. Dan olygiad... Owen Jones...
2 vols, x, 384; viii, 384 pp. 24 'highly-finished' engravings, 2 coloured.
Issued in twelve 2s parts, or four half-volumes at 7/6 each or 8/6 with gilt edges.

Mackenzie

1862–4
Taith y Pererin a Gweithiau Eraill gan John Bunyan... Dan olygiaeth... J R Kilsby Jones.
xxvi, 944 pp. 26 leaves plates, additional engraved title-page.
Possibly reprinted in 1868/9.

1866–7
Holl Weithiau... William Williams. Pant-y Celyn, dan olygiaeth... J. R. Kilsby Jones...
xxxiv, 816 pp. 5 steel engravings, additional engraved title-page.
Published in 1/- numbers.[92]

1868
Y Beibl Cyssegr-lan Gyda Nodau Esponiadol... Peter Williams. Dan olygiaeth... J. R. Kilsby Jones.
ii, 1166, 42 pp. Many steel engravings.
BIW 284.

1869–70
Argraphiad newydd o Eiriadur Beiblaidd... John Brown wedi ei ail olygu yn drwyadl gan... W. Brown... cyfieithedig gan J. R. Kilsby Jones...
vi, 594 pp. Many plates and maps.
Translation of *A Dictionary of the Bible* by John Brown of Haddington.

1873
Y Beibl Sanctaidd...
1172 pp. Steel engravings, some coloured.
Reprint of *BIW* 284 omitting preliminary matter, Apocrypha, etc.
BIW 303.

1871–4
Hanes y Brytaniaid a'r Cymry, yn Wladol, Milwrol, Cymdeithasol, Masnachol, Llenorol, a Chrefyddol, o'r Amseroedd Boreuaf hyd yn Bresennol. Gan Gweirydd ap Rhys...
2 vols, v, 528;
iv, 534 pp. Issued in six-shilling parts.

1879-80

John Peter and R J Pryse, *Enwogion y Ffydd: Neu, Hanes Crefydd y Genedl Gymreig, O'r Diwygiad Protestanaidd hyd yr Amser Presennol...*
4 vols in 2, [1] 512, [1] 514, vi pp. 16 plates.
Issued in sixteen two-shilling parts, each containing a steel engraving.

Fullarton

1864-7

Hanes y Ddaear a'r Creaduriaid Byw, gan Oliver Goldsmith; gyda Golygiad Arweiniol o'r Deyrnas Anifeilaidd gan y Baron Cuvier... A Bywgraffiad yr Awdwr, gan Washington Irving. Wedi ei gyfieithu a'i olygu gan R. E. Williams.
2 vols, vi, 105, 508; iv, 523 pp. Portrait, 73 hand-coloured steel engravings, additional engraved title page.
Issued in 36 shilling parts or 18 two-shilling parts, 2 (or 4) coloured engravings with each part.
Translation of Goldsmith, *An History of the Earth and Animated Nature* (1774).

1867-70

Credoau y Byd; neu Hanes yr Holl Grefyddau a'r Enwadau Crefyddol, eu Hathrawiaethau, eu Defodau, a'u Harferion, wedi ei gasglu a'i gyfieithu o Waith cyffelyb yn Saesnaeg, o eiddo... James Gardner... Dan olygiaeth... R. E. Williams...
2 Vols, 644, 640 pp. 40 steel engravings.
Published in twenty 2s parts.
Adaptation of Gardner's *Faiths of the World.*

Thomas C Jack

1874

Y Bibl Cysegr-lan... gyda Nodiadau Eglurhaol... Peter Williams... Matthew Henry; a Sylwadau Arweiniol i bob Llyfr, gan... R. T. Howell, Abertawe.
xvi, 1183 pp. Many coloured plates.
Sold as bound volume(s), not in parts but could be paid for by instalments.[93]
BIW 309.

1876

Taith y Pererin; y Rhyfel Ysbrydol, a Bywyd a Marwolaeth Mr. Drygddyn gan John Bunyan, gyda chipdrem ar Fywyd ac Amserau Bunyan gan... R. T. Howell. Cyfieithiad diwygiedig.
Lxxx, 736 pp. 12 leaves coloured plates.

1876

Y Bibl Cysegr-lan
xvi, 1184 pp. Many coloured plates.
Reprint of *BIW* 309, omitting editor's preface.
BIW 316.

1880-1

Meddyg y Fferm. Arweinydd i Drin a Gochel Clefydau mewn Anifeiliaid gan James Law… Mewn Dwy Gyfrol

xxv, 423 pp. 24 leaves plates. Also issued as 2 vols.

Translation of *The Farmer's Veterinary Adviser* (Edinburgh: T C Jack, 1879).

NOTES

1. John A H Dempster, *The T & T Clark Story: a Victorian Publisher and the New Theology, with an Epilogue covering the Twentieth-Century History of the Firm* (Edinburgh, 1992).

2. Agnes A C Blackie, *Blackie & Son 1809-1959: a Short History of the Firm* (London & Glasgow, 1959), 24-5.

3. G J Williams, 'Cyhoeddi llyfrau Cymraeg yn y bedwaredd ganrif ar bymtheg', *Journal of the Welsh Bibliographical Society* [hereafter *JWBS*], 9 (1958-65), 152-61 (156). Similar views (placing even greater emphasis on Scottish involvement) are expressed in his *Y Wasg Gymraeg Ddoe a Heddiw* (Y Bala, 1970). Quotations in italics, here and later, are translations by the author from the original Welsh.

4. Philip Henry Jones, 'A Golden Age reappraised: Welsh-language publishing in the nineteenth century', in *Images & Texts: Their Production and Distribution in the 18th and 19th Centuries*, edited by Peter Isaac & Barry McKay (Winchester & New Castle DE, 1997), 121-41.

5. Gomer Morgan Roberts, *Bywyd a Gwaith Peter Williams* (Cardiff, 1943), 61-80.

6. Roger J Williams, 'Hanes cyhoeddi *Y Gwyddoniadur Cymreig*', *JWBS*, 11 (1973-6), 54-67.

7. Although the title-pages of works published by these firms often placed London before Edinburgh or Glasgow as the place of publication, the books themselves were printed in Scotland.

8. Blackie, *Blackie*, 4-5.

9. *Report of the Committee Appointed to Inquire into the Condition of Intermediate and Higher Education in Wales and Monmouthshire*: Vol. II, *Minutes of Evidence and Appendices*, Parliamentary Papers, 1881, XXXIII, C.3047 [hereafter *Aberdare Evidence*], QQ 6275, 6277.

10. National Library of Wales [hereafter NLW], Cwrtmawr MSS 916 (6), John Peter, Y Bala, to Revd D Silvan Evans, 5 Nov 1875.

11. NLW, Cwrtmawr MSS 916 (9), John Peter, Y Bala, to Revd D Silvan Evans, 20 Sept 1876.

12. Vyrnwy Morgan, *Kilsby Jones* (Wrexham, [1897]), 25.

13. 'Rhagymadrodd' to William Williams, *Holl Weithiau…*, edited by J R Kilsby Jones (London, 1867), [1].

14. Letter from Owen Jones to John Jones, mis-dated 7 April 1870 [ie 1874], printed in 'Llythyrau Y Parch. Owen Jones, Llandudno, at Myrddin Fardd', *Traethodydd*, 62 (1907), 373-84 (379).

15. Charles Ashton, *Hanes Llenyddiaeth Gymreig, o 1651 O.C. hyd 1850* (Liverpool, [1893]), 646.

16. Raymond B Davies, 'Robert Edward Williams: cyfieithydd *An history of the earth and animated nature* gan Oliver Goldsmith', *National Library of Wales Journal*, 20 (1977–8), 312.

17. NLW, Add. MSS 302C (8), R J Pryse to A J Brereton, 22 April 1870.

18. The same.

19. *Y Genedl Gymreig*, 9 Oct 1889.

20. NLW, Add. MSS 302C (8), R J Pryse to A J Brereton, 22 April 1870.

21. The same.

22. Enid P Roberts, *Detholion o Hunangofiant Gweirydd ap Rhys* ([Aberystwyth], 1949), 190.

23. NLW, Cwrtmawr MSS 916 (8), John Peter, Y Bala, to Revd D Silvan Evans, 18 Sept 1876.

24. R Elwyn Hughes, 'Tasgau'r cyfieithwyr', *Y Casglwr*, 39 (Christmas 1989), 5.

25. Advertisement, *Baner ac Amserau Cymru* [hereafter *BAC*], 3 April 1867.

26. Letter from Owen Jones to John Jones, 5 Feb 1867, printed in 'Llythyrau', 376.

27. Letter from Owen Jones to John Jones, 9 April 1870, printed in 'Llythyrau', 379.

28. *Traethodydd*, 32 (1877), 439–40.

29. Letter from Owen Jones to John Jones, 22 April 1871, printed in 'Llythyrau', 381.

30. Rhianydd Morgan, 'John Peter (Ioan Pedr) 1833–77, ei fywyd ac agweddau ar ei waith' (unpublished MPhil thesis, University of Wales, Aberystwyth, 1990), 529.

31. *Caernarfonshire Record Office Bulletin*, 3 (1970), 14.

32. Edward Jones, 'Argraffwyr Cymru', *Traethodydd*, 56 (1901), 273–83 (282–3).

33. *BAC*, 26 Sept 1867.

34. *Beirniad*, 12 (1870–1), 364.

35. F Boase, *Modern English Biography*, 4 vols (Truro, 1892–1901), article 'Thomas Chater Jack'.

36. *BAC*, 11 Sept 1867.

37. *Drysorfa*, 34 (1864), 255.

38. *Traethodydd*, 22 (1867), 132.

39. *BAC*, 17 Feb 1869. For a judicious discussion of the authenticity of the portrait see Gomer Morgan Roberts, *Y Per Ganiedydd (Pantycelyn), Cyfrol 1, Trem ar ei Fywyd* (Aberystwyth, 1949), 183–7.

40. A rare exception was *Holl Weithiau... William Williams*, the last number of which had to be delayed because of problems in obtaining copy (*BAC*, 3 April 1867).

41. *BAC*, 1 Dec 1869.

42. *BAC*, 26 Jan 1870.

43. *Beirniad*, 8 (1866–7), 195–6.

44. The same, 99–100.

45. The same.

46. *Beirniad*, 9 (1867–8), 291–2.

47. *Diwygiwr*, 32 (1867), 178.

48. See, for example, NLW, Hughes & Son Donation 1958, Hughes letter-book 1862–73 (14), Richard Hughes & Son to James Burn, 7 Jan 1863.

49. *Diwygiwr*, 32 (1867), 178.

50. *Beirniad*, 9 (1867–8), 291–2 (292).

51. Evan Davies, 'Owen Jones: Meudwy Mon. Ail ysgrif', *Traethodydd*, 57 (1902), 161–74 (170).

52. *Traethodydd*, 29 (1874), 588.

53. *Beirniad*, 6 (1864–5), 267–8 (268).

54. *Beirniad*, 12 (1870–1), 363.

55. *Traethodydd*, 28 (1873), 508–11 (511).

56. *BAC*, 8 June 1870.

57. *BAC*, 31 July 1867.

58. *Herald Cymraeg*, 4 March 1870.

59. *Cymru*, 3 (1892), 269–70.

60. Thomas Edwards, 'Glan Menai', *Y Geninen*, 27 (1909 Gwyl Dewi), 35–8 (36).

61. *Traethodydd*, 23 (1868), 129–30 (129).

62. *Carnarvon & Denbigh Herald*, 3 July 1869.

63. Quotation from Caradoc Evans, *My People*, edited and introduced by John Harris (Bridgend, 1987), 110, with the kind permission of the Estate of Caradoc Evans.

64. *BAC*, 11 Sept 1867.

65. *BAC*, 18 Sept 1867.

66. *BAC*, 26 Sept 1867.

67. *BAC*, 30 Oct 1867.

68. *BAC*, 23 Nov 1867.

69. Based on accounts in *Carnarvon & Denbigh Herald*, 12 June 1869, and *BAC*, 26 June 1869.

70. Henry Curwen, *A History of Booksellers, the Old and the New* (London, [1873]), 363.

71. *Aberdare Evidence*, Q 6281.

72. Jones, 'Golden Age', 131–6.

73. NLW, Hughes & Son Donation 1958, Hughes letter-book 1862–73 (90), Richard Hughes & Son to Davies & Primrose, Leith, 26 Jan 1869.

74. The same (113[b]), Richard Hughes & Son to Miller & Richard, Edinburgh, 16 Sept 1869.

75. The same (49), Richard Hughes & Son to Ballantyne & Co, Edinburgh, 21 March 1865.

76. *The Ballantyne Press and its Founders 1796–1908* (Edinburgh, 1909), 155.

77. NLW, Hughes & Son Donation 1958, Hughes letter-book 1862–73 (66[a] and [b]), Richard Hughes & Son to Ballantyne & Co, Edinburgh, 15 Oct 1867.

78. The same (74), Richard Hughes & Son to Ballantyne & Co, Edinburgh, 4 April 1868.

79. NLW, Hughes & Son Donation 1958, Hughes letter-book 1912–22 (304), Hughes & Son to Ballantyne, Hanson & Co, 20 March 1916.

80. NLW, Hughes & Son Donation 1958, Hughes letter-book 1862–73 (108[b]), Richard Hughes & Son to Ballantyne & Co, Edinburgh, 29 July 1869.

81. The same (86), Richard Hughes & Son to McCorquodale & Co, Liverpool, 15 Dec 1868.

82. The same (119[b]), Richard Hughes & Son to Straker & Son, London, 1 Jan 1870.

83. The same (74 & 76), Richard Hughes & Son to Ballantyne & Co, Edinburgh, 4 April & 13 April 1868.

84. NLW, Hughes & Son Donation 1958, Hughes letter-book 28 Feb to 4 Sept 1887 (18), Hughes & Son to Revd Thomas Thomas, 28 March 1887.

85. The same (40), Hughes & Son to Ballantyne & Co, 5 May 1887.

86. NLW, MS 15518C, f 2^v.

87. NLW, MS 15517C, p 62.

88. NLW, MS 15518C, f 61^r.

89. NLW, MS 15518C, f 90^r.

90. Blackie, *Blackie*, 24.

91. *BIW* references are to item numbers in the standard bibliography, *The Bible in Wales...* (London, 1906).

92. Advertisement, *Y Cylchgrawn*, May 1867, back wrapper verso.

93. *Drysorfa*, 44 (1874), 179.

'Spreading the Hell-hounds of Jealousy and Discord': the Aberdeen Shaver *and its Times*

IAIN BEAVAN

THE *Aberdeen Shaver*, which lasted nearly six years from 1833, attracted a series of intensely hostile reactions, frequently culminating in legal proceedings. Indeed, the magazine's proprietors share the dubious honour of having a section of the *Black Kalendar of Aberdeen* devoted to the jury trial at which they were accused, and found guilty, of libelling Alexander Milne, a local merchant.[1]

This paper offers an initial survey into the significance of the *Aberdeen Shaver* as one manifestation of print culture in Northeast Scotland in the nineteenth century. Its importance lies in the topics it was prepared to discuss and the approach taken to them, the fact that it was shunned by the established 'trade', its evident popularity, and its relative longevity given the level of opposition it had to face. More explicitly, the magazine offers some insight into aspects of middle- and working-class culture of Aberdeen in the early to mid-nineteenth century that the so-called respectable press would not have so directly confronted. The span of subjects covered by the *Shaver* and its direct antecedents stretched from discussions of university medical lecturers, through to Chartist agitation, and from the abilities of local ministers, to houses of ill-repute, which, together, give some indication as to the breadth of readership the serial successfully addressed.[2]

The trial, *Alexander Milne v. the printers of the Aberdeen Shaver* was reported by the *Aberdeen Journal*.[3] The original article in the *Shaver* (December 1836) had referred to

> a certain Lime and Grain Merchant... a married man... keeps a 'Miss' in Commerce St, by whom he has had a couple of young 'chips'... We hear he was 'Milne'd' on his way home lately; 'tis a pity he did not get a sound drubbing.

It is unsurprising, then, that Alexander Milne, lime and grain merchant took the publishers to court. Prosecuting counsel, according to the *Journal*, claimed that

> Even in the metropolis, vicious as some part of the press was, which pandered to the inclinations of the public, there was not... a paper like the *Aberdeen Shaver*. It traded in slander; and made calumny its main and leading object.

The Shaver lost the case and damages of £150 were awarded – the heaviest inflicted on the publishers in their series of court appearances. The defendants, however, scarcely helped their cause by failing to put in an appearance, and should have considered themselves lucky, as a crippling £1000 damages had been sought.

In 1834, an attempt had been made, in a short-lived monthly, the *Quizzing-Glass*, to counter the *Shaver*, essentially by exposing its perceived vices, and to express disgust at its contents. Sarcastically, the *Quizzing-Glass* noted:

> It is quite refreshing, after having been fatigued... to throw oneself over on a sofa... and take up that elegant *bijou*... appropriately entitled *The Aberdeen Shaver* and read the... *multifarious* little elegancies it contains.

And with the invective starting to boil over:

> Utterly devoid of talent or wit, it contains nothing but the most fulsome and disgusting ribaldry. Falsehood, slander and obscenity meet the eye of the reader in every page. It is a common sewer, collecting all the filth and slander of the town, and a vehicle for the spleen of every vindictive scribbler who chooses to make it a medium of distraction.[4]

Almost certainly because of the essentially reactive nature of the *Quizzing-Glass*, it soon failed, probably leaving the *Shaver* grateful for the publicity, and with an increased readership. But the appearance of the *Quizzing-Glass* does raise an important question. It saw no purpose in the existence of the *Shaver* other than as a medium for salacious and damaging gossip, as a perpetuator of lies and as a wanton destroyer of personal relationships. But is there more to be said of the *Shaver*'s existence than the one implied by the *Quizzing-Glass*, that the contributors and publishers were merely pandering to, and profiting from, a taste for the scurrilous, and the sensational?

Earlier in the nineteenth century elements of the Aberdeen press had run into trouble, though principally over the expression of radical political opinions. In some contrast to the established, stamped, press (the ostensibly neutral *Aberdeen Journal* and the radical *Aberdeen Chronicle*) stood the unstamped *Aberdeen Star* of the mid-1820s, which described itself as a weekly and political miscellany, which openly paraded its distaste for the Tory party and spoke feelingly of the starvation of the working classes in parts of England. Inevitably it came to the disapproving attention of the Solicitor of Stamps in Edinburgh. A familiar series of events then unfolded: it was obliged to pay Stamp Duty, and within four issues it folded, having tried to retain its unstamped price of 6d per issue.

Pressure was also being exerted on local printers by influential individuals in Aberdeen, not to print any material seen as critical or unwelcome. The most explicit statement of this was made by Lewis Smith, a radical bookseller and publisher, who had attempted to establish three local magazines between 1825 and 1832.

In his autobiography Lewis Smith, writing of the *Aberdeen Magazine* in its last issue, December 1832, wrote (p 661):

This is now the third periodical which it has been the lot of the publisher to… follow with sorrow to the grave… It may seem strange, in these days of liberty, to speak of the bondage of the Aberdeen press, but let it be known that… the printer of the Aberdeen Chronicle [John Booth], notwithstanding his returning thanks at sundry Reform Dinners… refused to print the Aberdeen Censor, and the printer of the Aberdeen Journal refused to print the Northern Iris.

And, as Smith, later in his own autobiography, put it more trenchantly, these printers were defensive of their positions, 'declining the risk of offending somebody who might be made the subject of criticism'.[5] But, as Smith himself realised, if the established printers in Aberdeen either felt inhibited, or objected to publishing radical or apparently offensive material, then others would come along prepared to do exactly that.

THE *ABERDEEN PIRATE & HIGHLAND PLUNDERER*

The *Aberdeen Pirate & Highland Plunderer*, printed by [Robert] Edward & Co, Back Wynd, Aberdeen,[6] began in February 1832 as a weekly, unstamped, priced at 1*d*, and continued until perhaps April that year. Carrying articles on the election of the Police Commissioners, on political and moral instruction among the working classes, and on emigration, it was seen as a useful source of comment and information. A correspondent noted in April 1832 :

> Your publication is calculated to give knowledge at a cheap rate - did the inhabitants of Aberdeen patronize... the Pirate, much good would result... The Trades... have need to buy... such an undertaking. Ignorance on their part will not prevent designing men from imposing on them.

THE *ABERDEEN PIRATE: A WEEKLY MISCELLANY*

In its initial form, the *Pirate & Highland Plunderer* did not prosper, though the reason for failure is unclear. With a change of sub-title, an enlarged sheet size, and a different day of publication, it became the *Aberdeen Pirate: a Weekly Miscellany* which ran from July 1832 to August 1833, and then continued an attenuated existence as a series of unnumbered issues, or supplements, until February 1834. At the end of 1832 the imprint changed to 'Printed by John Anderson & Co., 5 Long Acre'; but this change was nominal only as the same individuals were involved in the production of the serial.

Reflecting the major preoccupations of 1832, the weekly carried extensive political comment, culminating in its celebration of the fall of the 'system of corruption' and the (unopposed) election of Alexander Bannerman for the city in December that year.

'Political Union', the leading article of July 1833 distanced itself from the Whig government, and observed that, 'The present Ministry are now almost Tories, and if we may judge from the conduct of the Aberdeen Political Union, we, Aberdonians, ought to be considered radicals: this certainly looks well'. And, indicative of what was to come, the *Pirate* had widened its purview of matters of legitimate concern, to include a section entitled 'Mirror of Folly' which commented humorously on the hypocrisy and behaviour of private individuals.

THE *ABERDEEN SHAVER*

In September 1833, the *Aberdeen Mirror* appeared (known only from internal references), seemingly the *Pirate* in a different guise, to be followed by the final – and longest lived – transformation into the monthly *Aberdeen Shaver*,

2d, usually 8 pages, which ran until April 1839. The *Aberdeen Shaver* was published, like its immediate predecessor, in two columns, and largely without illustrations, though it did carry a woodcut of a barber's shop in its masthead.[7] It also was printed and published by John Anderson & Co until autumn 1837, when it seemingly changed hands, the imprint subsequently given as George Leith & Co at the same Long-Acre address. Again, however, the change of business name was almost certainly a matter of expediency, as it is probably no coincidence that this took place under the shadow of the impending court case over Milne's alleged adultery, which presumably concentrated thoughts sufficiently for the then existing partnership (John Anderson & Co) publicly to announce its dissolution.

With the *Journal*'s report of the libel trial, and the uncharitable characterisations in the *Quizzing-Glass*, the group primarily responsible (in publishing and distribution terms) for the *Shaver* can be identified.

Robert Edward, 'Big Bob', was described as having been a souter and then a bookseller, and latterly a 'bankrupt tea-dealer and flying stationer'. John Anderson,[8] 'Old John, first man of the scandal mongers' firm', and 'ex-bully to Mary Power', at his death in 1839, had been a printer for over forty years, previously in the *Aberdeen Chronicle* Office. William Chesser, 'Maunting Willie, a nondescript with a red nose', worked as a pressman. The *Quizzing-Glass* hints that Chesser, too, had worked for the radical *Chronicle*. Assisting them was William Edward, 'Master Message Boy – and Professor of Impudence... Big Bob's promising son'. It is perhaps significant to note that the occupations of all three proprietors – Anderson, Chesser, and Edward – had situated them essentially amongst the articulate skilled working class. Robert Edward's background, in particular, is interesting: once a shoemaker, one of the trades which along with the local handloom weavers, had witnessed a decline in living standards and increasing unemployment in the 1830s, he had become a dealer in tea and books. In this respect, his employment closely parallels that of John Mitchell, originally a shoemaker, later a bookseller and newspaper agent whose shop became the headquarters of one of the main Chartist organisations in Aberdeen.[9] However, Mitchell and his colleagues were pilloried by the *Shaver*. There is, nevertheless, every reason to assume that Edward was acutely aware of the distressing results of economic and technological change, as addresses (from the 1820s and 1830s) for the Edward family[10] placed them in Gilcomston and Denburn, localities within the city where rents were relatively low, and where the artisan weavers and shoemakers had clustered.[11] Indeed, the *Pirate*, in commenting (July 1833) on the radicalism of the Aberdeen Political Union, had regretted the fact that it had never held 'a meeting in Gilcomston, the very place where the principles which they propagate had the best chance to take root'.

Who wrote for the *Shaver* and its antecedents? The character 'Lord Shaver', alias 'Dr Suds' has been identified as Robert Brown, a grocer. But perhaps more remarkable is the individual satirised by the *Quizzing-Glass* as the 'Laird O'Cockpen'. This is John Ramsay, graduate of King's College, one time secretary to Joseph Hume, radical MP, then teacher, mathematician, and, from the mid-1830s, at the same time as writing for the *Shaver*, was a journalist for the *Aberdeen Journal*.[12] 'Drunken Morty the bookbinder', is almost certainly William Mortimer, active in Aberdeen at that period. 'WR', clerk in one of the textile mills, and apparently a steady contributor, remains unidentified. Other casual informants included 'a Union Street Bookseller, a Broad Street Clothier, [and] an Ironmonger'. It is also very clear that other contributors had some measure of medical knowledge: the paragraphs on university lectures attest to that. And it is equally obvious that some of the writers had considerable insights into the manoeuvrings of the town council.

One important feature to note in the *Pirate* and especially the *Shaver* is the very restricted universe in which they operated. Each issue was given over largely to events, institutions or individuals from North-east Scotland, or else presented national events interpreted in a local context. Moreover, the style and apparent knowingness of the *Shaver* sometimes makes the text nigh on impenetrable, given the number of allusions and references within it.[13]

Anderson & Co had obviously been nervous about the Stamp Act and its requirements, but nothing untoward happened until a late issue of the *Pirate* was brought to the authorities' attention. The Stamp Office in Edinburgh, deemed the *Pirate* a newspaper, and insisted that stamp duty be paid. Anderson & Co chose not to defy the law and join the growing number of illegally unstamped periodicals, but rather changed frequency of issue, and name, to the *Aberdeen Shaver* to appear monthly, to avoid the duty. There was nothing

THE Aberdeen Shaver.

SHAVING PERPETRATED **HERE** ON THE MOST APPROVED PRINCIPLES.

LADIES' MATTERS **TRIMMED** WITH PRECISION AND DISPATCH.

"'Tis my vocation, Hal—every man must labour in his vocation."—FALSTAFF.

No. XII.] SEPTEMBER, 1834. [PRICE 2d.

HOUSE OF LORDS.

IT is needless, we see, for us or any other body to begin and | Coroners' Court shall be open to the public being determined to keep up the close system. The Commons would not agree—the Lords would not give up the r unusual in their course of action, and their protestations of innocence that followed were entirely to be expected: they complained that the *Pirate* had been harshly treated, in that 'hundreds of weekly periodicals issue from the British press, bearing a much greater resemblance to a newspaper than ours ever did'.

The fact that the unstamped *Aberdeen Shaver* remained legal only if it held to a monthly issue, formed the basis of an attempt to entrap it, by trying to wheedle out of the pressroom, copies of the *Shaver* before the permissible publication date. The pressroom, however, detected the trick (reported, January 1839) and refused to give out a copy.

The politics of the *Pirate* and *Shaver* were never fully articulated, though a general ideology can be made out. The editors consistently claimed that they supported no party, but there is a thread of reformism and radicalism running through both serials which assumed a high degree of political awareness, particularly at the local level, on the part of their readership.

In September 1832 the *Pirate* extolled 'the great cause which had led to the agitation of reform and to its glorious completion', though political disillusionment soon arrived. In August 1834 the plight of the handloom weavers was brought out by 'Textor':

> Why weeps the poor Weaver, why pale his face,
> Why ragged the garment he wears;
> Has Heaven decreed that our miserable race,
> Should languish in want and in tears?

And, by July 1838, the hopes of some were shattered:

> The dreams of happiness which had come over our spirits during the [Reform Bill] agitation, we have never realised... we have found the Whigs much severer task-masters than the Tories, and much more deceiving.

That same year (1838) witnessed the formation of the Aberdeen Working Men's Association. Nevertheless, the *Shaver* could not bring itself to embrace the demands of the Aberdeen Chartists, and in September had to defend its stance:

> It has been asserted... that we are endeavouring to sow dissension among the labouring classes. This is a delusion. We have on all occasions advocated... the true interests of the operatives... we need not be reminded that the aggregate of moral power and influence is composed of units, and that union is strength. But let these units be free and voluntary, for when once

public opinion is coerced by powerful organised bodies, liberty... is either gagged or strangled.

The *Shaver* last appeared in April 1839, probably because of further legal difficulties, and in that final issue listed those matters that it had not supported: the paper had been abused for not advocating the People's Charter, for not campaigning against the corn laws, and for not wholeheartedly pursuing tee-totalism. And goes on:

> We no more believe in the People's Charter as a remedy for our political grievances than we do in Morison's pills as a cure for all corporeal maladies. If the Universal Suffrage boys would give up hunting after a chimera, and begin reform at home, by sticking to the duties of their proper station, and learn to keep their own place, and prepare themselves by self-cultivation, and the acquisition of good habits and useful knowledge, for the exercise of that for which they are daily proving themselves disqualified, if instead of listening to insane or crafty demagogues, they would commence legislating within the little republic of their own families...

The *Shaver* did not dispute the validity of working-class grievances, but it did not advocate Chartism as a solution. The underlying argument advanced by the *Shaver* supports the primacy of moral improvement, personally and within the domestic sphere, backed by educational improvement, and the seeking after a status of respectability (however defined), as a means of achieving, earning perhaps, greater political involvement, and leading to a lessening sense of exclusion.[14]

A further striking feature of the *Shaver* (developed from the *Pirate*'s 'Mirror of Folly') was the number of personal attacks, which went far beyond those in the political domain. Accusations of cant and humbug levelled against the politically active were bad enough, but it was the criticism of private individuals that distinguished, regionally at least, the *Shaver*, and made it so infamous. To return to the *Quizzing-Glass* (December 1834):

> The feelings of parties are never considered – the sole and exclusive object... is the sale of this collection of trash... sacrificing the characters of individuals and families to the caprice of a trio of professional defamers... On more occasions than one, has the baneful influence of this vile publication been felt at the domestic hearth. It has been the instrument of making breaches that can never be closed.

But the *Shaver* consistently claimed the high moral ground, that essentially they were acting as a scourge to promote an improvement in individual behaviour, by exposing such lapses, and by pointing out infidelity, sexual laxity, hypocrisy, corruption, exploitation, deception and generally uncouth behaviour amongst the inhabitants of Aberdeen. Implicit in this was a high value placed on education, on independence, and on moderation and restraint.

The language used to illuminate the personal behaviour of those disapproved of by the *Shaver* was uncompromising, acerbic and sometimes coarse, though intentionally so for effect. Parody was frequently used to launch a satiric attack, and appeared in mock book reviews and advertisements. The 'Chronicles of Ellon', for instance, parodied the Old Testament text to expose the cruelty of a tailor towards his apprentice.[15] The means, essentially, justified the ends, and the *Shaver*, though sometimes prepared merely to laugh at aspects of individual behaviour, had a fundamentally serious purpose.

Occasionally a joke at an innocent party's expense misfired. Comments that John Niddry was 'averse to matrimony', that he was 'two stones lighter than most men', and that he had 'stipulated that no ladies should be in the coach with him to Ballater', were apparently intended as a harmless squib, but cost Anderson & Co £5 damages in court.[16] More serious, and more consistent with the role of the *Shaver* as moral censor, were two separate claims that 'a terrible fellow' 'drum by name and drum by nature' had visited the 'Dundee Establishment'; and that John Stuart, surgeon, was the father of a Mrs Anna Clark's boy, and that he and Mrs Clark were lovers behind the cuckolded husband's back.

Libel actions ensued, both of which were lost by the *Shaver*. The case involving James Drummond the bootmaker apparently attracted considerable local attention was published in October 1833 as an unnumbered 1*d* issue of the *Pirate* . The defendants admitted that Drummond's character had been damaged, but believed (they claimed) the article must have referred to someone else. They were perhaps treatedly lightly in having to pay only 50*s* damages, as the the libel was not trivial: the Dundee Establishment was a brothel. Dr Stuart also won his case – the proceedings also published at length[17] – and was awarded somewhat over £8. This sum, the *Shaver* noted with malicious satisfaction, was immediately seized by the court, in order to help pay off an outstanding debt owed by Dr Stuart.

Two regular columns provided the opportunities for some sharp observations. 'Literary and Scientific Notes' was merely a parodic vehicle for a number of barbed comments:

Speedily will be published, a short Essay on "Good Breeding." Written expressly for the perusal and personal application of a young *lady*, sole heiress to a female China and stoneware merchant, residing not a great distance from the foot of Queen Street.[18]

'Razor Cuts' also offered short but damning paragraphs. Quite how Henry Walker reacted to seeing his name in print can only be imagined:

A Tertian student of King's College, who is a great WALKER, and who would have equalled HENRY in his best days... and another [student] lately had some dealings with a fish-wife... The woman was unable to give them any muscles, as she had sold them at the market, but we are informed she treated them to a good supply of 'crabs'.[19]

And the discussion in the Watts household was probably quite animated:

G–e W–tts, flesher... is in the habit of attending a Dancing School at Bridge of Don, and passing himself off as a single man. He has deluded several girls already... Let him attend to his wife and large family at home, and leave off this infamous conduct.[20]

The radical demonstration in Aberdeen on Coronation Day in June 1838, gave the *Shaver* opportunity to launch a stream of criticism against Charles Logan, flaxdresser, local Chartist leader, and proceeded in following issues to attack his beliefs, his abilities and what the paper perceived as his pretensions. In September 1838, the *Shaver* carried a letter accusing Logan of being totally inebriated and publicly bawling out for Universal Suffrage along the streets of Aberdeen. (The accusation of drunkenness may indeed have been accurate; nevertheless its mischief lay in the fact that most of the Chartist leaders in Aberdeen advocated total abstinence.) In a 'Just Published' section the next month, they inserted a fabricated review of an equally fabricated title: 'A Disquisition on the Causes of the Retardation of Liberty... by Charles Logan, corresponding secretary of the Aberdeen Radical Association... a flood of light is thrown upon various topics... some entire paragraphs deserve to be written in gold... it is enough that an age should produce one such work'.

The *Shaver* still had not finished with the Aberdeen Chartists, as the February 1839 issue danced with glee on the grave of the *Aberdeen Patriot*, a locally produced paper for such views. Condemned as 'the very best specimen of pure drivel that has yet disgraced the Aberdeen Press', its death was noted 'at the tender age of two months, occasioned by a special visitation of public contempt'.[21]

It would be entirely unfair to characterise the *Shaver* as purely destructive. It was prepared to stand up for workers' interests, as in its publication of a letter, perhaps indicative of the tension between customary practice and factory discipline, from the 'slaves of the Donside Millocracy', which argued for the continued recognition of operatives' traditional rights and customs, essentially, occasionally to shorten their working day to go to a local fair.[22] The monthly also dropped hints regarding discreetly maintained trade restrictions. In a paragraph in December 1835, headed 'anti-Cheap knowledge' the *Shaver* referred to the cartel of local booksellers formed to guard against retail underselling.

The health of the local population was equally a genuine concern: during the 1832 cholera outbreak, the *Pirate* had issued warnings against quack doctors trying to make a quick profit; and indeed, concerns about the efficacy of patent medicines, and the extent to which they were pushed, made a number of appearances in its pages.

It seems likely that the specific matter which led to the production of the *Quizzing-Glass* was Dr Suds's morality. The controversy had started with an article in the *Shaver* of September 1834, which raised the question as to how assiduous the city authorities should have been in shutting down the local bawdy houses. In a splendid piece of pragmatist, and doubtless intentionally provocative, argumentation, the *Shaver* suggested that it was perhaps better to leave the brothels where they were, rather than close them down, as forcible closure would bring the prostitutes onto the streets and actually increase the occurrence of the activity. Indeed, the *Shaver* concluded that an unholy war was being pursued against the local prostitutes and brothel-keepers.

The *Quizzing-Glass* was morally outraged. 'Is it a most unholy war to put down houses which are the nurseries of every vice, debauchery, drunkenness, robbery and murder itself?'. Suds, the *Quizzing-Glass* summarised, must be afflicted by 'the deepest moral degradation'. And, as a counter to the *Shaver*'s line of thought, they argued that if the local brothels were forcibly closed, then the opportunities for prostitution would be reduced.[23]

THE *ABERDEEN NEW SHAVER*

Those who were affronted by the *Shaver* must have been horrified by the appearance of a second such publication. What prompted the publication of the *New Shaver*, the first issue of which appeared in July 1837, the second slightly over a year later, thus overlapping slightly with the *Shaver;* it then ran monthly, and was printed and published first by William, and subsequently by William and Robert Edward, both of whom had been intimately involved with the publication of the original satirical production?

There is no obvious answer: indeed the very existence of the *New Shaver* still requires an adequate explanation, given that both serials were similar in style, and appealed to essentially the same or closely overlapping market.[24] And there is no clear answer as to why there was a hiatus of slightly over a year between the first and second issues of the *Aberdeen New Shaver*.

Concerns over the impending libel trial of September 1837, and a wish, on William Edward's part, to dissociate himself from the *Shaver*, and start an independent career, in the expectation that the *Shaver* would collapse as a result of the court case, might account for the first issue.

The *New Shaver*, like the *Shaver*, was an effective satirist and critic, and made a point of attacking preferment in post, referring to the 'monstrous job of saddling... John Angus on the city as a principal Town Clerk'. The article, 'Whig Jobbing – Faust's Professorship' of June 1839 related to the appointment of John Blackie, advocate, to the Chair of Humanity at Marischal College. Blackie's abilities were questioned, he being described as 'a very infant in the classics, a very fool when labouring on the Circuit in his profession', and continued, ' All hail lucky son of a whig father! Good it was for thee that thy father... attended at Broad hill radical meetings, and acted as political pimp to our city member!'.

The *New Shaver* also gave wide publicity to the controversy surrounding James Robertson Reid, who, in publishing a pamphlet, was exposed as having plagiarised an earlier piece of writing by Daniel Dewar, Principal of Marischal

College. It was an effective disclosure, and destroyed Reid's credibility, for the magazine that he had just started to edit, immediately collapsed.[25]

In April 1839, the *Shaver* closed down, and William Edward was joined in the business of running the *New Shaver* by his father, Robert. But the *New Shaver* lasted little longer, the last known appearance being a 1*d* supplement for June 1840. Refusing to give names, the *New Shaver* stated defiantly that 'Blessed are they who are persecuted for the truth's sake', and never reappeared.

Both the *Shaver* and *New Shaver* made claims about their circulation figures. The *Shaver* maintained (September 1833) that it sold 'upwards of one thousand copies in Aberdeen alone' assessing that to be, 'more than double the town circulation of any of our newspapers'. Indeed, the size of the *Shaver*'s readership was presented by prosecuting counsel as an aggravating feature of the libel suffered by Alexander Milne. And in January 1839, the *New Shaver* claimed upwards of 1750 customers, each issue. The general question was clearly a sensitive one, as the previous year (February 1838) the *Shaver* had accused the local newspapers of manipulating their issue figures by procuring 'a few cartloads of stamped paper, for the purpose of making their circuiation [*sic*] appear to be many thousands more than it actually is'.

Sales themselves were achieved without recourse to the established book trade and copies were sold either from the back door of the office, or else through the papers' own system of agents.[26] Income was generated entirely from the sale of copies as neither paper carried advertisements. On occasion, donations helped, as the *Shaver*, at least, was quite prepared to accept gifts of money to help pay off libel damages.[27]

The claim (April 1835) that the *Shaver* had a greater circulation in the north of Scotland than any of the other newspapers published in Aberdeen, and that it thus offered an unparalleled medium for advertisers was, not surprisingly, studiously ignored by the commercial interest in the city.

Other, independent evidence also supports a widespread readership:
Even in Aberdeen, it is plain that Chambers's Journal... is not generally read by the working classes. Of the seven thousand individuals who are said to have signed the National Petition in this city, there is reason to think... that not one in twenty purchases a copy of it. It is too much to be feared that

a periodical of another description, peculiar, I believe, to Aberdeen, is much more extensively circulated among the labouring classes, and read with far greater avidity.[28]

What of the papers' geographical spread? The great majority of sales were undoubtedly in Aberdeen itself, but it is significant that the 'Country Cuts' section of the *New Shaver* referred to events and individuals as far south as Edinburgh, and as far north as Dingwall, Ross-shire.

REFORMED CHARACTERS?

Although the *Shaver* closed in 1839, it appears that the premises and equipment lay idle for a while. Moral improvement was at hand, but perhaps not in the form ever anticipated by the proprietors. In the course of a discussion (1841) on intended educational improvements within Greyfriars Parish, the clergy noted that

Employment within doors… for the boys, it may be mentioned… that a periodical paper of the most immoral and degrading tendency was lately published in the parish, within two yards of the Parish Church,[29] and had a fearfully wide circulation both in town and country. The Minister has bought up the press and other printing materials… and intends employing them in the publication of Christian school-books, and… works of a religious, moral and interesting nature… to exert a beneficial influence on the whole population.[30]

Possibly with monies obtained through the sale of the *Shaver* stock and equipment, Robert Edward & Co was able to restart business as printers. The imprint, 'printed and published for the proprietors by Robert Edward & Co' appears on the *Bon-Accord Reporter*, 1842–44, again with a local focus, and showing the same broad working-class sympathies. However, the tone is more guarded and moderated, and it lacks the level of sharpness and incisiveness of the earlier magazines. It is almost inconceivable that the *Bon-Accord Reporter*'s article on the accomplishments of music (December 1843) would ever have appeared in the *Shaver*. It is equally difficult to imagine the *Shaver* publishing an apology such as that given to Lady Burnett in September 1843 for daring to suggest that she disapproved of her workforce joining the Free Church.

ACKNOWLEDGEMENTS

To Colin McLaren, Librarian, Aberdeen University, for permission to quote from material under his charge. Also to Aberdeen City Library, Lawrence Aspden, David Ritchie, and Barbara Ross-Hadley.

The illustration on p 143 shows (much reduced) the first version of the 'barber's shop' woodcut incorporated into the masthead of the *Aberdeen Shaver*.

NOTES

Aberdeen Shaver is abbreviated to *AS*; *Aberdeen New Shaver* to *ANS*; the *Quizzing-Glass* to *Q-G*. The title of this paper is taken from the *Q-G*, December 1834.

1. *The Black Kalendar of Aberdeen from... 1746 up to... 1878*. 4th edn (Aberdeen: James Daniel & Son, 1878), 227-9.

2. The *AS* and other journals of the 1830s are discussed by J M Bulloch in an important series of articles, `Comic journalism in Aberdeen', in *Bon-Accord*, September 1891 to January 1892. Bulloch's articles do not pay much attention to the broader social and political background, but, usefully, they identify individuals connected with the *AS*.

3. *Aberdeen Journal*, 27 September 1837.

4. *Q-G*, December 1834 to February 1835. Three issues only. Printed for the proprietors by John Watt, Aberdeen. Quotations from front-page articles, Dec 1834, Jan 1835.

5. Lewis Smith, 'Autobiography', 21. (Aberdeen University Library. MS 9452)

6. The local radical press did not necessarily support publications of similar political stance. The *Scots Champion & Aberdeen Free Press*, October 1832, ignored the *Pirate*, and advised readers to 'avoid the very trash published in Aberdeen. There is not here a single vehicle of intelligence worth the time spent in reading, much less paying for'.

7. The *AS*'s woodcut is imitative of that used for the *Figaro in London*. The play of meanings between 'shaver' as barber, and as 'joker' or 'wag' is clear. Louis James, *Fiction for the Working Man* (London: OUP, 1963), 17, notes the appearance in the early 1830s of provincial versions of *Figaro in London*. I am grateful to Philip Jones for drawing my attention to the radical *Figaro in Wales*, 1835-6, set up to counteract possible Tory advances on local councils; and *Figaro the Second*, 1843-4. Both journals faced (and lost) libel actions. See Thomas Richards, 'Hen bapurau newydd', *Journal of the Welsh Bibliographical Society*, 5 (1937-42), 213-29. There is clearly scope for more research on the radical provincial press.

8. His death noticed in *ANS*, May 1839.

9. Robert Duncan, 'Artisans and proletarians: Chartism and working class allegiance in Aberdeen, 1838-1842', *Northen Scotland*, 4 (1981), 56-8.

10. Members of the family all traded (in various combinations) as tea dealers, book agents and printers.

11. Robert Duncan, *Textiles and Toil: the Factory System and the Industrial Working Class in Early 19th Century Aberdeen* (Aberdeen: Aberdeen City Libraries, 1984), 2.

12. John Ramsay, *Selected Writings...* (Aberdeen: John Rae Smith, 1871), xxii–xxiv.

13. Whosoever lived in Keith at the time was expected to appreciate the full significance of the paragraph (June 1835):

> Will be published shortly... a treatise on the art of watching rats, by a young gentleman residing... in the town of Keith. In the Appendix the author will give a... description of the manner in which he made the art of 'watching rats' subservient to the most congenial of all passions, love.

See also Donald J Gray, 'Early Victorian scandalous journalism: Renton Nicholson's *The Town* (1837–42)', in *The Victorian Periodical Press: Samplings and Soundings*, edited by Joanne Shattock and Michael Wolff (Leicester: Leicester U P, 1982), 323, where he encounters the same problem in his discussion of the *Age* and the *Satirist*.

14. Such views had been expressed elsewhere, eg in a Working Man's *Letter to the Members of the Aberdeen Working Men's Association* (Aberdeen: printed G Mackay, 1838). On p 23, the writer argued that universal (male) suffrage was no political panacea, and that in order better to exploit an extension of the franchise, 'We [the working classes] should place our chief hopes of better days on a higher cultivation of our moral and rational powers... on our advances in temperance, foresight and self-control; and on greater powers of self-denial, in enabling us to forego present gratifications for the sake of future good'. The franchise was to be 'a prize to incite you to progress in knowledge and improvement'.

15. *AS*, June 1835. On parodic expression, see Marcus Wood, *Radical Satire and Print Culture, 1790–1822* (Oxford: Clarendon Press, 1994), ch 1.

16. *AS*, October 1833, wherein the report noted 'the infinite amusement of the audience' at the trial.

17. *AS*, November 1833.

18. *AS*, September 1834.

19. *AS*, February 1836.

20. *AS*, October 1838.

21. Amongst the mourners was Rory M'Bean, 'small-beer poet and knight of the rueful countenance', probably identifiable as John Mitchell, the local Chartist leader and bookseller. The second publishing attempt by the local Chartists, the *Northern Vindicator*, was (cruelly but accurately) commented on by the *ANS*, as 'a short-lived abortion'.

22. *AS*, November 1834.

23. Aspects of the argument still resonate. See the articles (eg 28 February 1995) by Severin Carrell in the *Scotsman* on the controversy recently faced by Edinburgh District Council.

24. There is one point of difference. The *AS*'s stance on Chartism was unsympathetic, whereas the *ANS* asserted, 'We are radicals of the first water. It was only the other day we signed the great national petition'. However, the *ANS's never developed its Chartist sympathies to become a prominent feature.*

25. *Aberdeen Universities' Magazine*. Single issue, November 1838.

26. *AS*, June 1834.

27. *AS*, November 1833.

28. *Letter to the... Aberdeen Working Men's Association*, 13.

29. A reference to Long Acre, which ran beside Marischal College. The print shop was therefore easily accessible to the students.

30. *Parochial Churches and Schools in Large Towns* (Aberdeen, 1841), 1.

William Ford, Manchester Bookseller

BRENDA J SCRAGG

WILLIAM FORD has some claim to be the most prestigious bookseller Manchester has ever had, but his career has been unjustifiably neglected.[1] He was born in Manchester in 1771, the son of Ann and John Ford who had a prosperous business as tin merchants and braziers. William was baptised at Cannon Street Independent Chapel. Manchester was a considerable centre for the Independents and this chapel counted among its former ministers the Rev Timothy Priestley, brother of Dr Joseph Priestley.[2] At the demise of the Independent chapels some joined the Congregational Union as did this one. Other chapels were absorbed by the Unitarians. Ford was educated at Manchester School, now Manchester Grammar School. His name appears in the Manchester School Register[3] with a lengthy biography by James Crossley, a lawyer, book collector and local historian, who must have been personally acquainted with Ford. Crossley tells us that William intended to follow a medical career, but no other evidence of this has been discovered. On leaving school he may have joined the family business, but both Crossley and the Manchester Directory of 1800[4] describe him as being 'in the Manchester trade' which implies some aspect of the cotton business.

It is not clear when he first became interested in books and art, but he was an avid collector of both. Some financial setback seems to have arisen in 1802 which forced him to sell his pictures. Christie's sale of 1 May 1802 was described in *A Catalogue of a Small and Valuable Collection of Italian, French and Dutch Pictures, the Property of a Gentleman in the North of England*. Ford is identified as 'the gentleman' by the catalogue's inclusion in the Ford Scrapbook preserved in Chetham's Library Manchester.[5] The sale realised £3570, but years later Ford bemoaned the small prices some of the pictures had fetched. 'Never was a collection of paintings so shamefully sacrificed through the ill-humour and mismanagement of the auctioneer'.[6] That this setback was only temporary is evidenced by his continued collecting of books. He was eventually persuaded by his friends to compile a catalogue of his collection. This formed his first catalogue as a bookseller when he set up his business at

14 Cromford Court in 1805. In the Manchester Central Library is a scrap-book[7] containing the following note:

I call it Mr. Ford's *private* collection because it is well known (to his friends at least) that it had been accumulating for a series of years, activated by a prudent love of these pursuits without the most distant prospect of being intended for sale...

Ford's advertisment in the *Manchester Mercury*[8] announced

This day is published, price 1/- Observations on National Defence... of Great Britain.[9] Printed for W. Ford, Bookseller 14 Cromford Court who has on sale some beautiful and valuable paintings... and a large curious collection of books in various languages. Literary works of every description on sale as soon as published. Libraries or parcels of books catalogued and valued.

A manuscript note in Ford's own hand in a copy of his first catalogue formerly in the possession of J P Earwaker states[10]

This catalogue has become very rare... When I began to print it, with a view to the sale of the collection, I circulated the sheets *as they were printed* amongst my friends at a distance, who applied for and obtained it, *as far as it was printed, but neglected... to complete* it which means, out of 150 copies... not 50 complete copies remaining when the catalogue was published for sale.

Earwaker's copy of the catalogue had also been marked with the prices realised which show that the books sold for £2500. With hindsight Ford is reputed to have said 'Had I only had the good fortune to have kept the collection a few years longer I should have realised at least £10 000 by its sale'. His catalogue was widely distributed as the cover states that 'It may be had... at Mr. Robert Bickerstaff's, corner of Essex-Street, Strand London'. This undoubtedly accounts for the well-established collectors who were among his first customers. The copy in the John Rylands Library belonged to James H Markland[11] who bought many items from it, at least seventeen being marked. Not all the items were priced by Ford and in some cases a price has been filled in by Markland. The catalogue listed more than 3000 items and included many rarities. The most interesting item was lot 396 Shakespeare's *Venus and Adonis*, 1593 bound with Fletcher's *Licia, or Poems of Love*, 1593.[12] The two items were split, the *Venus and Adonis* being sold to Malone for £25;[13] the

Licia was acquired by Richard Heber. Ford's manuscript note in Earwaker's copy of the catalogue[14] describes the interest this item aroused

I received letters by the same post from Mr Heber, Mr Bindley, Mr Nassau, Mr Gifford, Mr Kemble, and many others – nine or ten I think; and several of them doubted the date being correct, as Mr Malone observed though there was an entry in the Stationers' books of this date, yet he had never been able to see, or even hear of, a copy, although he had been in search of it all his life.

Heber was also the purchaser of lot 435 Byshop's *Blossoms* (1577) for which he paid £1.11s.6d. Ford's note for this item says 'At page 54 of this very curious work, is to be found the remarkable story upon which the late Horace Walpole's play the Mysterious Mother is founded'. Also included was a special section devoted to books of prints and engravings and a smaller section of manuscripts, the most interesting item being a *Missale Romanum* 'MS on vellum containing seventeen large miniatures and sixteen small ones, most beautifully painted and illuminated… the whole coloured and gilt in a stile [*sic*] of magnificence, of which the most elaborate description would convey but a very feeble and imperfect idea'. It is not priced but Markland has inserted the price £10.10s.0d. and the buyer as F Twedale, Esq. In Ford's catalogue of 1820 he describes his 1805 catalogue as 'very rare'.

In 1805, William Ford was a founder member of the Portico Library in Manchester, a subscription library still flourishing today. Ford also supplied books to the Portico.[15] The earliest invoice I have seen dates from July 1808 and is for the supply of books and journals. Amongst these were *Antiquarian Repository*, Parnell's *Apology for the Catholics*, Aiken's *Biography* Vol 7, *Gentleman's Magazine*, and *Critical Review*. As evidence of his trade as a stationer he also supplied 100 quills. Invoices continue intermittently until 1812, when it would seem he no longer supplied the Portico. It is interesting that none of Ford's transactions were on printed letterheads, but were all handwritten, usually by Ford himself, on any suitable paper that came to hand.

By 1808, when Ford's next catalogue was issued, he had moved to 85 Market-street-lane. This catalogue contained 'A small, but elegant and valuable collection of manuscripts and printed books, in the Persian, Arabick, Turkish, and other oriental languages'. It was available from Longmans in London, Mr Parker in Oxford and Mr Deighton in Cambridge. It consisted of 255 lots and not every item was priced. Ford does not give the source of his stock, but for the manuscripts says 'Most of the following valuable collection are enumerated by Dr. Ad. Clarke in the Suppl. to his Bibliog[raphical] Dict. [1802] Tome 1. p.299 etc'. Another catalogue was issued in 1808 describing itself as 'Part First'. This had 5277 lots all priced but without annotation. The note at the beginning 'To amateurs and collectors of prints' announces the imminent availability of a collection of engravings and etchings.

One of Ford's customers was the Rev Thomas Frognall Dibdin (1776–1847) the prolific bibliophile, whose patron was the second Earl Spencer, and for whom he published catalogues of the many rarities to be found in the Library at Althorp. His several tours on the Continent in search of books for the Earl occupied Dibdin over many years. Dibdin gave Ford an inscribed copy of his *Specimen Bibliothecae Britannicae* (1808). It is preserved in the Manchester Central Library.[16] Only forty copies were printed. Ford has added many annotations to Dibdin's descriptions and also added items which he thought ought to have been included. It bears Ford's bookplate. Ford comments that at Mr Gosset's sale this work produced £3.4s.0d.

In 1808 excavations were taking place around the Roman fort in Manchester, and during the course of these excavations Ford was able to use his experience gained from his parents' business, as John Harland records[17]

> In 1808 a number of Roman *paterae* or dishes were found in Castle Field… the workmen… sold them as old metal to a brazier, at whose place they were fortunately seen by the late Mr William Ford, bookseller of Manchester, who rescued them from the melting-pot, and presented them to the British Museum.

The first part of his catalogue for 1810 listed 6608 items and once again not all were priced. Ford was now trading from Commercial Exchange Buildings, which had been erected in 1806. Lewis[18] writing of Manchester says

> Above the news-room, and resting on the pillars which support the ceiling, is a circular range of building, fifteen feet in breadth, and two stories high (originally forming part of the extensive establishment of Mr W Ford, bookseller), of which the lower contains the Exchange Library…

The second part of his catalogue published in 1811 was his most extensive with more than 15 000 items. In the preface to the catalogue Ford wrote

Of the collection which is now offered for public inspection and sale, I can speak with confidence, that it will not be thought unworthy of notice and attention, as it comprises many works which lay claim in a peculiar degree, both to scarceness and intrinsic merit: and at a period when the Literature of past Ages is sought after, and cultivated, with an unprecedented degree of avidity, the number, rarity, and intrinsic value of many of these volumes will certainly not pass unnoticed, as they combine many of the inestimable productions of our *early English Poets,* many of the laborious undertakings of our ancient Historians and numerous Tracts, which throw considerable light upon the Civil, Religious and Literary Antiquities and Biography of this Country.

In 1809 William Carey in his *Letter to I.A. Esq. [i.e.* Colonel J A Anderdon], a connoisseur in London, tells of his visit to Ford's premises in Manchester:

In the public rooms of Mr. Ford, the principal 'English & Foreign Bookseller', who is a zealous lover of the arts, I saw many fine prints and drawings. He has lately removed his imense stock of rare and curious books, to a noble range of apartments on the first floor of Commercial Buildings.

In 1811 Ford started an additional business in Liverpool. His announcement in the *Liverpool Mercury* [19]

Respectfully informs the lovers of literature and the arts; that for the purpose of forming a similar establishment here... he has removed a considerable part of his... stock in trade from Manchester to his rooms in Lord-Street, Liverpool, and which selection is now open for inspection.

Ford's business in Liverpool was short-lived. In 1813 the *Liverpool Mercury* [20] announced the sale by Winstanley & Taylor of Ford's books from his premises at Lord Street Chambers. It included furniture as well as books as Ford was giving up his establishment in Liverpool.

By 1814 Ford had moved yet again, this time to St Ann's Square. All his premises were located in a small area of the town, where by tradition booksellers and printers had their business. [21] The most interesting item from this catalogue is No 4 'Antiquarian Repertory'. Large paper fine impressions of the plates, 5 vols. Russia. eleg. gilt edges. £126'. Ford's description says

This unique copy of a very curious and valuable work is much enlarged by the insertion of many appropriate and rare prints, drawings, etc. and an entire fifth vol. has been added, composed of curious and original materials, of which the most laboured description would convey but a very imperfect

idea. It consists of early illuminations, manuscripts, fac-similes, rare portraits, curious antiquarian prints, very scarce (printed) historical tracts, and
original drawings, altogether equalling, if not exceeding in curiosity and interest the work itself, to which it is an appendage.

We do not know whether Ford himself had assembled this item or to whom it
was sold.

In 1815 and 1816 a series of articles appeared in the *Manchester Exchange
& Herald* under the heading 'Bibliographiana, by a Society of Gentlemen'.
Amongst the contributors were F R Atkinson, Nathan Hill and William Ford,
and the auctioneer Thomas Winstanley. The members met from time to time
in Ford's rooms for discussion where one would present a paper upon some
rare or meritorious publication. Ford's financial situation no doubt accounts
for the short life of the society. These articles were reprinted in May 1817 in an
edition of twenty-four copies only. Two copies are preserved in the Manchester Central Library, one being Ford's own copy.[22] The first item is devoted to
the sale of John Leigh Philips's collection (reprinted from 7 March 1815); the
writer says

> A great portion of those books, which rank amongst the *curious and rare*,
> were purchased within the last 7 or 8 years, out of the catalogue published
> by Mr. Ford, whose judgement and information in this department have
> been frequently & justly esteemed by those conversant in bibliographical
> pursuits.

Of the selection of ninety-four items, seventeen are said to have come from
Ford's stock with in most cases Ford's price given as well as that realised in
Philips's sale. In every case the auction price was greater than Ford's price,
sometimes by as much as four times. They were continued in the *Stockport
Advertiser*, but only ten copies were printed; an annotated copy is to be found
in the Manchester Central Library.

In July 1816 Lord Spencer (the second Earl, one of the leading bibliophiles
of his time) had been on a visit to William Roscoe (1753–1832), a prominent
Liverpool businessman, poet, book collector and perhaps best-known as the
author of *The Butterfly's Ball* and *The Grasshopper's Feast*. Spencer had been
to view some of the items included in Roscoe's sale and in passing through
Manchester he writes to Dibdin[23]

At Manchester I visited Mr Ford's warehouse for about an hour & selected about thirty pounds worth of odd out of the way things, none of which were of any considerable consequence. He is calling off, as I suppose you know for the benefit of his assignees & seems to have a large collection of goodish books, & some very fine copies; but there are unfortunately two bookbinders, one at Liverpool, & the other at Manchester, who [pride] themselves upon their <u>scavoir faire</u>, & and who have been employed on Mr. Roscoe's & upon Mr. Ford's books respectively much to the detriment of their appearance, to eyes accustomed to the works of Lewis & Hering.

The catalogue for 1816 somewhat curiously was published in Macclesfield, a small town some twenty miles south of Manchester. The more than 1000 items included many volumes of tracts bound together. Considerable space is devoted to listing Ford's publishing activities. Greswell's *History of Chetham's College* has a list of subscribers to fifty large-paper copies priced 16/- each and 101 subscribers listed to the ordinary issue. There are 100 large-paper copies of the *History of the Free Grammar School,. Old Mansions, Halls, etc in Lancashire and Cheshire* published in parts, each containing at least three prints for 7/6 per part. Specimens of engravings were available for inspection at Ford's. Some sixty pages are devoted to listing portraits and prints either published by, or available from, Ford.

In 1816 Ford suffered a financial setback, possibly as a result of expanding his business and a decline in book buying by his more important customers. As early as 1811 Ford was writing to Dibdin[24]

... I have sold a good number of your 'Bibliomania' here; though, to my sorrow, the disease does not exist in any great degree. But indeed it may be very readily accounted for, from the prevalence of a *more fatal* disease, which has absorbed every other, and rages with a more extended influence than was ever known before; I mean POVERTY - if it may be allowable to call it a disease, and which no ranks are free from. I assure you that I feel the effects of it most lamentably.

Ford was declared a bankrupt in June of that year and his name was published in the *Manchester Magazine*.[25] *Cowdroy's Manchester Gazette*[26] announced 'conclusion of bankrupt is awarded and issued forth against William Ford, of Manchester... bookseller, dealer and chapman'. This is the only time he has been described as 'chapman'. His stock of books was auctioned in three parts from December 1816 to February 1817. The catalogues contained very brief descriptions and had no bibliographical notes. There were 5405 lots and the sales took thirty-one days. The auctioneer, Mr Winstanley, was well known with establishments in both Manchester and Liverpool, and had in fact been the auctioneer at the closing sale of Ford's short-lived Liverpool venture. The sales took place at Ford's premises in St Ann's Square. A separate auction of his prints took place in December 1816 and though the catalogue listed only 518 lots, the first seventy-one items were multiple lots which totalled 1070 prints. Two further sales in March 1817 included the remaining pictures and books and his fixtures and fittings. His misfortune extended to his house at Cheetwood, an area on the northern edge of the city near Strangeways, then a good residential area but today an industrial wasteland, where in April 1817 Winstanley sold the household furniture and other effects, which comprised the entire contents, carpets, kitchen pans, etc. As Ford continued to live in the same house it would seen that he only rented the property.

In spite of his financial difficulties it is clear that Ford was still actively engaged in buying stocks of both prints and books. His next catalogue in 1818, gives his address as Bottom of Chapel Walks. He advertises 'A list of the numbers and prices of the valuable library and collection of prints, drawings and pictures of W. Roscoe, Esq which were sold at Liverpool in 1816'. It is priced at 7/-, which seems an emormous price and one wonders why Ford undertook such a publication. Ford also advertises for the first time that he will undertake binding in all its branches. The John Rylands Library has two copies of the 1818 catalogue, one containing an appendix and addenda. The 1818 and the further catalogue of 1819 are much more scrappy than his earlier ones. The entries are brief, without notes and the number of rare and interesting items is much reduced. In January 1820 we are told that he had transferred his business to his son John Ford, 'who has commenced in the same line, and also that of stationer'.[27] John Ford also carried on the profession of lithographer and many of the prints published by Ford were lithographed by his son.

Two catalogues were issued in 1820 by John Ford, the first listing 933 lots all priced, and extensive descriptions of many items were given. The second part listed only 305 lots, and the descriptions were very brief with no bibliographical notes.

Ford's catalogue for 1820 though printed in Manchester was issued from 4 Spring Gardens, Westminster. This seems to have been an additional place of business as there is no evidence that he ceased trading in Manchester, though it would appear that his son was managing the Manchester shop. 3525 lots are listed with good bibliographical descriptions. A separate section is devoted to 'Works relative to Lancashire'. The last unnumbered item is *Varnishando, a poem*, sewed, very scarce, 5/- (Manchester, 1808). Another section is included consisting of sale and auction catalogues of books and prints. Here Ford offers 'Complete set of W Ford's cats. from 1805 to 1816 inclusive 7 vols. £2.10s.0d'. Ford shared his Westminster premises with J Harris junior who is described in his advertisment at the front of Ford's catalogue as a 'miniature and heraldic painter; supplier [of] deficiencies in early MS and printed books, by accurate facsimiles'.

A catalogue, part the first, for 1825 of a *Curious and Valuable Collection of Books by Will Ford* was issued from yet another new address, 6 Merchant's Square, Market Street, Manchester. Ford takes this opportunity to inform the public that he still continues the profession of auctioneer and in a two-page advertisement headed 'Literature and the Fine Arts', preserved in Chetham's Library, Ford says 'he also offers his services, in the sale of Estates, Land, Buildings, etc'. The leaflet is undated but is issued from the Merchant's Square address. There is no evidence that he ever entered the property market. The catalogue contains a list of works published by Ford which includes John Palmer's *History of the Siege of Manchester, in 1642... to which is added... Complaints of Colonel John Roseworm Against the Inhabitants of Manchester* 6/-; Ford says original copies of Roseworm's tract had become so scarce that it had been fetching between £4 and £5. Ford published an engraving of Roseworm done by Walter Geikie, whom Ford tells us was born deaf and dumb, from a picture in his possession but formerly in the Utkinton collection. Ordinary prints cost 5/-, or on India paper 10/6. The list of works being prepared for publication included *Bibliographiana* and *Varnishando* a new edition with notes explanatary and illustrative, by the author. This had originally been published in 1809 as *Varnishando, a Serio-Comic Poem: Addressed to Collectors of Paintings By an Admirer of the Arts*. The author was Francis

Dukinfield Astley of Dukinfield Lodge, Cheshire. In his memoirs[28] Astley wrote that

His fondness for the arts, particularly for painting, led him like many others into society of several disreputable dealers in pictures, who took advantage of his liberal disposition, and want of sufficient caution to resist their allurements. Whatever might be his pecuniary losses to be placed to this account, he took a well-merited revenge on this tribe of fraudulent dealers, in a poem he addressed to John Arden, Esq. entitled *Graphomania*, and more particularly in *Varnishando*, a poem of great force and asperity, exposing the character of some notoriety in that class of dealers.

The poem was a defence of honest dealers and a criticism of a dishonest one called Varnishando. Ford was named as the main seller of this book. Neither of these reprints ever appeared. The 1677 items in the catalogue were only briefly described with very few bibliographical notes. At least one item is said to be from the J L Philips collection.

A catalogue was issued from Liverpool in 1832. It is described as the first part, but no further part was issued. It listed 800 items of miscellaneous literature. Of more interest is the 'Collectio Selecta' included at the end which consists of paintings and drawings together with a list of 'Lancashire Portraits, Views, etc., Published by W. Ford'.[29]

Ford died on 3 October 1832 and his 1833 posthumous catalogue published in Liverpool, but with no address of shop premises, lists in very brief form some 1730 items with no special rarities.

There is some evidence of the sources of Ford's stock. In May 1796 T Vernon sold by auction *A Catalogue of Original Pictures... Prints and Drawings... a Library of Books...* Amongst the items listed are Macklin's *Bible*, Martyn's *Shells*, 4 vols, in morroco, Ehret's *Plants*, etc.[30] In 1805 the *Manchester Mercury*[31] announced a large book and print sale of the bankrupt W M Willet (a liquor merchant of Shudehill). Items listed include Bayle's *Dictionary*, Ireland's *Views on Rivers Thames, Avon, Wye and Medway*, and the *Repository of the Arts*. A further large book sale by the same auctioneer took place in August 1805.[32] In Chetham's Library[33] a note by Ford dated 1804 reads

At this time I was on a visit at Browsholme Hall, the seat of Thomas Lister Parker, Esq. and purchased the old part of the library which had been more than two hundred years in forming, and contained among its black letter treasures four black letter Caxtons (one of which, the *Book for Travellers* was unique, and though containing only a few pages was sold to Earl Spencer for £70). The collection loaded one large four wheeled wagon and two carts and was the largest collection of books that had ever been brought into Manchester.

Ford was wrong in describing the *Book for Travellers* as unique and Dibdin states[34] that Spencer's copy was obtained from Miller for £105 it having been formerly in the collection of Mr Lister Parker. Ford's note must have been written some years afterwards, as he did not purchase the Parker library until 1808.

The extensive library collected by John Leigh Philips came under the hammer in 1814.[35] Ford bought 127 lots at a cost of £95.6s.0d. A few of the items were very recently published and might have still been available new. The total amount realised for the sale of all the books was £2880.6s.0d.

In 1816 *The Library of the late Robinson Foxley, M.D.*, an apothecary, was sold by auction at the Emporium in Exchange Street, Manchester by Mr Gasquoine.[36] The sale consisted of 949 lots, and included many seventeenth- and eighteenth-century items. The entries in this catalogue were very brief and there are no details of buyer or prices realised.

The most important sale in the North of England in 1816 was that of William Roscoe's books and prints.[37] The *Liverpool Mercury* was advertising the sale for many weeks in advance and altogether the sales including the prints lasted from 19 August to 20 September 1816. In spite of being declared a bankrupt in June 1816 Ford was nevertheless able to invest large sums of money in both books and prints at these sales. Of the books he purchased 191 lots at prices ranging from 4/- to 36 guineas. Three lots are singled out for special mention. Lot 1785 Thomas Martyn *Figures Of Nondescript Shells and Universal Conchologist,* large 4to, 4 vols. 1784. cost £34.2s.6d, lot 1811 *Biblia Sacra Latina. Vulgate,* Fol 2 vols, MS of the early part of the XVth century on the finest vellum cost 35 guineas, and lot 1812 described as a block book, *Historia S. Johannis Apocalypsis, Figuris Ligneis, Coloratis* cost £32.11s.0d. His total expenditure on books at Roscoe's sale was £423.18s.4d. Roscoe's drawings and pictures were sold on 23 September and five following days. Again Ford invested heavily and purchased 114 lots at prices ranging from a few shillings to several pounds. His most expensive items were lot 100 *History of the Prodigal Son* by Hans Holbein, 24 guineas , and lot 152 Gerard Terburgh *A Lady Practising Music With Her Master* £27.6s.0d. His total expenditure on prints was £185.10s.0d.

We do not know if Ford was bidding on behalf of customers or whether the items were for stock. It was not these purchases which were the cause of his financial embarrassment, as his bankruptcy had already been announced.

In 1823 the books belonging to the late John Arden of Underbank, Stockport, were sold on the premises by Mr J E Turner.[38] 412 lots were listed with the briefest of entries. Most were eighteenth-century with just a very few earlier. There was nothing outstanding and most subjects were covered. It has been suggested that Ford had already purchased the most important items while Arden was still alive.[39] No buyers names are given. The pictures consisted of 107 items, all very ordinary and perhaps unlikely to have interested Ford. Two copies of this catalogue are preserved in the John Rylands Library, and form part of the Hale Bellot Collection, the interest of the Bellot family being that some of the portraits listed as unidentified in the catalogue were recognised as members of the Bellot family and purchased by them.

A further Manchester sale, which Ford would almost certainly have attended, was that by Mr Gasquoine of the Library of the late Charles Lawson MA, formerly Master of the Free Grammar School, Manchester.[40] The catalogue is not dated but Lawson died in 1807, and the sale took place in the Master's house. Ryland's copy bears the signature of W Thackray.

These are just a few of the sales which Ford would certainly have attended because they were local. We do not know if he attended sales in other parts of the country, but three other sales, all of which took place in London while Ford was in business, are worthy of mention. In June 1813 the library of the Rev Isaac Gosset was sold by Leigh & Sotheby. In 1818 Mr Saunders at his Great Room, 39 Fleet Street sold *The Library of an Eminent Collector,* [identified as James Midgeley] *Removed from the North of England.* In 1821 the very interesting *Library of a Gentleman, Deceased, Singularly Rich in Topography* was sold by Mr Sotheby. Copies of these catalogues are all in the John Rylands Library; I draw attention to them as they all bear the signature of W Thackray, 1843, as do most of the copies of Ford's own catalogues in the Library, and it is interesting to surmise that they had once belonged to Ford himself, though they came to the Library from a later Manchester collector Dr Thomas Windsor. Thackray was a bookseller in Manchester for many years in the middle of the century. The very fact that a bookseller so many years later thought it useful to acquire Ford's catalogues shows the continued value of his bibliographical descriptions and notes.

Dibdin in his *Bibliomania*[41] says

> It is not because Mr. Ford of Manchester, has been kind enough to present me with one of the six copies of his last catalogue of books, printed on strong writing paper – that I take this oportunity of praising the contents of it, – but that his catalogues are to be praised for the pains which he exhibits in describing his books, and in refering to numerous bibliographical authorities in the description.

After examining a number of London sale catalogues in which the prices realised and buyers names have been added I have not come across any evidence that Ford purchased from London salerooms.

The Dunham Massey Papers in the John Rylands Library[42] give details of the services that Ford was offering to owners and collectors, and the charges he made for them. In 1822 he supplied 'Sundry books' at a cost of £19.4s.0d. This was made up of fourteen volumes Beaumont and Fletcher *Works*, Calf £9.16s.0d; nineteen volumes Richardson's *Works* £7.12s.0d and two volumes Gilpin's *Works*, £11.6s.0d. In December 1822 there were two bills of £12.2s.0d. each; 'Will Ford for his expenses at Dunham at various times' and 'To arranging the library at various times'. In the same month £27.1s.0d. was spent on binding from Ford. The prices range from 5/- to £14.14s.0d. Each item is separately listed and from a later catalogue of the Dunham Library we can identify many of the items mentioned by Ford.

While there are numerous references to Ford's book customers, by contrast, information about his picture-dealing activities is more difficult to find. The Manchester Central Library[43] has a volume of correspondence to Ford. One letter from John Britton, dated 31 October 1806, thanks Ford for his information and reminds him of his promise to supply details of all aspects of the cotton trade in Manchester. This was presumably to be included in Britton's *Beauties of England and Wales*, vol 8 *A New Topographical History and Description of Lancashire*; Britton acknowledges Ford's help in that volume. In

September 1807 Britton invoices Ford for prints supplied and also offers Ford a 10% commission on the list price of any of Britton's collection, but asks for their return in a fortnight. In November Britton is again writing to Ford asking him to negotiate the engraving of Dukinfield Hall with Mr Astley.[44] This cost 10 guineas, and Ford received a guinea commission. This portrait is listed anong those published by Ford priced 6/- or 10/6 on India paper. At the sale of prints belonging to the late John Leigh Philips,[45] which took place in Manchester, Ford bought no less than eighty-two lots at a total cost of £60.9s.4d. Prices ranged from 2/6 to £4.10s.0d. The total amount realised for the prints was £2880.16s.0d. Ford purchased even more heavily at the Roscoe sale in 1816.[46] Sixty-nine lots were bought costing him £179.6s.0d. While prices ranged from 5/- to £3.16s.0d., most items were £1 or more.

In 1825 a portrait of Ford was etched by Henry Wyatt. Wyatt was one of the lesser-known members of the prolific artistic family of that name. He was a portrait and subject painter, born in 1794, who came to Manchester some time after 1819 and remained there until 1825. The whereabouts of his studio have not been traced as he does not appear in any of the Manchester directories covering that period. He returned to Manchester in 1837 and lived there until his death in 1840.[47]

An undated book in the Manchester Central Library[48] *Character of the Different Picture Collectors in, and about Manchester Faithfully Delineated by Wm. Ford with Poetical Sketches of the Manchester Amateurs of the Portrait* consists of short verses followed by prose comments. The artists' names usually designated only by initials, have here had the full name filled in in red ink. The comments were not always complimentary, for example the description of John Greaves 'This niggard is so *mean* and *selfish,* He's as contracted as a shellfish'. The names are not well known, with the exception of B A Heywood, but one presumes they were Ford's clients.

Ford was also a contributor to the *Retrospective Review.* The first series was issued in twenty-eight parts from 1820 to 1826, with a second series in 1828. Authors of the first series were George Robinson, W Gray, Serjeant Talfourd, Joseph Parkes, etc; it was edited by H Southern. The second series was edited by Southern and Nicholas Harris Nicolas.[49] Although Lowndes does not mention Ford we know from the Ford Scrapbook in the Manchester Central

Library that he was a contributor as the text of some of his contributions can be found there. All contributions were unsigned, and in the first series even the editor's name was not given. The discursive seventeen-page introduction is unhelpful about the aims of the journal. It does, however, include the statement 'The design of this review... is an attempt to recall the public from an exclusive attention to new books, by making the merit of old ones the subject of critical discussion'.[50]

Ford died on 3 October 1832 and was buried in St. James's cemetery Liverpool. An obituary notice appeared in the *Liverpool Mercury* on 9 November 1832.

NOTES

1. Anthony Lister, 'William Ford (1771–1832) the universal bookseller', *Book Collector*. 38 (1989), 343–71. This is the only article devoted entirely to William Ford.

2. *The Manchester Guide*, 1804.

3. *The Admission Register of the Manchester School* (Chetham Society Remains, 73, 1868), 79–81.

4. Bancks's *Manchester and Salford Directory*, 1800.

5. Chetham's MS A.4.27.

6. Chetham's MS A.4.27.

7. Manchester Central Library, Ford Commonplace Book 091F.

8. *Manchester Mercury*, 24 September 1805.

9. This item has not been identified.

10. Details from the *Manchester Courier*, 16 July 1875. Quoted in *Local Gleanings Lancashire & Cheshire*, July 1875.

11. James Heywood Markland (1788–1864); see *DNB*.

12. For a contemporary description of the history of these items see William Beloe, *Anecdotes of Literature and Scarce Books* (1807) 1, 363.

13. It now forms part of the Malone Collection in the Bodleian Library, Oxford.

14. Quoted in the *Palatine Notebook*, December 1882.

15. Early invoice volumes in the Portico Library.

16. Pressmark 010.4 D6.

17. John Harland, *Collectanea Relating to Manchester and its Neighbourhood at Various Periods* (Chetham Society Remains, 68, 1866), 61.

18. Samuel Lewis, *Topographical Dictionary of England* (1831), 3, 237.

19. *Liverpool Mercury*, 27 September 1811, 102.

20. 30 July 1813.

21. Brenda Scragg, 'Some sources for Manchester printing in the nineteenth century', in Peter Isaac & Barry McKay [ed] *Images and Texts; their Production and Distribution in the 18th and 19th Centuries* (Winchester: St Paul's Bibliographies, 1997), 113–19.

22. Pressmark BR 010.5 B22.

23. Rylands Library English MS 71 No.161.
24. T F Dibdin, *Reminiscences of a Literary Life* (1836), 317.
25. *Manchester Magazine*, 2 (1816), 284.
26. *Cowdroy's Manchester Gazette*, 1 June 1816.
27. Letter of Ford quoted in RW Proctor, *Memorials of Bygone Manchester*, (1880), 36–7.
28. *Some Memoirs of the Late Francis Dukinfield Astley* (Manchester, 1828).
29. For more information about these prints see *Palatine Notebook*, April 1883.
30. A copy of this catalogue is in the John Rylands Library.
31. *Manchester Mercury*, 8 July 1805.
32. *Manchester Mercury*,14 August 1805.
33. Chetham's MS A.4.27.
34. Dibdin, *Bibliotheca Spenceriana*, 4, 319.
35. *Catalogue of the... Library of John Leigh Philips, Esq. Deceased... Sold by Auction by Winstanley & Taylor at the Large Room in the Exchange, Manchester Monday 17th October 1814 and 8 following days.*
36. *Catalogue of the Library of... Robinson Foxley M.D. which will be Sold by Auction by Mr. Gasquoine on Monday February 5th 1816 at the Emporium, in Exchange-Street.* Manchester.
37. *Catalogue of the... Library of William Roscoe, Esq. Sold by Mr. Winstanley*, Liverpool, 19 August to 20 September 1816.
38. *Catalogue of Books, Prints and Pictures the Property of the Late John Arden, Esq at his Mansion in the Underbank, Stockport. Wednesday October lst. 1823.*
39. *Cheshire Notes and Queries*, Saturday 15 June 1889.
40. *A Catalogue of the Late Charles Lawson, M.A Sold by Auction by Mr. Gasquoine Thursday, June 18th.*
41. T F Dibdin, *Bibliomania*. New and enlarged edition (1876), 123.
42. EGR7/12/8 items 47,48,49.
43. Letters to William Ford, BRq 091F5.
44. Francis Dukinfield Astley of Dukinfield Lodge, Cheshire.
45. *Catalogue of... Prints & Etchings of.. John Leigh Philips Sold by Auction by Winstanley & Taylor Monday 31st October 1814 in the Large Room in the Exchange, Manchester.*
46. *Catalogue of the prints, books of prints... of William Roscoe. 9th September, 1816.*
47. Samuel Redgrave, *A Dictionary of Artists of the English School* (New edition, 1878), 492. He does not feature in Evans's *Catalogue of Engraved Portraits*.
48. Shelfmark MS 827.79 Fl.
49. W T Lowndes. *Bibliographer's Manual.*
50. For a critique of the *Retrospective Review* see *Blackwood's Magazine*, LIX (December 1921), Part II.

At the Fall of the Hammer:
Auctioning Books in Manchester 1700-1850

MICHAEL POWELL & TERRY WYKE

A UCTIONS HAVE long been acknowledged as an important feature of the history of the book trade. Indeed some auctions have become defining dates in that history: the year 1812 recalls the Roxburghe sale rather than the assassination of the Prime Minister or the military exploits of Napoleon. Yet whilst the role of the book auction has been recognised, the broader economic and social history of the auction trade remains lightly sketched. In spite of the pioneering work of McDonald and Swaim,[1] our view of the book auction continues to be shaped by the sales of important collectors and of the activities of a small number of metropolitan-based firms which displayed an atypical ability to survive in a trade where the majority of businesses had a short existence.[2] Understandably, attention has been directed at relatively accessible sources such as individual sales catalogues even though their representativeness is problematic. When we turn to assess the role of the auction in the secondhand book trade questions still outnumber answers. The need for further detailed local research would seem self-evident. This paper presents some preliminary evidence on book auctions in Manchester before 1850. In particular it focuses on the extent and organisation of the auctioneering trade and the role that auctioneers played in the local book trade. As in most provincial towns book auctions in Manchester have not been systematically studied. Our knowledge of even those auctioneering firms with a long pedigree remains superficial.[3] Similarly, historians have paid scant attention to those sales for which catalogues have survived. For Manchester we have no more than a few dozen examples of book-auction catalogues for the years 1700–1850. In the first section of the paper we set out to clarify the role of the auction in the book trade and indicate the major changes occurring in the trade during the industrial revolution. The second section gives a brief outline of the development of book auctions in the city before presenting some provisional data, derived from an examination of newspaper advertisements and commercial directories, on the extent and dynamics of book auctioning in the first half of the nineteenth century. First-hand evidence of auctions is surprisingly scarce and in the final section we use the reminiscences of the Manchester secondhand bookseller, James Weatherley, to provide a more direct view of the organisation of auctions and the conduct of those individuals who actually peopled the provincial auction room.

ROLE OF THE AUCTION

The ascending-bid or English auction in which the buyer was the person making the highest bid for the item offered for sale quickly established itself as the chief form of auction in the book trade. It had a number of positive features for sellers which help explain its establishment. Most importantly, it provided a comparatively simple way of selling an item whose real value was uncertain. Moreover a seller had the knowledge that items put up for sale would usually be sold and that the money would be paid by a certain date. The introduction of reserved prices meant that sellers were not without some degree of control over price. Yet attractive as the auction was to the seller, there was no guarantee that the best price would be paid. Auctions offered the opportunity for a wide range of fraud and a popular view of auctioneering was of a trade that did not always serve the best interests of the seller. Auction rooms were depicted as 'temples of deception'.[4] One of the most serious problems arose from collusion among the bidders. The operation of buying rings among booksellers reduced the number of effective bidders, resulting in the seller receiving a lower price. In contrast, buyers accused auctioneers of inflating prices as they engaged in 'buying in' lots. Such practices prevented the auction from operating efficiently, and delivering the highest price from those who attended. Yet whilst some auctioneers behaved in ways which did nothing to instil public confidence and approval,[5] it was not always the auctioneer who was at fault; auctions required those who attended to possess a cool head. Even experienced members of the trade could find themselves in difficulty. At the sale of John Leigh Philips in Manchester in 1814 the bookseller William Ford bid the high price of £3.10s.0d for Taylor Combe's *Terracottas in the British Museum* (1810). This item had already been knocked down to a Mr Garnet of Salford for £1.19s.0d when a dispute arose and the lot was put up again. Ford bought it for the higher price thinking all along that he was bidding for the subsequent lot in the auction, Holbein's *Icones Historiarum Vetus Testamenti*, of 1538.[6]

The auction trade, with its low entry costs, inevitably attracted individuals of varying talents and probity. Given such conditions it was not surprising that there was to be a long struggle for auctioneers to develop those enforceable codes of conduct associated with the professions.[7] Paradoxically this was the case in spite of the fact that from a relatively early date auctioneering was a trade subject to government regulation.[8]

The most significant development affecting the auction trade in these years occurred in 1777 when the State searching for new war-time taxes, introduced a duty on land and goods sold at auctions. This fiscal initiative appears to have been influenced by the long-established system of taxing property and goods sold at auction in Holland, one of the Dutch taxes which Adam Smith had drawn attention to in his recently published study, *The Wealth of Nations*.[9] Books were one of the forms of property specifically identified in the act and initially they were subject to a tax of 6*d* in the pound (2.5 per cent). This rate was subsequently increased to 7*d* in 1787, 10*d* in 1797 and finally one shilling (5 per cent) in 1805. Under the 1777 Act auctioneers were also required to take out an annual licence and provide a bond to operate.[10] This legislation had important consequences on the auction trade, as it was the auctioneer's responsibility to collect and to pass on to the Excise the appropriate duties. Auctioneers had to notify the Excise of forthcoming auctions. This was done by presenting the Excise with a catalogue no less than three days before a sale was scheduled to take place. Following the auction, the auctioneer had to present, within 28 days, an account of the prices paid at the sale to the Excise, from which the duty payable was calculated. A sale catalogue with the prices of each lot marked proved to be a convenient administrative document for presenting this information. To what extent this measure may have encouraged the publishing of separate auction catalogues for book sales is unclear given the general assumption that the catalogue was already an essential feature of such sales, but it probably did increase the publication of catalogues for other types of sales, including general household sales, which may have included books among the lots on offer.[11]

Thus after 1777 the selling of books by auction in Britain (the duties were extended to Ireland in 1797) entered a new era which was to continue until 1845 when auction duties were abolished as part of Peel's rationalisation of the taxation system.[12] In theory, the 1777 Act significantly changed the position of the auctioneer. It was no longer possible to set up as an auctioneer unless a licence had been taken out and sureties found.[13] The need for presentation of accounts and payment of the duties were new responsibilities, requiring auctioneers to have a greater sense of business organisation.[14]

DEVELOPMENT OF BOOK AUCTIONS IN MANCHESTER

The first recorded book auction in Manchester took place on 4 October 1692, most probably the work of an itinerant auctioneer designed to trade stocks of unsold remainders rather than a book collector's library.[15] By the first two decades of the following century auction sales of secondhand books were becoming commonplace. One of the first Manchester auctioneers was the wig-maker Edmund Harrold. His manuscript diary for the years 1712–16 shows that he bought, swapped and sold books. In 1714 he conducted a number of auctions in Stockport, Rochdale and neighbouring towns, and held a series of auctions in Manchester all apparently carried on at night. In November of 1714 he organised the sale of books of Nathaniel Gaskill, one of the founders of the Cross Street Chapel, for which he charged five shillings a night. Clearly the life of an auctioneer was not without difficulty.

I bless God for enabling me to perform and govern myself so well as I did, considering that I was so much scoffed and derided and jeered, by the mob and other malicious persons, who offered to baffle me with opprobrious words. Indeed they told me of all my faults and more than all, of drunkenness, foolishness... and was very abusive.[16]

At the same time as booksellers became a feature of the retailing world in what was still a small, if busy, market town, auctioneers also began to establish themselves, though the line dividing the bookseller and auctioneer was frequently crossed. John Berry, publisher of a series of Manchester maps in the 1740s, was accounted a celebrated auctioneer alongside his other skills as a dealer in watches, jewellery, toys, grocery, tea and all kinds of patent medicines. Similarly Robert Whitworth, the Whig bookseller and publisher, also supplemented his income by auctioneering. His newspaper, *The Manchester Magazine*, advertised a 'catalogue of the library of the ingenious Mr Gore, teacher of mathematics, to be sold at a shop in the house of R Whitworth' on 26 August 1746, and the following year a sale of over 1300 valuable books, 'which will be sold cheap'.[17] It appears that the custom at this time was for the auctioneer to place a minimum price on each lot as a 'reserve price'. The conditions of the sale of another library sold by Whitworth in 1751 show that the reserve prices were actually printed in the catalogues.[18]

No book will be sold before the time fixed. The catalogue will be read expeditiously over, and to prevent disputes if two persons are for one book the highest bidder to have it.

Clearly the existence of printed prices in a catalogue does not always help to clarify the distinction between a bookseller's catalogue and that of an auctioneer.

The unprecedented increase in business activity that transformed Manchester by the end of the eighteenth century should have resulted in an increase in the number of auctioneering firms. Some idea of the changes in the trade in Manchester and Salford can be obtained from the commercial trade directories though, given the various problems surrounding the compilation of a comprehensive and accurate directory, the extant directories can provide only an approximate estimate of the numbers of licensed auctioneers.[19] Moreover, although these years saw the establishment of specialist auction rooms, auctioneering remained a trade in which individuals from other trades might take out a licence but not necessarily classify themselves as auctioneers in the commercial directories. Booksellers became auctioneers, either temporarily or permanently. William Ford is probably the best-known Manchester bookseller who turned to auctioneering.[20] His contemporary James Hopps, who, having sold his bookselling business to his brother, established himself as an auctioneer in Bridge Street, is less well known.[21] Table 1 provides evidence on the development of auctioneering in the first part of the nineteenth century based on the local commercial directories.

Two main trends are suggested by these data. In the first place it appears that the number of those individuals who regarded themselves principally as auctioneers did not increase steadily in numbers throughout the period surveyed, years in which the town was expanding rapidly. For many years their numbers appear to have not kept pace with population growth. Only in the 1840s was there a significant expansion in the numbers of auctioneers identified in the directories. But it is the second trend which is more revealing. A closer analysis of those businesses listed in the directories indicates that auctioneering in

Table 1: Auctioneers in Manchester and Salford, 1815-1850

Year	1815	1819-20	1824-5	1830	1836	1840	1845	1850
Nos	23	24	24	26	31	30	47	50
New entrants		12	12	19	15	10	30	26
Ratio to population	1:4075	1:4500	1:5209	1:5462	1:4934	1:5462	1:3732	1:3739

Manchester was marked by a high turnover of firms. As the number of new firms entering between the sample years indicate, the typical firm had a low chance of survival. Over each five-year period approximately one-half of the businesses disappeared. None of the auctioneers identified in 1815 was trading in 1850. Indeed, only a handful of firms – Jacob Goodier, James Drew, William Capes, John Morris – operated for more than twenty years. Auctioneering was for some a business that had to be combined, as in the previous century, with other trades if a living was to be made, whilst for others it was a precarious and transient business; the licences taken out one year were not necessarily renewed the next.

Commercial directories, however, provide no direct evidence on the actual business conducted by auctioneers in Manchester. Other sources need to be examined. In particular, local newspapers appear to offer the opportunity for acquiring more detailed information on the auction trade. To assess the usefulness of this source our preliminary research has involved an analysis of auctions advertised in the Manchester press in the years from 1800 to 1850. Advertisements were, of course, a primary source of profit for newspapers, and no newspaper could hope to survive without attracting advertisers.[23] Our methodology, following that of Scott Bennett's work on newspaper advertisements, involved the counting of advertisements for auctions in each issue of a Manchester newspaper in six sample years.[24] In each of the years a single newspaper was surveyed (the first issue for each month in the year) and the number of auctions of all types identified. These adverts were then classified. The classification was in two main sections: first, real property, capital goods and major enterprises; second, retail trade. The resulting data are presented in Table 2.

Even taking into account the fact that these figures represent only a sample, the evidence from newspaper advertisements would suggest that book auctions were not a major category of auction sales.[26] Books were but one of the 'several sorts of goods' advertised for sale,[27] and there was a wide range of sales that involved books. The survey confirms that most books were sold as part of general household sales rather than as part of specific libraries. In addition, books were auctioned as part of the stock of booksellers who died or who were made bankrupt or as part of the stock of related businesses such as printers or stationers.

The advertisements enable us to build up a much clearer picture of the activities of leading auctioneers. Whilst it is clear that many auctioneers sold books, mainly as part of the sales of household effects, there is evidence to suggest that a number of firms, notably those of Thomas and Robert Winstanley and Thomas Dodd in the 1820s and William Capes, Jasper Fletcher and William Fullalove in the 1830s and 40s showed at least some specialization in the sale of books, and other small works of art - pictures, prints, sculpture. Alongside this specialization, throughout this period there continued to be a number of sales organised in Manchester by outside auctioneers. At the beginning of the nineteenth century one of the main auctioneers, Thomas Winstanley, ran sales from his base in Liverpool and it was only after many years of business that he opened a branch in Manchester run by his son Robert. In June 1810 a Mr Wise of Bath held a grand sale of books, maps and prints at the Bulls Head, Market Place.[28] In May 1840 Mr Hodgson of Liverpool held a sale at the Picture Gallery, Market Street, to which he earnestly solicited 'public attention to this truly superb assemblage of books; a finer collection not having been offered in Manchester for many years'.[29] Evidence of itinerant

Table 2: Advertisements of Auctions in Manchester Newspapers 1800-1850[25]

	1800	1810	1820	1830	1840	1850
Property & land	113	149	141	121	120	171
Machinery & Equipment	17	16	26	27	52	93
Livestock, carriage, etc	18	15	17	11	21	59
Textile goods	6	8	10	9	23	32
Pictures	1	3	0	3	9	16
Household goods (without books)	15	20	24	37	58	99
Household goods (with books)	1	4	2	4	8	14
Books	0	2	6	7	11	8
Other	2	4	14	19	40	80
TOTAL	173	221	240	238	342	572
Booksales as percentage of total	0.6	2.7	3.3	4.6	5.5	3.8

auctioneers and their sales could not be found from a study of Manchester trade directories and their activities are yet another area that requires further study.

A further point arising from a survey of advertisements is that they confirm that large numbers of sale catalogues have simply not survived. Virtually all advertisements for the sales of libraries and household effects point out that catalogues of the sales may be had from the auctioneer in advance of and on the date of the sale. Few of these have found their way into public collections. In the absence of sale catalogues, the advertisements do at least provide us with important information about the type of books that were sold. Although the advertisements vary in the amount of information they offer, most contain some details about individual titles or runs of books. The sale of 'magnificent, illustrated and embellished books', by Robert Winstanley advertised in the *Manchester Guardian* on 6 November 1830 is by no means unrepresentative:

A Splendid Collection of Books, comprising, among others of high importance, *an unique large paper copy* of the Beauties of England and Wales, *illustrated* with upwards of 5,400 engravings, and half bound, in 114 vols.; *Boyer's* folio edition of Hume's England, *with the addition of* Houbraken's Heads; Meyrick and Smith's Ancient Costumes, &c. in 10 vols.; fine copy of Macklin's Bible, 6 vols. folio; Bryant's Dictionary of Painters and Engravers, inlaid in large 4to paper, and *illustrated* with about two thousand engravings; Henault's Chronological History of France, inlaid in folio paper, *enriched* with two thousand portraits and plates, bound in 7 vols.; an *original copy* of Pennant's London, inlaid on folio paper, *illustrated* with a profusion of engravings, and bound in 6 vols.; Galerié du Museé de France, 10 vols. 4to. L.P. *Proofs before the Letters* with the *Etchings*; Piranesi's Works. 14 vols. brilliant Roman impressions; Museé Français. 5 vols. atlas folio. *Proofs* before the letters; Voyage Pittoresque des Isles de Sicile, de Malta, let de Lipari, 4 vols. folio et de Naples, et de Sicile, 5 vols. folio et de la Swisse, 4 vols, folio; the Staoffrd [*sic*], Forster's, and Tomkin's British Galleries, *proofs*; Grose's Antiquities, Whitaker's Leeds, Smith's Ancient costumes, Camden's Britannica, by Gough, 4 vols. 4to., with select copies of *Pocoke's Description of the East,* Cook's Voyages, Philosophical Transactions, abridged, 18 vols., Transactions of the Society of Arts, Manufactures and Commerce, Rees's Cyclopaedia, in parts, Lavater's *Physiognomy*, 5 vols. imperial 4to., Perry's Conchology, and other works of considerable value.– The books are principally in *elegant, substantial, and appropriate bindings.*

Although the evidence from newspaper advertisements makes clear that the main business of auctioneers was in selling property and goods other than books, adverts relating to books do provide insights into the book trade. Above all they suggest that when individuals wished to sell books for whatever reason, they were more likely to take them to a bookseller than an auction room. This is best illustrated by the fact that many of the sales of household effects which do not contain books, do contain bookcases, but books, as small portable commodities, could be excluded from the sales of entire household goods. Indeed one may speculate that given the time and expense required to compile a catalogue auctioneers might well have directed those individuals seeking to sell books to booksellers rather than sell the books themselves, presumably receiving some sort of commission for this recommendation. This may explain, if it is true, the low numbers of individual sales in the auction room. Of course, unlike those seeking to sell some goods, the very existence of secondhand booksellers did give the seller an alternative to the auction room.

JAMES WEATHERLEY AT AUCTIONS

As the recollections of the Manchester secondhand bookseller, James Weatherley, suggest, the auction was an important part of the bookseller's world. Although a bookseller might still organise an auction as a means of selling books in a town poorly served by other booksellers,[30] for most booksellers an auction sale was organised by a professional auctioneer, and offered them the chance to replenish stock, to pick up a particular volume for a regular customer, the opportunity for a bargain. The books offered for sale varied greatly in quality and what was dismissed as little more than wastepaper by one dealer would have been a profit opportunity for another. But whatever level of the trade one was from, success at an auction required a cool business head. Lots had to be examined, their condition noted. To rush into buying books unseen was to court disaster. When Weatherley attended a crowded auction in Liverpool, he was foolish enough to give up a good seat which would have enabled him to scrutinize the lots. He recalled:

the moment I got in the room there was a hundred & three vols of the Gentlemans Magazines going to be knocked down at one shilling pr vol with coming from Sharps and no little vexed at myself for being such a fool to give up my seat at the table where I could see and handle every book that was brought up the Magazines were just going I said fifteenpence Pr Vol when a bid of one penny Pr Vol advance would have done but I was put out of the way with Sharps there was 17/- flung away on his account and all through the sale after I could not get a book to look at the time of selling which made me suffer most awfully.[31]

Auctions were also used by booksellers to sell their own stock. When it proved impossible to meet the demands of creditors by other means, booksellers might dispose of part, if not all, of their stock, in the auction room. Weatherley was thus both a seller and buyer in the Manchester auction rooms. The financial pressures on him must have been especially severe in 1840, as he not only auctioned his entire collection of books but also the fittings of his shop in Church Gates including 'counters, shelving, gas meter, pipes, burners, oven and grate, large kitchen dresser'.[32] Such sales were an opportunity for those still trading to profit.

Collusion between booksellers at auctions was frequently asserted, though how extensive it was is difficult to assess given the nature of the practice and the understandably jaundiced comments of sellers who felt cheated.[33] Weatherley provides first-hand evidence of such rings and, indeed, he clearly participated in them though as a bookseller whose fortunes fluctuated, his interest must have been confined often to the less expensive lots and residual volumes. At its most basic level, collusion only required an understanding between two booksellers. Weatherley recalled one such occasion when a local bookseller James Nuttall was compelled to sell some 800 volumes in order to raise immediate cash. The venue for the sale was Dodd's Auction Rooms in Exchange Street.[34] The sale, however, coincided with another one outside of Manchester so that the only other bookseller attending was James Wroe, whose Ancoats bookshop was a well-known centre for political radicalism. An arrangement was made to divide the lots:[35]

> I said to Wroe it is of no use of you and me opposing each other I said you take all the odd numbers in the Catalogue such as 1 3 5 7 9 11 to the end and I will 2 4 6 8 10 to the end of the Catalogue it was agreed on most of the lots were knocked down at 6d and 9d a lot they run from four to eight in a lot... a few days after the Sale Nuttall found great fault with me and Wroe he called him radical Wroe, he said we had robbed him of his Books in buying them so low, we told him we had the Public to contend with and that him or someone should have been there to Protect them...

Auctioneers could only have connived at such practices.

Nuttall's experience was a reminder of the care needed in organising sales, preparing a catalogue, arranging publicity, and ensuring that they were held at a suitable venue and time. To overlook these elementary arrangements meant sellers struggled to obtain fair prices. Poorly organised sales were an opportunity for bargains. The sale of the Revd Moses Randall's considerable library in 1834 was another such Manchester sale, 'Attorney Heslop had the management of the estate', remembered Weatherley, but 'it was a bungling job altogether the property was flung away'.[36] Another sufferer was the bookseller Edward Bayliss whose circumstances did not allow the preparation of a proper catalogue when he sold his books.[37] Even the simple act of organising titles into broad groups might ensure that larger sums were realised.

If the operation of rings at auctions had obvious consequences for the seller, it was not without repercussions on the booksellers themselves. Booksellers needed to be part of the ring if they were to obtain profitable volumes. To be outside of the ring placed one in a vulnerable position. Recalling the sale of Dr George Tomlinson's library in 1827 Weatherley underlined the competitive nature of the local book trade. The auction was conducted by the Liverpool auctioneer, Thomas Winstanley. Weatherley arrived at the Manchester Exchange with his fellow bookseller, John Gleaves, expecting to be part of the ring.[38]

... but when we got in the room the other Booksellers knowing we were short of cash some of them thought to drive us from the Sale by refusing to let us Join with them, well as soon as Patten Baylis saw us go in the room he came up to John and me and said that himself and Matthew Thakery Bill Newton Brother to Tom of Liverpool, and the other Booksellers objected to our Joining with them in the knock I said well its all right we shall make you pay dear for what you buy, the first lot Put up was the Armanian Magazines from one to five of the first vols of the Magazine they were then searched after and very scarce well the lot was started by Baylis at 6d per Vol they would have been knocked down for that, but just as the hammer was falling I said 2/9 for the lot. Bill Newton shouts out in an Instant 3/- and looked as black as thunder at me, I let the hammer just be falling I said 3/3 Matthew Thackery shouts 3/6 they were all getting botherd just as the hammer was again falling I shouts out £3-15-0 for them Mr Winstanley stared besides the rest of the Company and Winstanley said do I understand you right I said yes Sir £3-15-0 Matthew Thackery shouts quite in a pet £4 - - I then said let the Gentleman have them he deserves them (a laugh) so much for the first Lot they would have gone for 2/6 if we had Joind a many of the lots through the Sale I worked the same way...

Evidently, as long as such rings operated, it must have been difficult for many booksellers not to participate. In the short term it might have been possible to make life less profitable for those inside the ring, but in the longer term such aggressive practices were hardly sustainable. Such bidder collusion at auctions, of course, distorted the market, producing lower prices than when all bidders competed for a lot. Such practices need to be acknowledged when explaining wide variations in the prices of comparable books sold at auction. In such circumstances it would be wrong to assume that auctions necessarily settled the price of a book, providing other members of the trade with a reliable indication of its true value.

Auctioneers, as we have suggested, needed to have particular talents if they were to survive. Apart from the skills needed to run a small business, they also required a strong personal presence, the ability to command the auction room. It was an art to set the tone and pace of an auction, to know just how much to say about each lot.[39] One could not be long-winded. John Hopps, another Manchester bookseller turned auctioneer, was considered wearisome as he 'had too much to say about the Books which was very tedious to hear and losing a deal of time'.[40] Though as Hopps had, according to Weatherley, once cheated him at an auction, Weatherley's assessment may not have been entirely reliable.[41] An auctioneer also required an equable temperament, especially if disputes occurred over particular lots. Tactfulness was not one of the qualities always evident in the Irish-born auctioneer, William Howe.[42]

I recollect when he was selling at Lark Hill there was an old small Quarto Vol of Poems in Black Letter without covers he knocked it down to me at 6/-, but Ebenezer Thomson Bookseller of Market St claimd it he said he gave Mr Howe a nod, Howe denied it they soon got to high words which was often the case when they came in contact for both of them were short temperd men I ever met with, the lot was put up again and I made Thomson pay £1-1-0 for it which nettled him very much he called me a bread and Cheese Bookseller he said a lot of the Booksellers went to London and lived on Bread and Cheese Howe said Mr Thomson I wont allow such Language to be used here and if you persist in it I shall not take another bid from you Thomson said if you dont mind what you are about I will inform your Employers, Howe said pointing towards Kersall Moor you may go and tell the man on the mountains for what I care.

To what extent auctioneers themselves attempted to mislead customers or benefited from the operation of the ring is difficult to estimate. As in any trade there were those who were dishonest. Practices such as inflating prices by ghost bidders and the buying in of lots on behalf of the vendor were aspects of the trade which could be abused. The printing and reading of the rules governing auctions helped to establish the probity of the auction but these were not always followed. Sharp practices might be tried to mislead and cheat the customer. On one occasion Weatherley found himself in dispute with John Morris, an auctioneer whose business address was in King Street, after buying a lot which had been presented as a good run of the *Gentleman's Magazine* (the lot was sold by weight).[43]

> ... he then said now Gentlemen that is a fair sample of the lot and I will sell them by the Pound I said to Mr Morriss what weight do you suppose there is of them he said Perhaps there may be three or four Hundred weight the lot was started at threepence per Pound it kept advancing untill the lot was knocked down to me at 1/1 Per Pound when I came to examine it I found all that was put on the Counter as a sample was the whole of the Gentlemans Magazines all the other was very bad damp and dirty I told Mr Morris I would not have them for they were not what he had represented them either in Quantity or Quality and I would not have them.

Weatherley insisted that Morris had misrepresented the goods but Morris delivered the volumes with an invoice for £18.12s.6d and demanded his money. Weatherley refused to pay and, eventually, he turned to another auctioneer, William Heywood, for help to resolve the dispute.[44]

Of course, there was another side to such disputes and allegations, auctioneers were understandably keen to ensure that once goods had been sold they remained sold, resisting what they considered to be unfair attempts by purchasers to withdraw from a contract of sale. After the introduction of the Auction Tax this could also mean the payment of two lots of tax if a lot was returned and later re-auctioned. But it would be misleading to see all auctions as riddled with deception and sharp practice though such practices may have been more in evidence at the lower, more transient end of the trade. Not all auctioneers fitted Bierce's celebrated definition of 'a man who proclaims with a hammer that he has picked a pocket with his tongue';[45] close business links existed between auctioneers and booksellers. Auctioneers provided a vital line of credit to booksellers. How widespread this was and how the terms were decided is unclear though we know that Thomas Dodd, one of the auctioneers who features most frequently in Weatherley's recollections, provided credit of two months, a generous term given the need to pay the seller and the Excise.

There is little information on the attendance of private collectors at auction sales and whether they were successful in bidding against the dealers. Individuals, of course, could commission bookdealers to bid for specific lots on their behalf. In such arrangements the need for precise instructions was paramount. In most cases there was little difficulty, but there was always the possibility of misunderstandings. When Weatherley was asked by William Yates, a local collector, to buy a scarce Manchester tract – Robert Bradbury's *Immortality of the Soul* – the instructions were of little use as Yates had also engaged another dealer to buy the same lot. The outcome was a predictable farce with a lot which should have gone for 2*s*.6*d* selling for 16 shillings.[46] It was not only the operation of the ring which meant that the prices paid at auction were not necessarily a reliable guide to the true value of books.

CONCLUSION

The selling and buying of books at auction was an important – if elusively quantifiable – part of the book trade in the eighteenth and nineteenth centuries. From this preliminary investigation into Manchester book auctions we would emphasise that although elementary work still needs to be completed on those extant auction catalogues, it should be recognised that they can only provide us with a partial view of the role played by auctioneers in the book trade in Manchester. The disposal of the leather-bound volumes of local bibliophiles, was important but it only represented one part of the many books disposed of at auction. As we have argued, it is also important to acknowledge those auctions for which catalogues have not survived, the sales of the libraries of less eminent individuals, the sale of stock by booksellers keen to raise funds when cash flow problems threatened to embarrass, and the disposal of books in general household sales. Paradoxically, given the impetus to produce printed catalogues following the introduction of the auction duty, catalogues for the majority of such sales have not survived. Newspaper advertisements help to reduce our ignorance about this part of the secondhand book trade.

Our preliminary analysis of auction advertisements during the first half of the nineteenth century, although not drawing on all of the available Manchester's newspapers, suggests that such advertisements can provide a considerable range of information about the different types of books auctioned in the town. They also provide, unlike the commercial directories, more precise evidence on which auctioneers specialised in the selling of books. Although not without their problems of interpretation – nor were all auctions advertised in the press – such advertisements represent a vital if time-consuming source to analyse. Their use should not be confined to studies of the eighteenth-century trade.

The lack of detailed records of such sales should not prevent us from recognising that considerable numbers of volumes passed through the auction rooms. Auctions were an integral part of the secondhand book trade, though as Weatherley's reminiscences suggest, this was a dangerous world for the uninitiated or the unconnected. Not least of the problems arose from the apparent widespread collusion among buyers. The existence of the ring appears to be virtually omnipresent and many booksellers must have found it difficult not to take part, unable to withstand those pressures which their fellow booksellers could exert when working together. The removal of competitive bidding removed one of the vital features of the auction, with the consequence that the prices obtained for books did not represent their true market value.[47] Auctioneers must have been aware of such practices. Efforts may have been made to strengthen the rules governing auctions in an attempt to drive out sharp practices, but the provincial auction room in the first half of the nineteenth century was certainly not a place for the unworldly.

ACKNOWLEDGEMENTS

We would like to thank the Bibliographical Society for its financial support of our research on James Weatherley and the Manchester book trade.

NOTES

1. W R McDonald, 'Book-auctions and book-sales in the Aberdeen area, 1749–1800', *Aberdeen University Review*, 42 (1967-8), 114–32; Elizabeth Swaim, 'The auction as a means of book distribution in eighteenth-century Yorkshire', *Publishing History*, 1 (1975), 49–91.

2. Among the best-known accounts of auction firms selling books are Frank Herrmann, *Sotheby's: Portrait of an Auction House* (London, Chatto & Windus, 1980); H C Marillier,

Christie's 1766 to 1925 (London, 1926); *One Hundred Years of Book Auctions, 1807–1907: Being a Brief Record of the Firm of Hodgson and Co* (London, 1908). They were, of course, based in London.

3. The collection of auction catalogues of Capes & Dunn, including sixteen for the years before 1850, have been little used by historians of the book trade. They are deposited in the Arts Library, Manchester Central Library.

4. *The Ruinous Tendency of Auctioneering...* (1812) quoted in Robin Myers, 'Sale by auction: the rise of auctioneering exemplified: in the firm of Christopher Cock, the Langfords, and Henry, John and George Robins (c.1720–1847)', in *Sale and Distribution of Books from 1700*, edited by Robin Myers and Michael Harris (Oxford, 1982), 126–163 (131).

5. In part the poor public image was based on the activities of unlicensed auctioneers and the holding of mock auctions, see Felix Folio, *The Hawkers and Street Dealers of the North of England* (Manchester, [1858]), 87–90.

6. Manuscript note by J T Allen in Chetham's Library copy of *A Catalogue of the Valuable, Extensive, and Well-Chosen Library, of John Leigh Philips, Esq... which will be sold by auction, by Messrs. Winstanley and Taylor, of Liverpool,... on Monday the 17th of October, 1814, and eight following days...* (Manchester: J Aston, 1814). The Holbein item is incorrectly printed in the catalogue as *Historiarum Veteris Instrumenti Lugduni*, a mistake which can only be explained by the fact that auction catalogues were often compiled by one person dictating the titles to a colleague who wrote them down.

7. F M L Thompson, *Chartered Surveyors: The Growth of a Profession* (London, 1968), 47–50.

8. *Select Committee Report on Laws Relating to Auctions* PP 1818 (360) III, 1–3.

9. S Dowell, *A History of Taxation and Taxes in England* (1884, 1965 edition), vol 2, 170, 329.

10. 17 Geo. III c. 50. The annual licence for provincial auctioneers was 5s; more importantly the bond required was £50.

11. The PRO reports that no local excise papers have been deposited.

12. Dowell, *History of Taxation*, vol 3, 19–20.

13. In 1845 the licence duty was increased to £10 (8 & 9 Vic. c.15).

14. See Joseph Bateman, *Law of Auctions* (first published in 1843); P F Evans, *Bateman's Law of Auctions*, 7th edition (London: Sweet & Maxwell, 1895); and the various editions of Robert Ritson, *The Auctioneers' Manual* (London: Estates Gazette Ltd).

15. Fragment in Manchester Central Library, see G Pollard & A Ehrman, *The Distribution of Books by Catalogue from the Invention of Printing to 1800* (Cambridge: Roxburghe Club, 1965), 235.

16. Chetham's Library Manuscript, Mun. A.2.137. Quoted from 'Diary of a Manchester wig maker', *Collectaneae Relating to Manchester and its Neighbourhood at Various Periods...* compiled and edited by John Harland (Manchester: Chetham Society, o s 68, 1866), 204.

17. Quoted in a report of a lecture given by C W Sutton on 'Book auctions in Manchester in the eighteenth century' to the Lancashire & Cheshire Antiquarian Society on 10 December

1909; see *Transactions of the Lancashire & Cheshire Antiquarian Society*, 27 (1909), 189–91.

18. The same, 190.

19. J E Norton, *Guide to the National and Provincial Directories of England and Wales, excluding London, published before 1856* (1950) remains the best starting point to a large literature discussing the problems associated with the interpretation of commercial directories.

20. On Ford's work as an auctioneer, see Anthony Lister, 'William Ford (1771–1832) "the Universal Bookseller"', *The Book Collector*, 38 (1989), 343–71 (368–70), and the previous chapter herein by Brenda Scragg.

21. James Weatherley, *Recollections of Manchester and Manchester Characters and Anecdotes Relating to Manchester and Lancashire Generally from the year 1800 to 1850 by James Weatherley, for Nearly Half a Century a Bookseller in the Locality of the Manchester Exchange*. Chetham's Library MS Mun A.6.30.

22. Based on the commercial directories for those years, see G Tupling, *Lancashire Directories 1684–1957* (Manchester, 1968).

23. Ivon Asquith, 'Advertising and the press in the late eighteenth and early nineteenth centuries', *Historical Journal*, 18 (1975), 703–24. For an introduction to the Manchester press in this period see D Read, *Press and the People 1790–1850* (London, 1961).

24. Scott Bennett, 'Victorian newspaper advertising: counting what counts', *Publishing History*, 8 (1980), 5–18.

25. The newspapers surveyed were *The Manchester Mercury* for 1800 and 1810, *Wheeler's Manchester Chronicle* for 1830 and the *Manchester Guardian* for 1830, 1840 and 1850.

26. For an important examination of the role of auctions in agriculture see J R Walton, 'The rise of agricultural auctioneering in eighteenth and nineteenth-century Britain', *Journal of Historical Geography*, 10 (1984), 15–36.

27. Advertisement in *Prescott's Manchester Journal*, 22 January 1780.

28. *Manchester Mercury*, 5 June 1810.

29. *Manchester Guardian*, 2 May 1840.

30. In 1823 Weatherley organised such an auction at the Reed Inn in Rochdale. Books and prints were sold for marked prices during the day whilst in the evenings he auctioned his stock, Weatherley, *Recollections*, 42.

31. In the direct quotations from Weatherley we have followed the original spelling, capitalisation and punctuation (Weatherley, *Recollections*, 70–1). For further information see Michael Powell & Terry Wyke, 'Penny capitalism in the Manchester book trade: the case of James Weatherley', in *The Reach of Print: Making, Selling and Using Books*, edited Peter Isaac & Barry McKay (Winchester, 1998), 135–56.

32. *Manchester Guardian*, 23 May 1840. Our thanks to Neil & Sue Richardson for drawing our attention to this advertisement.

33. Ford's anger over a 'villainous Cabbal of Picture-dealers' must have been repeated by many sellers in auctions where the expected prices were not realised; see Lister, 'William Ford', 344.

34. On Thomas Dodd and the part he played in founding the Royal Manchester Institution see C P Darcy, *The Encouragement of the Fine Arts in Lancashire 1760–1860* (Manchester: Chetham Society, 3rd ser 24, 1976), 64–6.

35. *Recollections*, 34–6.

36. *Recollections*, 67.

37. *Recollections*, 33.

38. *Recollections*, 54.

39. For a general discussion of such skills see 'Auctions', *Chambers Journal*, 3 November 1866, 698–9.

40. *Recollections*, 21.

41. *Recollections*, 21.

42. *Recollections*, 54–5.

43. *Recollections*, 64.

44. *Recollections*, 64.

45. Ambrose Bierce, *The Devil's Dictionary* (1991 edn), 11.

46. *Recollections*, 56–7.

47. To what extent in these years booksellers followed auction prices in marking up their own stock is unclear, 'How the value of books is estimated', *Book Lore*, 4 (1886), 165–8.

Niche Marketing in the Nineteenth Century:
The Shepherds' Guides of the Northern Counties

BARRY McKAY

IN AUGUST 1835 or 1836 (the final digit of the date on the imprint is obscure) Mary Tyson of Ulverston printed a poster offering a reward of five guineas for information leading to the conviction of sheep rustlers operating in the South-West corner of Cumberland.[1] The poster is typical of its type and time, and the text in general would have been found in any part of the country where a similar problem occurred. However several lines at the bottom of the poster are unusual, if not unique, to Cumbria. These lines contain a code which would enable anyone with an understanding of the terms used, to identify the specific ownership of the stolen sheep:

BLACK HALL STOCK.– A red smit stroke down the near side; and both ears cropped and upper Key bitted.

GAITSCALE STOCK.– A red smit mark over the Shoulder; and some of them also a red pop on the near Hook Bone, as a gathering mark for a particular part of the pasture; and both ears cropped and under Key bitted.

This code describes the daubed designs on the fleece of the animals: the smit marks; and the pieces cut from their ears: the lug marks. These marks, together, occasionally, with a mark burnt into the horns of suitable breeds of sheep, have for a great many years been used to identify the individual flocks of sheep which grazed the unenclosed uplands of the region. Each combination of marks is unique to a particular farm and, allowing for no duplication, means that any lost or stolen sheep can be identified and returned to their rightful owner.

Although the various combinations of marks which identified a specific flock would have been known to neighbouring shepherds it is unlikely that any shepherd would have been familiar with those from outside his immediate neighbourhood. Following the printing of the first *Shepherd's Guide* in Penrith in 1817 it became possible to refer to a reference book of marks in order to identify the owner of any lost sheep. For these guides are not books of advice on the management or breeding of sheep; they are extremely accurate directories of flock ownership.

In order to understand the situation which brought about these guides, it is perhaps necessary to have a modest understanding of the sheep-grazing practices in the upland areas of the region. The valleys of the Lake District have been extensively farmed for centuries and the dry-stone walls which enclose the fields are an essential feature of the area. However, the enclosed fields rarely extend far up the fell sides and above the wall-line the fells are generally unenclosed. The open-ranges of the higher parts of the fells provide grazing to those breeds of sheep suitable to the unforgiving environment. By-and-large this means the Herdwick, Swaledale, and Rough Mountain breeds, or cross-breeds with significant elements of one or other of these in their genetic make-up. One of the characteristics of these breeds is that once they are used to a specific locality, 'heafed' to use the technical term, they rarely wander far from their native area. It has been said, particularly of the Herdwick breed, that they never stray off the fell where they were born. I suggest that the existence of these guides disproves that old tale, for if they did not stray then there would be no need of a guidebook in order to identify their owner and return lost sheep to him!

The smit marks which are applied to the fleece, were originally done with rudballs made from red haematite ore, or of graphite from the Seathwaite lead mines in Borrowdale. Although chemical dyes are used today, many farms used to make their own ruddle by boiling grease, Stockholm tar and Venetian Red pigment, well into the twentieth century.[2]

The ear, or lug, marks are pieces clipped from, or patterns cut into, the ears of the sheep when they are lambs. These marks follow prescribed patterns and each has its own style-name: fold bitted, ritted, sneck bitted, and so forth.[3] Horn burns, more commonly found in the east, generally have the initials of the farmer or farm name branded in. Furthermore these marks remain part of the freehold of a farm and even today many upland farms have the same, or remarkably similar marks, to those given in the earliest guides.

Two distinct groups of *Guides* were issued in various editions over 170 years between 1819 and 1990. One group covers the farms lying within or adjacent to the present-day Lake District covering Cumberland, Lancashire North of the Sands, and Westmorland west of Shap Fell, while the other covers the eastern side of present-day Cumbria (Westmorland east of Shap Fell) and parts of Northumberland, Durham and Yorkshire.

In 1817 Joseph Walker, a 'statesman' of Martindale near Penrith, issued the first guide.[4] It is reputed that he 'first sketched a sheep on a piece of paper, with his own mark, and sent the paper to his neighbour, William Jackson, who sketched his sheep facing the other way, and showing the reverse side… this paper was sent round till it resulted in the first Shepherds' Guide.'[5] The method, arrived at more or less accidentally, of showing two sheep, face to face, to display both sides of the animal, was adopted by Walker as the best method to illustrate his *Guide* and has remained the standard method of displaying the marks up to the present day.

Even quite late editions of the guides are uncommon and the earliest examples are of near-legendary rarity, so I have been unable to locate a copy of the first Walker's *Guide* to examine personally. Fortunately a copy is described in Garnett's *Westmorland Agriculture* which quotes the title as *The Shepherds' Guide or a Delineation of the Wool and Ear-marks of the Different Stocks of Sheep in Martindale, Barton, Ashkam, Helton, Bampton, Measand, Mardale, Long Sleddale, Kentmere, Applethwaite, Troutbeck, Ambleside and Rydal.*[6]

The coverage it offers is therefore of quite a small area of the Lake District, which may be defined as the parishes from just below Penrith in the north to just above Windermere in the south, and from Long Sleddale in the west almost into Langdale in the east

The book was printed by William Stephens, printer, bookseller and bookbinder of the Market Place, Penrith, who operated from *circa* 1817 to 1825 or 1827. Very little is known of Stephens beyond his printing of the early *Shepherds' Guides*, a sermon, and a couple of posters for Inglewood Races. However he was on the circuit of the travellers of the Edinburgh publishing house of Oliver & Boyd, whose ledgers record his credit rating as 'doubtful'.[7]

Although I have not seen the book I have seen an illustration of it.[8] This shows that the blocks of two sheep were printed three to a page, from wood-engravings, with letterpress descriptions of the owner's name, farm and the specific marks below each cut. This style of presentation, with only few exceptions, remained the norm throughout the history of these publications.

The smit and lug marks on the blocks appear to have been added by hand with pen and ink.

Joseph Walker died aged forty-one in 1820, and the next guide, also printed by Stephens, extended the area covered to include some 240 marks from farms in the north and central areas of the region. This was compiled by William Mounsey and William Kirkpatrick, both of whom had assisted Walker. They reprinted Walker's original introduction in which he had written

My object in bringing this work before the public is to lay down a plan by which every man may have it in his power to know the owner of a strayed sheep, and to restore it to him, and at the same time, that it may act as an antidote against the fraudulent practice too often followed, – in a word, to restore to ever man his own.

The 'fraudulent practice' referred to is probably that of cutting off the whole ear to remove the principal mark of ownership. The basic rule of thumb appears to have been that if a sheep lacked an ear, or ears, its provenance must be in doubt.

At about the same time Stephens printed a third *Guide*. Although the book was published anonymously it is accepted that the author was James Whineray, a farmer of Lowick, near Ulverston in Lancashire. Whineray's guide, substantially the largest yet produced, covered an extensive area and recorded the marks of some 587 farms in thirty-seven parishes to the west and south of the region.

Figure 1 Stephens's Cut

Stephens used a group of six wood-engravings, one of which carries the initials IN (perhaps Thomas Bewick's apprentice Isaac Nicholson) printed three to a page. However, in each of the Stephens printings a different method of presenting the information was used. Walker's *Guide* has the letterpress details printed below the engravings, Mounsey and Kirkpatrick's *Guide* has the text and engravings printed separately and numbered to relate to each other, while Whineray's *Guide* has the engravings on the recto with the letterpress descriptions on the facing verso. Where fleece and lug marks have been added they have been done by hand with pen and ink and, since not all the engravings have been so 'enhanced', it must be presumed that the owner of the volume added those marks which were desired.

Walker's idea was adopted by Chapelhow of Appleby, who produced a guide to the marks of the Eastern Fells, which extended coverage eastwards from the edge of Walker's *Guide*, across to Stainmore on the Durham border, and southwards into the Yorkshire Dales. Again no copy has come to light, but as no record of a Chapelhow farming in the Appleby area at that time can be found, it was presumably produced by John Chapelhow, the first printer in the town. If so, then this would considerably pre-date the hitherto earliest known substantial book printed in that town. Garnett describes it as 'an improvement on Walker's, for committees are named and places and times of meeting arranged'.[9] The committees referred to by Garnett are those which regulated the smooth running of the loose associations of shepherds, and drew up rules for the maintenance and return of lost sheep. These meetings are a long-established tradition where the shepherds from a district gather together to return lost sheep and enjoy a day's holiday. These 'shepherds' meets' frequently used to involve traditional country sports such as horse-racing, hound-trailing, and Cumberland and Westmorland wrestling. One site where a famed meet continued into the 1830s was on top of High Street to the west of Ullswater, where the site of the horse-racing is fossilized today on the Ordnance Survey map.[10]

In 1824 James Moore extended the coverage of the Eastern area to include Westmorland parishes east and south of Shap Fell and the Yorkshire Dales. He further improved the organisation of the still very loose shepherd's associations by naming the various men in each parish or township whose duty it was to see that all strays were gathered on two specified days each year on their respective commons.

Moore's book was printed by William Knipe of Ulverston; the only recorded book from his press. As with the Stephens printings, several wood-engravings of sheep are used but for the first time the compiler or printer has undertaken the task of illustrating all the marks recorded. The blocks used by Moore have been pierced to allow for the insertion of a letter or symbol in order to represent the smit marks. These were possibly added individually from a single slug of type or, more probably, by dropping the appropriate letter into the hole left in the wood block in the manner of a seventeenth-century factotum, any strokes or other symbols being added by hand. Even though these blocks used by Knipe are split and may have been either of poor-quality wood or have been used on a *Guide* I have been unable to locate.

In 1827, an anonymous guide to the marks of the Saddleback and Skiddaw ranges was issued, but again, I have been unable to locate a copy to examine. It was printed by James Brown of Penrith who also issued an anonymous extension of the Eastern-Fells guides, which was unillustrated and relied entirely on printed descriptions of the marks. In 1839 Brown also printed an updated edition of Walker's original *Guide* which was revised by William Kirkpatrick; Richard Mounsey, the son of Kirkpatrick's former co-compiler, and J Mattinson. In 1848, Brown's widow, Hannah, printed a revised edition of the 1827 Saddleback and Skiddaw *Guide* in which she used the blocks which Stephens had employed in the *Guides* which he had printed.

My original suspicion that by then the illustrations would be printed from stereotypes is disproved by this edition. As is usual the illustrations are printed three to a page and one, the top block on the recto of each leaf, is severely split. This damage to the block was presumably present before printing began as it appears thus throughout the book. There is also some lesser damage to the middle block (which is the one in the group with the initials IN) which first appears on page 33 and continues thereafter to the end. The presumption must be that this block was damaged in the course of printing the book.

Coverage of the Lake-District region was now virtually complete and some revisions had been undertaken. The time was ripe for a compendium of all the recorded marks. This was compiled by William Hodgson of Corney, and printed in 1849 by Stephen Soulby of Ulverston.

Soulby was the youngest son of John Soulby and furthermore is the man who can, with some conviction, be claimed as the inventor of the printing press later known as the 'Wharfedale'. Hodgson's *Guide* was by far the largest yet produced; it ran to 751 pages covering seventy parishes or townships, and recorded over 1100 marks – a quite remarkable undertaking given the difficulties of communication in the region at that time. Soulby used a new block, now almost certainly printed from stereotypes, printed three to a page on the rectos, with the descriptive text printed on the facing versos. The lug and smit marks, in red or black, are once more added by hand. Although this is the first comprehensive guide its coverage remains firmly the preserve of the Lake-District shepherds, for although twenty-three Westmorland parishes or townships are included they are very firmly west of Shap Fell. No Eastern Fells Association parishes are included and it is quite clear that the breed and regional cultural differences marked by the Shap Fell divide is rigorously maintained.

In 1853 Benjamin Thomas Sweeten of Penrith produced a revision of the 1835 Eastern Fells *Guide*. This is printed from stereotype blocks similar to the earlier Penrith guides. In 1869 Robert Bailey of Keswick produced a new edition of the 1827 and 1848 Northern Fells *Guides*. The engravings used by Bailey are copies of the earlier Penrith blocks; however there are differences of detail on them and so I presume that he had had half-a-dozen new ones cut.

By 1879 thirty years had passed since the first comprehensive guide to the Lake-District Fells, and a new revision was needed. This was undertaken by Daniel Gate, a Keswick agricultural merchant, and finally we have some documentation which sheds light on the production of these books.

Gate took as his model Hodgson's *Guide* of 1849, but retained the traditional form of three blocks to a page with letterpress descriptions underneath. There may have been a charge made for entry as Gate writes in the preface: 'There are several entries still unpaid; but trusting to the honour of the Parties concerned, I have inserted them in order to make the work as complete as possible'. The coverage, like Hodgson thirty years before, was restricted to the Lake-District Fells and recorded some 1500 marks from ninety-eight parishes or townships.

Gate had new line-blocks made by G E Oliver of Edinburgh after a photograph by Thomas Mayson of Keswick, of sheep in the flock of Edward Hawell of Lonscale, Underskiddaw, near Keswick. The blocks were pierced to take the lug marks which were printed from specially prepared slugs and the smit marks overprinted with type or printers' rules or, where they were more complex, washed in by hand in either black, red, or green.

Production was obviously under way in April 1878 when Gate wrote to the Brash Brothers of Cockermouth:

I find that the old Book contains 752 pages[11] but with the letterpress under the prints that number would be reduced one half to which you must add the same number of pages as are contained in the book I lent you & say 30 more pages for extra blocks. Should there be any more required we can arrange hereafter if necessary. The cuts are pierced <u>ready for slipping in the luggs with their different marks</u>. (*Gate's underlining*) Mr Gate provides the cuts & ears with their separate marks. Letterpress similar to the old book give estimate (soon) for 300 500 or 700 copies of 400 pages with red and black pops letters &c and also without smits. & how much per page after & how much per page for Adverts. The different smits will have to be put on by hand, the luggs will be printed & not marked with pen as old book. Send estimate to me Cloth binding will do or clothback with paper (simulating cloth) sides, letter back "Shepherds Guide" I do not want an expensive paper or binding, if it is pretty substantial [*annotated in pencil* 'say cloth'] State particularly price per page for advertisements & make you estimate out for 300 500 or 700 copies complete. Also without the smits (red & black) so that I may know the differences. Put any other particulars in you may think proper.[12]

In an undated draft from their Lancaster office, Brash Brothers estimated £35 for three hundred copies; £50 for five hundred (with a pencilled cross placed by this figure) and £63 for seven hundred copies. The run-on cost ranged from an additional 1*s*.0*d* (five pence) for 300 copies to 1*s*.6*d* for 700; while if advertisements were included these would range from 1*s*.9*d* to 2*s*.3*d* per page. On the reverse of this draft estimate is written:

The binding in above estimate would be cloth boards turned in and letter on back 'Shepherds Guide' They would come in 3d or 4d cheaper in cloth boards cut flush. With respect to the red marks, letters, &c we should charge according to the time it took about 6d per hour and as we have no idea how many of them are to be marked, we of course can't tell how long it will take.

The printing, marking, and binding of at least part of the edition had been completed before the middle of August 1879, when the bookbinders, Leighton, Son & Hodge of London, sent three delivery notes to Brash Brothers in Cockermouth, all dated 14 August, which account for 103 copies. Leightons wrote again on 21 August stating that they had 'this day sent to Cockermouth 80 copies of the "Shepherds Guide" making in all 188 copies (*sic*) – the remaining 12 are imperfect and shall be kept here as per your instructions'.

In August 1879 Brash Brothers prepared a draft invoice whick showed a printing cost of £55.10s.0d which is altered in pencil to £50 with other small sums for red ink, &c. £3.13s.6d for 'cutting blocks for ear and other marks' and £3.15s.0d for adding smit the marks. This figure being altered in pencil to £36.5s.0d (presumably to 'hide' the true printing cost which was over the estimate). The cost of printing specimen pages and order forms added a further £4.2s.6d to give a final (draft) figure of £99.4s.6d.

Therefore it appears that the printing, binding and marking, together with the costs of printing notices, specimen pages, order forms, &c brought the book to Gate at a unit cost of around four shillings per copy. To this sum must be added the unknown costs of producing the blocks, any newspaper advertising, and the cost of posting out specimens and order forms. However as, apparently, a regular visitor to the agricultural shows which proliferated in Cumbria in the later summer months, Gate doubtless handed order forms to his potential subscribers, thus reducing the cost of postage of this important means of selling copies of his book. Furthermore his costs in gathering the details of marks for insertion in his book were probably minimised by distributing some sort of form for the recording of marks to the shepherds he met at shows in the preceding year, or years. Since the retail price was 10s.6d it would appear that the unit cost per copy was around half the retail price.

Gate does not seem to have relied overmuch on the Cumbrian book trade for orders. No trade orders survive in the documentation, but this may be misleading as the only orders which do survive are four orders dated either 12 or

15 December 1879. Three are annotated 'no money – not sent'. One however, is further annotated '?send a/c'. This is firmly crossed out!

An undated memorandum, which from other evidence is dateable to shortly after 12 December 1879, suggests that 154 copies had been accounted for. Of these seventy-three copies had gone to subscribers, Gate himself seems to have had eighty-six copies in several small lots, while one copy had been sent to the British Museum Library (where it has the not inappropriate shelfmark: 7293.k.9).

One copy went to William Ritson of Wasdale Head. Ritson, onetime landlord of the Wasdale Head Hotel, was famous for winning lie-telling contests – indeed once his reputation was well established he won one contest by claiming he was ineligible to take part as 'he could not tell a lie'. Ritson wrote to Brash Brothers on 12 December 1879

to inform you that when Mr Gate was at Wasdale Head he got 3/6 in debt and he said that he would allow it when he sent the Guide Book and if you will allow the 3/6 you may forward me a Book at the same time as you send Mr Tyson's and I will send you 7/- being the difference.

Despite his reputation, Brash Brothers obviously took Ritson at his word as the letter is annotated: 'Book sent'.

Both Gate and Brash Brothers seem to have been responsible for receiving orders and sending out copies of the book. This seems to have led to some confusion. In October and December four people wrote complaining that they had subscribed to the book but not received copies, while H Parkin of Penrith wrote to complain that he had received a copy of the book, but had neither paid in advance nor been invoiced.

Gate's credit-rating with Brash Brothers may have been a trifle 'doubtful'. On 5 September 1879 he wrote from the George Hotel, Keswick: 'Please bring or send a fresh supply of books to-day, I have sent them all out though I have got pay for only part yet. Off to otter hunt in haste'. And on 10 October wrote for more: 'Please forward tomorrow Saturday, without fail, as I want to attend Ambleside Sheep Fair on Monday & it is a very important fair. 40 or 50 more Books at least'. The letter is annotated '20 sent'.

Various receipts and waybills suggest that the railway was a favoured means of sending out the books. Ones from the Cockermouth, Keswick & Penrith Railway Company show that in December 1879 copies were despatched to

Torver, Ravenglass, Troutbeck, Bootle, Ulverston, Penrith, Seascales, Broughton and Shap, and to Ravenglass again, Newby Bridge, Ireleth, Gosforth, Egremont, Shap again, and Eskmeals. This means of distributing the copies was obviously efficient as on 27 December 1879 Daniel Braithwaite of Bootle wrote to order seven copies for himself and friends. He wrote again on the 31 December to acknowledge receipt and to state 'I dare say that I could get you an order for some more, but I should expect some commission for my trouble'. There is no further correspondence from Mr Braithwaite in the archive, and so perhaps his hopes for commission went unfulfilled.

On 28 and 29 June 1880 Leighton, Son & Hodge wrote twice more to Brash Brothers announcing that they had sent off a further 363 copies in five boxes and a tea-chest. Since they had already delivered 188 copies they appear to have bound-up somewhere around 550 copies of a the book.

So despite 1000 notices and order forms, and some 1400 entries (which presumably meant 1400 potential purchasers) only around one third of the edition had been sold in the first ten months. This perhaps helps to explain the final two letters in the archive. On 5 August 1880 Gate wrote to Brash:

Enclosed please find Bill duly accepted on the terms you mentioned which will be attended provided you let me have all the blocks & marks & Books in your Possession to make up the number. I have not yet recd. The copyright which you will oblige by sending.

Gate wrote again on 2 November 1880:

The Bill is due today & I am unable to meet it as I have not yet got my money in. I am sorry you did not remind me of it so that I could have it so that it could be [?remitted] as I have sent a lot of Goods away this week & I have also commenced delivering Books with Horse and Trap. Kindly renew the bill if possible to give me time.

Gate was in debt to Brash Brothers for some part, if not all, of a bill of £99.4s.6d for over 500 copies of a book of which a copy was offered for sale in Cumbria several years ago at £285.

On the East of the county two of the associations united in 1863 to publish a joint *Guide* which was separately printed and diversely illustrated, but issued bound together in a single volume;[13] again I have been unable to locate a copy to examine. Ten years later they were joined by the third association to publish a single guide. Again I have been unable to find a copy, but, of this edition, Garnett writes:

The wood cuts of the sheep in the issues of the amalgamated Associations were mere outlines and compared unfavourably with the early editions of the West Fells, with their well-engraved sheep, smits in colour, and croppings correctly shown.

Recording in West Fells guides of wool and ear marks is extended in the Amalgamated Associations guide to include horn burns, and Garnett notes that 'out of 1578 entries only 44 use no horn burn or the horn burn is uncertain'.[14]

From this date guides to the marks of Amalgamated Association members (*ie* those on the East of Cumbria, &c) are issued much more frequently, usually at intervals of around a decade.

The 1885 edition, the first published outside present-day Cumbria, was printed by William Ward in Barnard Castle. The title page shows the extent of coverage of the Amalgamated Associations to include *certain parts of unenclosed lands, lying and being within the counties of Yorkshire, Westmorland, Cumberland, Durham, and Northumberland... Extending from Bowes and Wensleydale, to Sedbergh, in Yorkshire; from Ravenstonedale and Brough, to Gillumholme, in Westmorland; from Cross Fell and Kirkoswald, to Castle Carrick, in Cumberland; from Knaresdale and Allendale, Hexhamshire, to Blanchland, in Northumberland; from Lanchester and Stanhope, to Middleton, in Durham; and from thence to Bowes, in Yorkshire.*

New editions of the Amalgamated Associations' *Guide* appeared in 1907, 1919, 1929, and an undated edition, probably printed in the 1930s. These were all printed in Barnard Castle by William Ward's successors: A & E Ward in 1907, Harry Ward in 1919 and E J Ward in 1929, and the 1930s. The next three Amalgamated Associations *Guides* were all printed in Consett, by Ramsden Williams. The first was undated but apparently around 1950, with other editions in 1960 and 1970. The last edition, printed in Haddington, Scotland, was published in 1990. For this edition entries cost £10 each with a reduction if two or more marks were recorded to a particular farmer. Each contributor received a free copy and so, presumably, the fees for insertion, together with the proceeds of the trade suppliers' advertisements, covered the production costs and made the publication a self-financing venture.[14]

The geographical coverage remains uniform throughout the hundred years since the first Amalgamated Associations' *Guide*. Although a new block is used, the same simple outline is retained, with no colour, other than black used to represent the fleece marks, and no attempt whatsoever to represent the lug marks. Since the horn burns were generally the initials of the farmer it was presumably felt unnecessary to illustrate them; however, since a hornless breed of sheep is used for the illustrations it is perhaps just as well. One feature of the Amalgamated Associations' Guides is that each edition contains several pages which illustrate all the patterns of lug-marking used in their areas.

In the Lake District there was only a revision of the 'small Skiddaw' book in 1892 before the next major revision of the whole region. This was instigated at the Buttermere Shepherds' Meet in 1906, and their suggestion was supported at several other meetings. Thomas Wilson of Keswick was appointed to undertake the task. During 1907 Wilson visited many of the fell farms in the district and by the Mardale Shepherds' Meet of November 1907 he had obtained over 1300 entries. At that meeting, and at others, Wilson spoke in favour of a central association to take up both the interests of the sheep farmers and to prosecute sheep stealers. Printing seems to have begun shortly afterwards, initially by R Brash of Lancaster.

Brash reused the blocks and lug marks of Gate's *Guide* of 1879; so presumably Gate did not 'get back all the blocks' he had requested from Brash in August 1880. For this edition the fleece smit marks and letters shown in black appear to have been overprinted by letterpress with the occasional pop mark perhaps added by hand. However any red smit marks also appear to have been added by hand.

Wilson died in the midst of these labours and production appears to have ceased in 1908, and John Simpson of Borrowdale and Thomas Bennett of Threlkeld took the matter in hand. They came to an arrangement with Wilson's representative to purchase the part already printed, and George Watson, who had assisted Wilson, completed the work and brought it up to date. For some reason Brash was unable to complete the printing which was taken over and completed by Easton & Bulfield in Lancaster. The book finally appeared in 1913.

This is the first guide I have seen to contain a subscribers' list which shows that 284 copies were taken up. While this may perhaps seem a poor response for a guide with around 1600 entries, it does reflect the initial sales of Gate's *Guide*.

Furthermore, and it is perhaps an interesting point when one considers that it is frequently held that Lake-District farms stay in the same family for generation after generation, a comparison of the names and farms which are listed in Whineray's *Guide* of 1819 and Wilson's of 1913 show that of 1204 names listed, only around twenty-four farms appear to be still in the ownership of the same family.

R H Lamb produced a revision of the 'small Skiddaw' guide, the most frequently updated, in 1927, before undertaking the next comprehensive edition in 1937. In an article in the *Whitehaven News* of 25 April 1935 Lamb discussed the problems associated with the printing of the guides.

The method of recording is to have a series of pictures from the one block showing two sheep presenting the near and far side, but without ears. On these are overprinted the fleece marks in colour, the ears being stiffly overprinted in solid black, with the appropriate cuts represented in diagrammatic fashion... The printing of these uncommon books is an exceedingly difficult and tedious task, so much so, in fact, that some of the few who have been through its throes declare that it nearly broke their hearts. Three separate operations are necessary and only a few pages are done at a time, while considerable care is needed to place every mark in its proper position; and then the compositor has to grapple with the strange language of the shepherd.

Lamb's *Guide* was so well regarded that is was not superseded until 1985 although the South Westmorland area of the National Farmers Union produced a guide in 1967 which 'for reasons of economy was printed in black and white and did not show illustrated ear marks. It also suffered from being in paperback only and had not stood up well to even the limited use it had on many farms'.[15]

The most recent Lake-District guide, compiled in 1985 by G F Brown and W Rawlings, took into account the problems of the 1967 guide. Once more the lug marks are present, overprinted in black, while the smit marks, in either black, red, blue or green, appear to have been overprinted lithographically.

For nearly two centuries the various marks of ownership of the northern flocks have been recorded. These books represent an example of localized and remarkably specific appeal. They also have, as I hope I have shown, other points of interest. The methods of production, even in times of comparatively cheap labour, were labour-intensive and therefore relatively expensive. If Gate's *Guide* of 1879 can be taken as typical, then the cost of adding the smit marks accounted for around a third of the entire production costs.

Today they remain of use to the agricultural, property or family historian, as they allow the identification of the occupants of many, if not all, of the farms in the upland areas. They have a certain charm and, certainly to local collectors, considerable interest and financial value. Finally, as my wife put it when she first looked at one 'they are, *surely*, the ideal bedside book for insomniacs'.

ACKNOWLEDGEMENTS

I am grateful to Tom Clarke of Howgill Castle and Andrew Humphries of Ivegill for their suggestions and corrections; also to John Garbutt of Grange-over-Sands, David Wise of Keswick, and John Mattley of Phenotype Books, Penrith, for furnishing me with details of various editions of the *Guides*; and to the staff of Cumbria Heritage Services in Carlisle and Kendal for drawing my attention to the Gate archive and to copies of *Guides* in an un-catalogued collection.

NOTES

1. Whereabouts of an original unknown but reproduced in William Rollinson, *Life and Tradition in the Lake District* (London, 1974), 86.

2. Rollinson, *Life and Tradition*, 85–6.

3. Lakeland lug marks are illustrated in Rollinson, *Life and Tradition*, 85 (figure 19).

4. William Rollinson, *The Cumbrian Dictionary* (Otley, 1997), 155, defines a statesman as 'an independent tenant farmer who held land by customary tenure rather than by copyhold and who, until the Act of Union, was obliged to take up arms in any border warefare'.

5. Miss [?Mary] Powley, 'Past and present among the northern fells', *Trans of the Cumberland & Westmorland Antiquarian and Archaeological Society*, OS II 1876, 355–56. & note.

6. Frank W Garnett, *Westmorland Agriculture 1800–1900* (Kendal, 1912), 178–9.

7. *Oliver & Boyd Travellers' Logbook*, (National Library of Scotland Acc.5000/78) I am grateful to Bill Bell for a copy of his transcription.

8. Rollinson, *Life and Tradition*, plate 52.

9. Garnett, *Westmorland Agriculture*, 180.

10. OS Outdoor Leisure: *English Lakes North East Sheet*, grid reference 111441.

11. The page count suggests that Gate was referring to William Hodgson's *Guide* of 1849.

12. Cumbria Record Office, Carlisle: DB20/9, which reference covers all the correspondence, orders, carriage slips, &c. concerning Gate's *Guide*.

13. Garnett, *Westmorland Agriculture*, 181–2.

14. I am indebted to John Taylor of Low Howgill, Milburn, for information concerning the most recent Amalgamated Associations guide.

16. G F Brown & W Rawlings, *Lakeland Shepherds' Guide* (Ennerdale Bridge, 1985), xii.

The Edward Clark Collection
at Napier University Library, Edinburgh

GRAEME S FORBES

T HE COLLECTION has its genesis in the will of Edward Clark, who was born in Edinburgh, to Robert and Emma Clark on 11 December 1864. His paternal grandmother Isabel was sister to Adam Black, Lord Provost of the City of Edinburgh from 1843 to 1848, and a Member of Parliament from 1854 to 1865. More relevant to our interests, however, is that he began business as a publisher in Edinburgh in 1815, taking his nephew Charles into partnership and thus founding the firm of A & C Black. Black published the *Edinburgh Review* for many years, and also acquired the copyright in the *Encyclopaedia Britannica* when the business of Archibald Constable & Co was dissolved in 1828.

Edward's father, Robert Clark, came to Edinburgh from Montrose, and at the age of thirteen, was apprenticed as a compositor to William Burness. After completing his apprenticeship he went to London to gain further experience, working there for two years[1] before returning to Edinburgh where, with the modest sum of £200, he set up as a small-scale law printer in George Street. With his own hands he set up the type and printed a circular which he sent to those connected with the Law in Edinburgh, 'soliciting their attention' to his services. Slowly the business increased and in due course he moved to larger premises in nearby Hanover Street. However, Clark was not wholly satisfied with the progress of business and so travelled to London during the 1850s, seeking work from book publishers. He was particularly successful in establishing contact with the firm of Macmillan, who at that time were changing from bookselling to book publishing, and were moving from Cambridge to London.

This venture led to the close connection between Edinburgh printers and London publishers, as Robert Clark's enterprise was copied by other Edinburgh printers. In 1861 the abolition of the duty on paper gave the opportunity for his London work to be increased. In December of that year R & R Clark employed only twenty-one compositors, a number exceeded by eight other printing firms in Edinburgh, but the number of employees rapidly increased. This expansion was aided by Clark obtaining from his uncle, the aforementioned Adam Black, the contract for the printing of Scott's Waverley Novels.

It was during this period of expansion that Clark's claimed the distinction of having the first female compositor in Britain. Following a major strike of compositors in 1871, Clark engaged and trained women to do the job, the first being Fanny MacPherson who remained with the firm for over sixty years.[2]

By 1882 further expansion was required and a move was made to a new site at Brandon Street. In 1880, James Kirkwood had been assumed as a partner, and in 1887 Edward Clark, the only son of Robert Clark, also became a partner. The second R Clark in the name of the firm was Richard Clark, who was a cousin of Robert, but he was never more than a sleeping partner, having provided finance for the founding of the firm. The driving force was always Robert, whose ambition and determination is aptly encapsulated by some words from his diary 'to do work of the best possible quality, to give the most efficient service and to charge the highest possible prices'.[3]

The printing of books for London publishers continued to expand after the opening of the Brandon Street works. It was said that on any day during the fortnight following Lord Tennyson's death in 1892 at least twenty-nine machines could be seen printing the works of the Poet Laureate. It is believed that such a concentration of the work of any author is unprecedented in the history of printing. By the time of Robert Clark's death in 1894, R & R Clark were employing between five and six hundred people.

Such, then, was the position when Edward Clark inherited the responsibility for the firm. He was twenty-nine years old and had been a partner for about six years. James Kirkwood was still alive when in 1895 the firm became a limited company with Edward Clark as Chairman and Managing Director. Though he had inherited a thriving business, Clark was not content to allow the company to rest on its laurels. From about the year 1910 several additions were made to the premises and many tens of thousands of pounds were spent in installing up-to-date machines. The company continued to flourish up to and beyond the Great War.[4]

Outside his business interests Edward Clark was apparently a jovial man and was popular in his social life, both in London and in Edinburgh, though, like his father he eschewed public affairs, preferring to delegate. Also like his father he was a keen sportsman, running a string of racehorses, and playing an enthusiastic round of golf, though less skilfully than his father. It is recorded that after one unsuccessful wager on the course he remarked that his loss would mean the printing of more Bibles – whether for financial gain or moral penance is not recorded.

I stated earlier that the Collection was born out of Edward Clark's will. The will is in fact a most remarkable document. Handwritten, it was begun on 17 October 1917 and with alterations, additions, deletions and codicils it was amended up to, and including, 5 August 1926. Clark left a considerable number of personal legacies to staff employed at his house at North Berwick, to staff at R & R Clark, and to personal friends, including one recently married daughter of a golfing partner 'as a token of my deep affection for her and for all her kindness to me free of tax'. One assumes it was the legacy, and not the affection which was free of tax!

In addition, there was some £50 000 left to specific charities, including the following two significant legacies. Firstly: 'To endow a Printing School for Edinburgh I leave Ten Thousand Pounds. W Maxwell R & R Clark to manage same and whom failing Robert Wilson Printer Edinburgh.' Secondly: 'I, Edward Clark, Printer, Edinburgh, Do Hereby Make this Codicil; I bequeath to the Managers for the time being of the Heriot-Watt College, Edinburgh to be held in trust by them or their successors in the management of that College such a sum, being not less than Five thousand pounds and not more than Ten thousand pounds as my Trustees may fix free of duty to be paid without interest as soon as convenient for the purpose of furthering the teaching of typography under the auspices of that College. My wish is that it should be regarded as a capital sum so that if any expenditure be made on plant etcetera a depreciation and obsolescence fund should be provided out of future annual income so as to replace what is so spent and keep the fund intact.'

The legacies are dated 5 August, six days before Clark's death on 11 August 1926.

As there was a certain amount of ambiguity about the objects to which these funds could be put, legal counsel's opinion was sought, and the Clark Trustees were advised that the term 'typography' could be interpreted in its widest form, namely printing from relief printing surfaces (as opposed to lithography

and intaglio processes), and that this could include electrotyping and stereo-
typing as well as machine composition for relief-printing processes. As a result
of this ruling it was possible to meet from this legacy the main cost of the
Monotype and line-composing equipment as well as typesetting frames and
letterpress machines which were installed in the Edward Clark Wing, part of
the extension of the Heriot-Watt College opened on 22 January 1935 by the
then Secretary of State for Scotland, Sir Godfrey Collins, who was also a
member of the well-known family of Glasgow printers and publishers.

This equipment accounted for much of the Capital Fund and, therefore, in
accordance with the terms of the Bequest, the Governors of Heriot-Watt College allocated the income from the remaining funds to bring the total Capital
back to £10 000 as instructed by Edward Clark's Will.

In view of the fact that there was already a Printing School at the Heriot-Watt
College, counsel was asked whether the words 'to endow a Printing School for
Edinburgh' could be applied to any purpose connected with the existing
printing school. Counsel was specifically asked to express a view as to whether
the income from the Trust could be applied to the purchase of books illustrating the development of printing and of printing processes, as a means of dem-
onstrating to students how printing had developed over the centuries. The
opinion of Counsel was favourable to this idea and the Edward Clark Collection was conceived.

WILLIAM MAXWELL & THE BUILDING OF THE COLLECTION

William Maxwell, to whom the task of managing the income of the Trust Fund
was given, was born at Leith on 3 April 1873. He began his working life as an
assistant in a grocer's shop in Edinburgh, but soon realised that there were few
prospects in this trade and so he decided to learn shorthand. When he was
qualified in this subject by attending evening classes, he left the grocer's shop
and at the age of about nineteen he became confidential clerk to Edward Clark.
This was a little time before the death of Robert Clark, but Maxwell soon won
the confidence of his employer, and his position extended at times beyond the
immediate interests of the Company, as the following anecdote illustrates.

I have already remarked that Edward Clark owned a string of racehorses
which he often ran at meetings in the north of England. As well as being an
owner, howvere, Clark had earned a reputation for being a successful punter,

and became suspicious that bookmakers, seeing him coming, would shorten the odds. Accordingly, he despatched the young Maxwell to a race meeting in the north of England with betting instructions. Needless to say Clark's wagers were successful, but Maxwell later recalled having spent an anxious evening in a strange hotel with several hundred pounds in cash.

As Maxwell's career in the firm developed, Clark entrusted 'W.M.', as he became known, with considerable powers and gave him shares in the Company. At the time of Edward Clark's death in 1926, William Maxwell was a Director and Secretary of R & R Clark Ltd., and in accordance with Edward Clark's will he received a sum of money, further shares, and the Executors were instructed to make him Managing Director of the Company. He also became the prime mover in assembling the Collection.

William Maxwell began collecting the books as early as 1931 (or perhaps before that), but difficulties of space made it impossible to store these books at Heriot-Watt College, and so the early purchases were kept by William Maxwell at his own house. It was not until the opening of the First Extension to the College in 1935 that books could be stored there, and even then they could not be displayed on shelves but had to be kept in locked cupboards in the Printing Department, although from time to time, exhibitions on particular subjects were mounted in display cabinets. By the time of opening Maxwell had assembled[5]

> over 120 volumes selected from the work of distinguished European and other presses from the sixteenth century to the present day, including such works as a copy of *Eusebius*, printed by Robert Estienne in 1544 in the Greek types of Claude Garamond, a copy of the large folio Baskerville *Bible* of 1763 in perfect condition, and excellent examples from the Kelmscott, Doves, Ashendene and other private presses.

I quote here from the 1934–35 annual report of Heriot-Watt College, which also stated that[6]

> It is hoped to make these books available for inspection by all those engaged or interested in printing in Edinburgh, and to exhibit them periodically in the display cases in the new building. The preparation of a catalogue is receiving attention.

More about this final remark later.

Maxwell continued to purchase fruitfully throughout the 1930s. In 1936, a leaf from the 42-line Gutenberg *Bible* was added, as well as a copy of the great folio Jubilee *Bible* designed by Bruce Rogers and entirely set on the Monotype, and the Nonesuch *Herodotus*. Maxwell also donated his own copy of the the Kelmscott *Chaucer*, arguably William Morris's greatest work. By 1937, the Collection had increased to 450 items and included an uncropped edition of the *Nuremberg Chronicle*, printed by Anton Koberger in 1493. The following year saw the purchase of Haebler's *West-European Incunabula*, and Geisberg's *Woodcuts from Books of the XVIth century*, both being large portfolios of mounted originals. Tuer's fascinating *Printers' International Specimen Exchange* complete in sixteen volumes, containing nearly 5000 examples of display work in letterpress and lithography, was also purchased.

Maxwell continued to make notable purchases into the 1940s: a fine folio Plantin *Bible* of 1483, the five-volume Nonesuch Press *Bible*, 1924–27, a fine Bodoni quarto *Horace* of 1793, a fifteenth-century Dutch manuscript *Book of Hours* on vellum, and a splendid copy of *Medailles de Louis le Grand* printed at the Imprimerie Royale in 1702. The College annual report for 1942–43 stated that due to Maxwell's purchases,[7]

This remarkable collection is now exceptionally representative from the aspect of typography... Attention is now being directed to the acquisition of representative examples of illustration and of bookbinding.

And, during the 1940s the Collection's direction was further diversified with the addition of early scientific and mathematical books, typical 'Keepsake' volumes from the nineteenth century, illustrated books for children, and examples of present-day book production. One outstanding 1947 acquisition was a copy of Bassandyne & Arbuthnot's *Bible*, the first printed in Scotland.

William Maxwell continued to purchase material for addition to the Collection up to his death on 12 October 1957, though around a year earlier the Clark Trustees had transferred responsibility for the funds of the 'Printing School Trust' to the Governors of Heriot-Watt College.

In 1964 the Printing School was transferred from Heriot-Watt College to the newly established Napier Technical College, built around Merchiston Castle, once home to John Napier, among many other things the inventor of logarithms. The Edward Clark Collection was handed over by the Governors of Heriot-Watt College to the Board of Management of Napier College, subject to the condition that items from the Library could be borrowed for the purpose of exhibition or for demonstration in classes, either by Heriot-Watt University (which Heriot-Watt College became in 1966) or by the Edinburgh College of Art.

In 1966 the opportunity arose to acquire a considerable number of books from the Library of the late Bernard H Newdigate, who had worked at the Shakespeare Head Press. This very valuable addition added appreciably to the books from private presses, not only from the Shakespeare Head Press but also from others. Bernard Newdigate had, in the 1930s, reviewed in *The London Mercury* books for their typographical content as opposed to their literary merit. Among the books so acquired were the copies which had been sent to him for review as well as scrapbooks containing the reviews themselves, and correspondence.

In the thirty years to date Napier College became Napier College of Commerce & Technology, then Napier Polytechnic of Edinburgh, and is now Napier University. During this period the Collection has remained within the institution, initially located in the Printing Department, but subsequently within the University Library, administered by the Library, with assistance from the Department of Print Media, Publishing and Communication, the latest incarnation of the Printing School.

Acquisitions have continued to be made to the collection which has not been frozen at any particular date. However, most of the recent acquisitions have been of secondary material, that is, descriptive and historical works on printing and typography. The exception has been some purchases of private-press books.

CATALOGUES

Earlier I quoted a remark from the 1934–35 annual report of the Heriot-Watt College that a catalogue was 'receiving attention'. In fact, by 1936 the first catalogue had been compiled by Frank Restall, then Head of the Printing Department of the College. Actually, the catalogue was no more than a hand-list prepared to assist William Maxwell with purchasing. The system was that William Maxwell did the actual purchasing, but that either he or Frank Restall would examine booksellers' catalogues and either one or other would suggest purchases. The hand-list would assist them in avoiding duplication.

As the Collection grew it was realised that the hand-list was insufficient; so, in 1939 William Beattie[8] of the National Library of Scotland was engaged on a part-time basis to prepare a preliminary catalogue. After the War this was revised and updated by R Butchart who had recently retired from the post of Librarian of Edinburgh Public Library.

Following William Maxwell's death the preparation of the catalogue passed to Peter Kilpatrick, then Chairman of the College Committee of Heriot-Watt College and also Chairman of the Printing Joint Advisory Committee. Kilpatrick consulted with Blair Maxwell, the Managing Director of R & R Clark and also a Governor of Heriot-Watt College. They discussed the catalogue with Beatrice Warde, typographical adviser to the Monotype Corporation and writer on typographical matters under the pseudonym of Paul Beaujon.

Beatrice Warde pointed out that the catalogue prepared by Butchart lacked full notes on the typography of the books and that this was essential if full use was to be made of it as a teaching aid. It was important, in her view, that attention should be drawn to the development of type faces, particularly in the earlier centuries. She suggested that Harry Carter, the archivist to the University Press at Oxford, would be most suitable for this task, and after obtaining permission from Charles Batey, Printer to the University of Oxford (and himself a former student and an Honorary Fellow of Heriot-Watt College), Carter was approached and consented to undertake the work. Kilpatrick assumed the role of general editor, and the project was under way.

Carter had completed his work by the time the Collection was transferred to Napier College in 1964, and in the following year composition of the text of the catalogue was begun. However, when the first galley proofs were considered at a meeting in May 1966 it was realised that insufficient attention had been given to books added to the collection purely because of their illustrations. It was at this point that Frank Restall, by then retired from the Printing School, agreed to write a history of the development of processes for the reproduction of illustrations using examples from the collection to demonstrate how these processes grew. He completed this work in 1970, two years before his death, and it forms a substantial part (117 pages) of the second volume of the catalogue.

Eventually, a full revision of the catalogue, coordinated and managed by Napier-College staff was published in 1976.[9] The two-volume catalogue, printed, appropriately, by R & R Clark, was distributed free of charge to printing schools, as suggested by Beatrice Warde. The catalogue, according to the Edinburgh typographer Neil Macmillan, 'In itself a magnificent reference book on the history and techniques of printing, this product of many dedicated people admirably complements a superb library of which Scotland should be proud'.[10]

Roderick Cave also notes its 'lavish' production, 'admirable points in its approach to the wide range of materials', 'comprehensive index' and the 'outstanding virtue of its typographical notes'. However, he also notes that 'the division of the catalogue into various sections is not faultless, so that one needs to know it rather well to use it to best advantage'.[11]

The fact that the catalogue was produced as a limited edition means that this advantage is available only to a few. A supplement listing new additions was published in 1980,[12] but this lacked typographical notes. From 1980 until 1996 new additions were noted in an Accession Register with little bibliographical, and no typographical information.

Following the Follett review of academic libraries,[13] which reported in December 1993, the higher-education funding bodies invited submissions for funding of specialised research collections in the humanities. Napier University Library applied for funds for the Edward Clark Collection and was fortunate to be awarded recurrent funding of £141 000 over a three-year period for cataloguing, conservation and housing.[14]

The cataloguing element of the project was begun in April 1996, the aim being to convert the material in the printed catalogue into machine-readable form and in so doing to improve and extend access. The nature of the Collection demanded that we give full consideration to each book as a physical artefact, as well as cataloguing and classifying its content. Napier has, since the automation of its catalogue in the 1980s, rigorously followed established international standards for cataloguing and classification; these standards are adopted for this work. As a result, information can be retrieved about all persons connected with the production and history of a volume, such as printer, engraver, binder and former owner as well as author and editor. Features such as binding, paper, and typography are recorded consistently, and a record of conservation work undertaken is incorporated into the catalogue record.[15] Three aspects of this cataloguing work may be of interest to scholars.

Firstly, we noted that several of the periodical titles in the collection were not covered by existing indexing or abstracting services, so we have enabled users of the Library's catalogue to search at article level for such information through the creation of analytical records attached to the parent record for the periodical.

Secondly, during the project the cataloguers came across correspondence 'hidden' between the pages of text. These letters, written by the author, printer or publisher of the work, often shed light on the history of the book's production. These letters have been placed in acid-free folders and referenced to the books in which they were found.

Thirdly, as an offshoot of the cataloguing work we created World Wide Web pages for the collection.[16] These pages can now be accessed directly from the Library's Web-based public-access catalogue, enabling us to provide links from bibliographic records to digitised images of material in the collection, and to other information relevant to the text.

Finally, though the target for the cataloguing element of the project is now almost complete, there still remains a considerable amount of work which we wish to undertake; this involves principally, the recording of over 6000 glass slides depicting printing and typographical processes, and the body of correspondence relating to the production of the printed catalogue.

CONSERVATION

As well as cataloguing, funds were also directed towards conservation and housing of the collection. Since its establishment the collection has been maintained through the years as a teaching resource, and many students have seen at first hand the splendid examples of typographers', printers', illustrators' and binders' art and craft. However, such familiarity has a cost, and in recent years there has been some concern about deterioration of the Collection.

Because of this we have operated a policy of restricted access, and this, in conjunction with the rarity of the printed catalogue meant that up to 1996 only a relatively small number of people knew of the Collection's existence. We did not however, wish to sustain this inaccessibility where, and here I quote from *The Name of the Rose:*[17]

only the librarian has... the right to move through the labyrinth of the books, he alone knows where to find them and where to replace them, he alone is responsible for their safekeeping.

As a librarian, I know from bitter experience the damage that can be done to collections by allowing too easy access. We tread at times a difficult path between access and conservation. Conservators work to preserve books for posterity, but it is easy to forget that posterity is here and now as well as in the future.[18] Napier's students, staff and indeed scholars worldwide are the posterity for which Edward Clark, William Maxwell and successive librarians have built and preserved the Collection. And so it is as a working Collection that we wish to conserve the stock.

To this end we have sought to stabilise and repair the stock to withstand (careful) handling. In 1992, using funds from the Trust and the University, an in-house conservation survey was undertaken, and preparations for a deacidification programme put in place. Following the award of funding in 1996, a full conservation audit was commissioned from the University of Dundee's Library Conservation Unit, and from this we planned a programme of conservation work. To date over 300 items have been treated, and a considerable amount of work is in hand.

In addition we were able to purchase equipment and materials to assist with the proper care and treatment of the Collection; these include tissue for the protection of illustrations, acid-free bookmarks, book snakes, cushions and rests, boxes, envelopes, and portfolios, dusters, air-guns and gloves.

Furthermore a project is currently under way, at the Merchiston Library, to improve the environment for the storage and study of the collection. This has been made possible through combining some of the Non-Formula funding referred to earlier, with funds from the Edward Clark Trust, the University, the Library, and the Department of Print Media, Publishing & Communication. Customised shelving has been purchased and building work, incorporating environmental controls and security, should have been completed in July 1998.

NOTES

1. With Messrs Clowes & Vizetelly.

2. See accounts in *A Reputation for Excellence: a History of the Edinburgh Printing Industry*. (Edinburgh: The Scottish Printing Archival Trust [&] Merchiston Publishing), 1990, and

in *Imprints in Time: Scottish Publishers Past and Present* (Edinburgh: Merchiston Publishing, 1991). Both are works compiled by students of the Department of Print Media, Publishing & Communication at Napier University.

3. Quoted in 'Clark's of Edinburgh: centenary of famous printing house', *The Scotsman* (22 November 1946), 5.

4. R & R Clark celebrated its centenary in 1946, and among many tributes received this one from George Bernard Shaw 'So the great printing firm of R. & R. Clark is 100 years old and I am only 90. They have been as natural a part of my workshop as the pen in my hand'. Quoted in 'R & R Clark: the great printing house's centenary', *The Bookseller* (November 1946), 3.

5. Heriot-Watt College. *Annual Report 1934–35* (Edinburgh: Heriot-Watt College, 1935) 21.

6. Heriot-Watt College. *Annual Report 1934–35* (Edinburgh: Heriot-Watt College, 1935), 21.

7. Heriot-Watt College. *Annual Report 1942–43*. (Edinburgh: Heriot-Watt College, 1943), 12.

8. Later Professor William Beattie CBE, MA, LLD, and Librarian of the National Library of Scotland 1953–1970.

9. P J W Kilpatrick [ed], *Catalogue of the Edward Clark Library*; With Typographical Notes by Harry Carter and an Essay on the Printing of Illustrations by Frank P Restall. (Edinburgh: Privately Printed for Napier College of Commerce & Technology [and] Lothian Regional Council, 1976), 2 vols.

10. Neil Macmillan, 'A tale of two libraries', *Scottish Print and Packaging*, 14 (March 1993), 21–2.

11. Roderick Cave, *Rare Book Librarianship* (London: Bingley, 2nd edn, 1982), 72–3.

12. *Catalogue of the Edward Clark Library. Additions to the Library since Publication of the Catalogue in 1976* (Edinburgh: Privately printed for Napier College of Commerce & Technology [and] LothianRegional Council, 1980).

13. *Joint Funding Councils Libraries Review Group: Report*. [Sir Brian Follett, chairman] (Bristol HEFCE, December 1993).

14. A full list of projects is given in *Accessing our Humanities Collections: a Guide to Specialised Collections for Humanities Researchers* (London: JISC, 1997).

15. Graeme Forbes, Sarah Forbes & Alyson Lochhead, 'The Edward Clark Collection cataloguing project at Napier University Library, Edinburgh: a brief note', *Rare Books Newsletter* 54 (Winter 1996) 35–9; Sarah Forbes, 'The Edward Clark Collection: Gutenberg and beyond', *Humanities Collections*, vol 1 no 1 (1998), 615.

16. http://www.napier.ac.uk/depts/library/clark/ecchome/html

17. Umberto Eco, *The Name of the Rose*. Translated from the Italian by William Weaver, (London: Picador, 1984), 37.

18. Adapted from the words of Peter Freshwater, 'Rare book collections as centres of excellence', *Library Association Rare Books Newsletter* , 29 (May 1987).

Index

219